# DICTIONARY OF
# ASTRONOMY

second edition

D1413170

We publish a wide range of specialist English and bilingual
dictionaries. For full details, visit our website:

**www.petercollin.com**

or contact:

Peter Collin Publishing Ltd
32-34 Great Peter Street, London, SW1P 2DB
email: info@petercollin.com

*In the USA, please contact:*
Independent Publishers Group
814 North Franklin Street, Chicago, IL 60610
tel: 312 337 0747  fax: 312 337 5985

# DICTIONARY OF
# **ASTRONOMY**

second edition

by Martin Ince

**PP**

PETER COLLIN PUBLISHING

Second edition published 2001

First edition published 1997

published by
Peter Collin Publishing Ltd
32-34 Great Peter Street, London, SW1P 2DB

Text    copyright Martin Ince 1997, 2001
Illustrations    copyright Tom Hosking, 1997

British Library Cataloguing in Publication data

A catalogue record for this book is available from the British Library

ISBN 1-901659-72-0

Text computer typeset by PCP
Printed and bound by WS Bookwell, Finland
Cover design by Gary Weston

# Preface

Astronomers are fond of claiming that their science is the oldest of all. Every culture in history has had ideas about the universe, and ancient carvings and other relics from prehistoric societies show that they, too, thought about the lights in the sky long before they wrote down words about them. As well as its inherent fascination, astronomy must have been one of a small number of sciences – like plant and animal breeding – which were vital to our ancestors' survival, because of its importance in predicting tides and providing information on the times for crops to be planted.

The sheer antiquity of astronomical thought is a joy for anyone with an interest in ideas. But it is also a severe problem for anyone trying to produce a comprehensive dictionary of astronomy which will both define the terms used by astronomers and give an idea of their importance. Many thousands of scientists have contributed to our astronomical knowledge, and only the most important can be mentioned here. But astronomy is above all a new science. In recent decades astronomers have acquired the ability to look at the whole range of radiation emitted from the sky, using radio and infrared telescopes on the Earth's surface, and satellites to observe the waves unable to penetrate the Earth's atmosphere. And as the tools available to astronomers have expanded, most spectacularly with the Hubble Space Telescope and the astounding missions to the planets of recent decades, so has the breadth of phenomena they are able to observe and theorise about. If this Dictionary does its job properly, it will transmit not only the content of this new astronomy but some of its excitement and its rapid rate of change.

The aim of this dictionary is to define the terms used by astronomers from their own subject and from other sciences, especially physics, optics, space science and astronautics, and the environmental sciences, in such as way as to make modern developments in astronomy comprehensible and to make clear their importance in the history and texture of the subject.

As well as technical terms, it discusses famous astronomers of the past and present, notable celestial objects such as the planets and satellites of the solar system, the constellations, bright and nearby stars, other bodies in the sky with some claim to fame, the instruments and methods used by astronomers to do their work, and past and future space missions of significance to astronomers. And it goes into the theories and ideas used by astronomers to make sense of the observations they perform.

Modern astronomy is a complex science, although it is still one to which dedicated amateurs make a tangible contribution. If this dictionary succeeds, it will make the complexity less daunting, and replace it with the wonder which is the only proper response to the beauty of the universe which is now known to us. Contemporary astronomy is not a finished subject, but a fast-moving one whose speed is likely to grow rather than diminish. And our current knowledge allows us a much fuller understanding of the universe and our own place in it than has been available to any previous generation.

This book comes with love and thanks to my father, Leslie Ince and my wife, Vicky Hutchings: neither have much interest in astronomy and both have tolerated my fascination for it when plenty of better priorities were being ignored.

*Martin Ince*

# Aa

## A (star classification)
Class of stars with surface temperature of 7500-10000°, and strong spectral lines due to hydrogen. Examples include Sirius, Deneb, Vega and other bright stars. A stars tend to be white or bluish in colour. Apparent in the spectra of A stars are ionised metals like magnesium and calcium

## AAVSO
THE AMERICAN ASSOCIATION OF VARIABLE STAR OBSERVERS
a well-known US body of amateur and professional astronomers

## aberration[1]
The difference between the observed and the calculated position of an astronomical body caused by the time taken for light, or other radiation, to get from it to the observer

## aberration[2]
The imperfect formation of an image by a telescope or other optical instrument. Varieties include chromatic aberration, the differential focussing of light of different wavelengths, spherical aberration, the imperfect focussing of light because of the use of spherical rather than parabolic lens or mirror surfaces, coma, the blurring of off-axis images, astigmatism, the distortion of images because of the irregular curvature of lenses, mirrors or the surface on which the images are formed

## absolute magnitude
The magnitude of a star or other astronomical object, seen from a distance of 10 **Parsecs**. The apparent magnitude of astronomical objects seen from the Earth depends upon their intrinsic brightness and also upon how far they are from us, so that the Moon can outshine everything else in the night sky by being the nearest astronomical object. Comparing astronomical objects as they would appear from a uniform distance removes this effect

## absorption line
A dark line seen in a stellar **spectrum**, caused by radiation passing through a cool medium on its journey to the observer. Absorption lines give information about cool matter such as interstellar gas clouds, planetary atmospheres and stellar atmospheres

## abundance
The relative amount of a particular type of star, galaxy, atom or other

item in an overall population. Elemental abundances, the amounts of different atomic species in meteorites, moonrock etc., yield information about the early history of the solar system. The abundances of different types and ages of stars in the galaxy tell us about the evolution of both stars and galaxies. Stellar abundances are the proportions of different atoms in different types of star, and provide information about their ages and development. In the Sun, every million hydrogen atoms are accompanied by 63,000 atoms of helium, the next most abundant type

## accretion
The accumulation of a number of objects to form a single larger one. Accretion is among the commonest of ways for astronomical objects to form. In particular it seems that the planets, including the Earth, were built up by the accretion of **planetesimals** which formed a cloud around the Sun almost five billion years ago. Most of the planetesimals were swept up in the accretion process, leaving a small number to appear as comets and other small solar system objects

## Achernar
The brightest star in the constellation Eridanus and the tenth brightest in the sky. Distance 118 light years, type B3, apparent magnitude 0.51, absolute magnitude -2.3

## achromatic
Of a lens or mirror, free from chromatic aberration, false colour caused by the different reflection or refraction of light of different wavelengths

## active galactic nucleus (AGN)
Zone in the central region of some galaxies where a mass of up to 100 million times that of the Sun is concentrated, emitting large and variable amounts of radiation. About one per cent of galaxies probably house an AGN. Extreme types include BL Lacertae objects and quasars

## active region
Disturbed area of the Sun which can exhibit sunspots, solar flares, faculae, prominences, and other phenomena associated with intense magnetic fields

## Adams, John Couch (1819-1892)
British astronomer expert in the dynamics of the solar system, now remembered mainly for calculations which should have led to the discovery of Neptune by astronomers in Cambridge, England, in 1846. The discovery was actually made in Berlin on the basis of French calculations

## adaptive optics
Optical systems capable of adjusting to compensate for atmospheric distortion. Adaptive optics were advanced during the 1980s and 1990s because of spending by the US on the Strategic Defense Initiative, which called for methods of firing laser beams accurately through the

atmosphere. Adaptive optics systems use an optical system to determine distortions to incoming starlight and compute the necessary alterations to optical surfaces to render the image as precise as possible. This must be done several thousand times per second. This method is now entering use with big ground-based telescopes such as the **Keck** telescope in Hawaii, from which images matching in quality those from the Hubble Space Telescope have been obtained.

## Adhara
22nd brightest star in the sky, found in Canis Major. Apparent magnitude 1.48, absolute magnitude -5.1, type B2, distance 680 light years

## Advanced Satellite for Cosmology and Astrophysics (ASCA)
Japanese satellite launched in 1993 for X-ray astronomy, especially the examination of spectra of very bright objects in the X-ray sky

## Advanced X-Ray Astronomy Facility (AXAF)
Original name for the NASA space telescope now called **Chandra**

## Aerobee
Type of sounding rocket used from 1957 to 1985 by US researchers for a wide range of astronomical, geophysical and other experiments in the upper atmosphere and on the edge of space

## aeroshell
Outer casing of a planetary landing spacecraft, designed to protect it from frictional heat generated by passage through an atmosphere

## aerosol
A suspension of solid or liquid particles in a gas. Aerosols are encountered in planetary atmospheres, including those of the Earth and Mars

## AGN
*See* ACTIVE GALACTIC NUCLEUS

## airglow
Faint glow in the night sky caused by fluorescence of air molecules in the upper atmosphere. The air at this height glows as the result of interaction with solar radiation, especially when ultraviolet radiation from the Sun forms nitrogen oxides with the emission of visible light. The airglow can exist at 600km or more above the Earth's surface. Although interesting in its own right, the Airglow can also hamper other astronomical observations

## Airy disc
Small disc of light produced by a lens or mirror forming an image of a point source of light such as a star, caused by the diffraction spreading the light out. Called after George Airy (1801-1892), British astronomer and Astronomer Royal

## albedo

The proportion of the light (or other radiation) falling on a surface which is reflected away from it. The higher the albedo of a surface the brighter it seems to outside observers. Albedos are usually expressed as percentages. Among the Earth's near neighbours, albedos run from Mercury's 6% to Venus's 76%, while the Earth's is 36%. Earth and Venus have high albedos because of their cloud-filled atmospheres

## Albireo

Noted triple star in the constellation Cygnus. Seen in telescopes as a spectacular double star

## alcohol

Ethyl alcohol, $C_2H_5OH$, is widely distributed in interstellar space, along with other molecules of abundant elements

## Alcor

Star in Ursa Major with a faint companion, Mizar, which can just be distinguished with the naked eye. Spectra of Mizar show that it in turn is also a double star. The two components of Mizar are a genuine double in orbit around each other while Alcor is not part of the system, but is merely aligned with Mizar in the sky as seen from Earth

## Aldebaran

13th brightest star in the sky and the brightest in the constellation Taurus. Type K5, distance 68 light years, absolute magnitude -0.7, apparent magnitude 0.86. Both are averages since Aldeberan is a variable star

## Alexis

US spacecraft launched in 1992 and initially assumed lost because of damage at launch. Its name stands for Array of Low-Energy X-Ray Imaging Sensors. It later proved possible to use the satellite for part of its mission to map the X-ray sky

## Algol

Noted variable star in the constellation Perseus, also called Beta Persei. Its brightness alters as two stars in orbit around each other cut each other's light off from the Earth, making it an eclipsing binary. Its brightness and the large amplitude of its variability, between magnitudes 2.3 and 3.5, make it a favourite observing target of amateur astronomers

## Alhazan

Arab mathematician and optical scientist of the 10th and 11th centuries AD (about 965-1040), born at Basra in present-day Iraq

## Alinda

Asteroid capable of making close approaches to Earth

## ALMA

The Large Atacama Array, a telescope planned for construction in the desert in Chile by the European Southern Observatory at the time of writing in 2000. It would consist of 64 12-m dishes designed to look at the sky at millimetre wavelengths, between the radio and infrared wavebands. It could be used to observe galaxy and star formation and would be one of the most powerful telescopes ever built.

## Almagest
**Claudius Ptolemy's** great work on astronomy, now known by its Arabic name. Written in the second century AD, it remained the classic text on astronomy until the time of Copernicus, a record unlikely to be matched by modern works. In **'The Sleepwalkers'**, the standard history of cosmological thinking, Arthur Koestler complains that its dominance was caused by the whole science of astronomy being sent up a cul-de-sac for one and a half millennia

## Alpha Centauri
The brightest star in the constellation Centaurus. It consists of three stars, including the faint Proxima Centauri, the nearest star to the Earth after the Sun, and a slightly more distant double star including the G2 type star which accounts for most of the light we receive from the system. The total magnitude of the system is 0.01 and its distance is about 4.3 light years

## Alpha Crucis
21st brightest star in the sky, distance 370 light years, type B0.5, apparent magnitude 1.39, absolute magnitude -3.9

## alpha particle
A nuclear particle consisting of two protons and two neutrons and having a positive electrical charge. An alpha particle is essentially the nucleus of a helium atom, the second most abundant atom in the universe, and alphas are common in nature, especially in cosmic rays and as a product of the radioactive decay of heavier atoms

## Alphonsine Tables
A book of tables of astronomical data, mainly planetary positions, published at Toledo, Spain, in 1273 and used throughout the middle ages in Europe

## Alpine valley
Noted topographical feature on the surface of the Moon

## ALSEP
APOLLO SURFACE LUNAR EXPERIMENT PACKAGE
A nuclear-powered package of scientific experiments left on the Moon by US Apollo astronauts to detect events such as lunar earthquakes and meteorite impacts on the Moon

## Altair
12th brightest star in the sky, and the brightest star in the constellation Aquila. One of the stars of the conspicuous 'summer triangle', along

with Deneb and Vega. Type A7, distance 16.5 light years, absolute
magnitude 2.2, apparent magnitude 0.77

## altazimuth

Type of telescope mounting which has two separate axes of movement,
one for altitude, controlling the angle of the telescope between the
horizon and the zenith, and one for azimuth, the point of the compass to
which it points. On small telescopes the controls can be manual but
some large modern telescopes have altazimuth mountings pointed by
computer

## altitude

In positional astronomy, the height of an object above the horizon
measured in degrees or some other unit of angle. Otherwise, the height
of an object above a surface, as with a satellite above the Earth

## Amalthea

160km-size satellite of Jupiter with a 12-hour orbital period just above
Jupiter's cloud surface

## amino acids

Complex organic chemicals which carry the genetic information used to
reproduce Earthly life forms and which are also found in meteorites

## Amor

Asteroid which has given its name to the Apollo-Amor asteroids, which
can approach the Earth at low velocities relative to the Earth's own.
This group constitutes a small but real collision risk for the Earth, and
has excited interest among visionaries who would like to use them as
raw material to mine for space colonies, since unlike terrestrial raw
materials they would not have to be dragged into space against the pull
of Earth gravity

## amplitude

The total range of variation of a quantity like the height of a wave, the
magnitude of a variable star, or any other measured amount. In
astronomy, amplitude measurements are most often made of light
curves, the graphs which show how the radiation received from stars
and other astronomical objects varies with time

## AMPTE

A joint US/UK/West German science experiment of the 1980s which
was designed to yield data on the Earth's electric and magnetic fields.
Its most spectacular feat was the release of an 'artificial comet' of
barium metal high above the Pacific Ocean

## analemma

The imaginary figure of eight shape traced out in the sky by the Sun at a
given time of day over the course of a year. The Sun is highest at noon
in midsummer and lowest at midwinter. The difference between the
spring and autumn positions of the Sun is caused by the fact that the

Earth's orbit is not circular

## Anaximander
Greek astronomer who lived approx 610-545BC and was one of Pythagoras's teachers. He developed one of the first non-mystical models of an essentially infinite universe, and made one of the first effective sundials

## Andromeda
Constellation of the northern hemisphere best known for containing M31, the Andromeda nebula
*(Genitive is **Andromedae**)*

## Andromeda nebula
Spiral galaxy M31 which is the nearest major galaxy to our own. M31 has played many vital roles in the advance of astronomical knowledge, especially the vital development of the idea that there are observable galaxies beyond ours. It is also the furthest object visible to the naked eye, at a distance of about two million light years

## Anglo-Australian Telescope
Large (3.9m mirror) telescope at Siding Spring in Australia, used for research on the southern sky by British, Australian and other astronomers

## Ångstrom
Unit of measurement used especially for wavelengths of light and equal to one ten billionth of a metre. Not an SI unit, the Ångstrom is falling out of official scientific favour

## angular measure
The angles between objects on the celestial sphere are the basis of all astronomical information, defining where to find objects and how they move in the sky and relate to each other. There are two main systems of angular measure. One uses degrees (360 to a circle), minutes (60 to a degree) and seconds (60 per minute) while the other uses radians, the angle formed by a length equal to the radius of a circle seen at its circumference. About 6.3 radians make a full circle. The Sun or the full Moon are about half a degree across in the sky

## angular momentum
The momentum a body possesses as the result of circular or other angular motion – in astronomy, usually encountered when considering objects in orbit

## angular velocity
The velocity of a body in its orbit, or other angular motion, measured either in distance per unit time (e.g. kilometres per second) or angle per unit time (e.g. degrees per second)

## annular eclipse
An eclipse of the Sun in which the Moon is too far away from the Earth

in its orbit to cover the Sun completely. Instead an annulus or ring of the Sun is left showing, so that the Sun's atmosphere does not become visible. Annular eclipses occur when the Moon is at its farthest from the Earth because of the eccentricity of its orbit

## anomalistic month
*See* MONTH

## anomalistic year
The year as measured by the time the Earth takes to revisit the apses of its orbit, and equal to 365.26 days.
*See* YEAR

## anorthosite
Type of rock widespread in the highlands of the Moon and also found on Earth. Anorthosite is a coarse-grained igneous rock formed at great depth

## ANS
*See* ASTRONOMICAL NETHERLANDS SATELLITE

## Antares
15th brightest star in the sky, in the constellation Scorpius. A variable star with average absolute magnitude -5.1 and average apparent magnitude 0.92. Type M1, 520 light years from Earth

## antenna
The receiving component of a radio device like a radio telescope or a satellite communications system. Possibly the largest single antenna is the huge dish at Arecibo in Puerto Rico. But aperture synthesis methods allow far larger antennae to be simulated than can be physically built

## anthropic principle
The idea that the universe is in its present form to allow life capable of observing it to evolve. The principle is the opposite of the commonsense view that life arises as a result of the structure of the universe. The anthropic principle is controversial because it involves a cause – life – coming after the effect – the universe. Some cosmologists claim that it is wrong, unnecessary or unscientific. Others look at the coincidences which are necessary for intelligent life (like ourselves) to arise and favour the Anthropic Principle

## antigravity
A postulated gravitational force in which mass repels rather than attracts other mass and radiation. Although never observed, antigravity has a role in modern physics and cosmology, where whole 'antigravity universes' are postulated. On a smaller scale, some astronomical objects including Kerr black holes seem able to drive light away from them instead of sucking it in as most black holes must, an example of antigravity in action. Unfortunately these examples provide little assistance to would-be mountaineers who might provide a ready market

for portable antigravity equipment

## antimatter
Matter of the opposite charge (or more rarely magnetic spin or other characteristic) to the equivalent particles making up the bulk of the mass of the present universe. Examples of antimatter include positrons – identical to electrons except for having a positive rather than negative electrical charge – and antiprotons, which are identical to protons except for having a negative rather than positive electrical charge. Little is known about why there is so little antimatter in the universe we see around us, but when matter and antimatter meet they annihilate each other with a release of energy

## anti-tail
Extension of the tail of a comet, pointing towards the Sun rather than away from it like a normal comet tail

## Antlia
Small constellation in the southern hemisphere.
*(Genitive is **Antliae**)*

## Antoniadi, E M
Italian astronomer best known for planetary observations in the early part of the 20th century. He is remembered especially for observations of Mars which undermined the idea of artificial Martian canals. A brilliant observer, he could not see canals and promoted the idea that the supposed canals were optical illusions caused by the observer's tendency, especially if the will was present, to see isolated details as lines and other extended features

## Apennine Mountains
Major mountain range on the Moon

## aperture
The effective light-gathering diameter of a telescope lens or mirror, or other devices used for other wavelengths. The amount of light or other radiation gathered increases with the square of the aperture, in other words with the total area of the light-gathering surface

## aperture synthesis
Process used mainly in radio astronomy whereby signals received by more than one telescope are combined mathematically to give the effect of using a single much larger one. Radio telescopes on separate continents have been used for aperture synthesis to create the effect of a planet-sized telescope, and the Soviet Soyuz space stations have been used as sites for antennae for aperture synthesis beyond the Earth, with one part of the aperture in orbit and the other on the ground. These experiments may be the precursors of astronomical instruments of astronomical size, in which perhaps one element could be on the far side of the Moon to avoid terrestrial radio pollution and the other in

orbit around Pluto, making a telescope effectively billions of miles across.

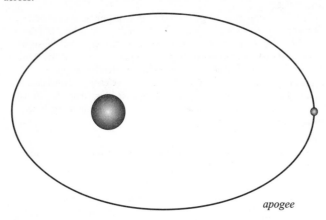

*apogee*

### apogee
The point in a satellite's orbit where it is most distant from the Earth. For orbits around other objects the terms aphelion (for the Sun), apluna (for the Moon) etc are used. *See diagram above.*

### Apollo[1]
Asteroid which has given its name to the Amor-Apollo asteroids, a group which can cross the Earth's orbit. Almost 100 are known although many more must exist. They are related to the Aten group, but Atens have orbits of under a year and Apollos more

### Apollo[2]
US space programme which placed people on the Moon for the first and so far only time, in 1969 and the early 1970s. Apollo and other lunar projects carried out by the US before the manned landings, Surveyor and Lunar Orbiter, led to a huge increase in knowledge of the Moon and the rest of the solar system, but did not lead to increases in the practical use of space technology, one of the main intentions behind Apollo. It now seems to have been a technical cul de sac and future Moon missions will rely little on Apollo technology

### Apollo-Soyuz Test Project
The only joint manned space mission to have involved the United States and the former Soviet Union. Held in 1975, the project involved docking a US Apollo spacecraft with a Soviet Soyuz craft, the two carrying a total of five people. The language problem was solved by having Americans speak only Russian and the Soviets only English

**apparent magnitude**
The brightness of an object in the sky as seen from the Earth, as distinct to absolute magnitude

**appulse**
A close approach of two astronomical objects as seen from the Earth. Their true distances in space may be very large even when they are almost aligned from the point of view of a terrestrial observer

**apse**
The line joining the two foci of an ellipse, such as the orbit of a planet or satellite, and the nearest and farthest points of the ellipse itself. Also known as the line of apsides

**Apus**
Constellation in the Southern hemisphere.
*(Genitive is **Apodis;** means the 'bird of paradise')*

**Aquarius**
Large constellation on the ecliptic and spread across the celestial equator.
*(Genitive is **Aquarii;** means the 'water carrier')*

**Aquila**
Constellation of the northern and southern hemispheres, crossed by the Milky Way and containing the bright star Altair.
*(Genitive is **Aquilae;** means the 'eagle')*

**Ara**
Small constellation of the Southern hemisphere.
*(Genitive is **Arae;** means the 'altar')*

**Arab astronomy**
Astronomy flourished in the Arab world especially between the decline of Rome and about AD 1200, after which the major emphasis of astronomical progress moved to Europe. Now Arab countries are taking a renewed interest in astronomy, with plans for large telescopes and observatories, although the accomplishment of such plans depends upon oil prices and other economic and political issues. As well as making their own astronomical discoveries (usually dismissed by Western writers), the Arab astronomers of the period up to the 12th century were the guardians of the work of Greek and Egyptian scientists like Aristotle, long forgotten in the West. Their own discoveries included work on planetary observations, and transmitting to the West the system of 'Arab' numerals (in fact of Indian origin) including the zero, which is the basis of all modern mathematics

**Arago, Dominique (1786-1853)**
French astronomer best known for research on the Sun (discoverer of the chromosphere) and for planetary observations. Also a member of the French national assembly and a gifted physicist

## archaeoastronomy
The study of ancient astronomy on the basis of writings and sites of astronomical significance. Archaeoastronomy has little contact with the conventional study of the history of astronomy. Instead it concentrates upon the search for astronomical significance in ancient artefacts like solar and other observatories in Europe, China, Latin America, North America and elsewhere. This work yields two main types of benefit – information on ancient cultures, and information on the sky at particular periods in the past, especially the appearance of comets, novae, eclipses and meteor showers in ancient skies

## arch filament
Structure seen in the Sun's atmosphere joining together parts of sunspots. The arches can be much larger than the Earth

## Arcturus
Third brightest star in the sky, and the brightest in the constellation Bootes. Colour orange, type K2, 36 light years from Earth, absolute magnitude 0.3, apparent magnitude -0.06

## Arecibo
Site on Puerto Rico of the world's largest single dish radio telescope, 305m in diameter, made by excavating an existing crater. As well as being powerful enough to warm the upper atmosphere or create an artificial **aurora** when used as a transmitter, it has been used as a detector and transmitter in attempts to communicate with extraterrestrial intelligence

## Argo
A huge former constellation of the southern hemisphere with a supposed resemblance to the ship in which Jason sailed to hunt the golden fleece. Now divided into component parts Carina, Puppis, Pyxis and Vela

## Argyre
Region of the surface of Mars marked by river beds and water channels, all now dry

## Ariane
Rocket launcher developed by the European Space Agency and first launched in 1979. The first launch of the Ariane V launcher, the largest in the series, ended in disaster on June 3 1996 with the destruction of the rocket and the **Cluster** satellites 40 seconds after launch.

## Ariel
700km radius satellite of Uranus, discovered in 1851, and orbiting Uranus in a retrograde 191,000km orbit every 2.52 days. Ariel's surface is cut by deep, wide channels like flood channels on the Earth. Ariel is an icy world with a comparatively uncratered surface

## Aries
Constellation crossed by the ecliptic and in the northern hemisphere.
Brightest star is Hamal
*(Genitive is **Arietis**; means the 'ram')*

## Aristarchus (of Samos)
Greek astronomer born around 310BC who attempted to measure
distances in the solar system and developed the idea of the planets
orbiting the Sun. Aristarchus's idea of the Sun, not the Earth, as the
centre of the universe, was eventually associated with the name of
Copernicus nearly 2000 years later

## Aristotle
Greek philosopher (384-322BC) whose Earth-centred astronomy
dominated the science for 18 centuries. The system set out by Aristotle
eventually collapsed under the weight of its own contradictions, because
it allowed only for uniform circular motions to preserve the perfection
of the heavens. This called for more and more complex models of the
universe, especially the orbits of the Sun, Moon and planets about the
Earth, until in the 16th century AD a system of Sun-centred orbits of
elliptical shape was adopted instead. His work in zoology, notably in
animal classification, was also notable

## Arizona Meteorite Crater
One of the best-known meteorite craters on the Earth's surface, and
outstandingly well-preserved because it is in the desert in the south
western United States. The crater is just over 1km across and seems to
be 20-50,000 years old. Iron meteorites in abundance are found nearby

## armalcolite
Mineral found in moonrock and named after the three astronauts of the
Apollo 11 expedition, Armstrong, Aldrin and Collins

## artificial intelligence
The capacity for creative or original thought in machines. Artificial
intelligence is a major field of computer research and of immense
importance in astronomy and space. It could help make deep space
probes, especially to other stars, practical by giving them the ability to
repair themselves, and could also have a role in space stations and
orbiting observatories of the future

## ASCA
*See* ADVANCED SATELLITE FOR COSMOLOGY AND
ASTROPHYSICS

## asterism
Archaic term for any close grouping of stars

## asteroid
Solar system body intermediate in size between planets and meteorites.
The largest are hundreds of kilometres across and the smallest only

hundreds of metres. When first discovered, asteroids were called 'minor planets' and, because they mostly orbit just inside the orbit of Jupiter, were thought to be material which would have formed a real planet were it not for the gravitation of Jupiter. Now the asteroids are thought to be related to comets and to the 'planetesimals' from which the planets formed, kept in orbits inside that of Jupiter by the effects of Jupiter's gravitation. Some comets have been observed to lose their tails in the inner solar system, at which point they start looking like asteroids. Asteroids are material from the earliest days of the solar system, so that information about them is of immense astronomical value. On the basis of occultation experiments, radar studies and spacecraft flybys, many asteroids seem to travel in pairs orbiting about each other. They are classified in groups on the basis of their albedo. The less reflective asteroids have albedos which seem to resemble those of chondritic meteorites, while the brighter S group seem to have properties like those of silicate rocks on the Earth. There is also a group M with metallic-type albedos. Now the classifications are being expanded as more data is obtained with modern instruments and spectral examination shows more links to meteorites and other objects. Infrared observations from orbit are a particularly powerful tool for this work. In the 1990s our knowledge of the asteroids was expanded by the visit by the Galileo spacecraft to asteroids 243 Ida and 951 Gaspra, en route to Jupiter. (Asteroids are given a number in order of discovery, as well as a name chosen by the discoverer. Number 5,000 was reached in 1989, 1 Ceres having been found on the first day of 1801.)

### asteroid belt
The region between the orbits of Mars and Jupiter where most asteroids are concentrated

### Astro[1]
Astronomy observatory designed to be flown on the Spacelab module carried into space by the US Space Shuttle. It flew first in 1990 and for the second time in 1995, carrying a range of instruments for ultraviolet astronomy

### Astro[2]
Series of Japanese satellites for X-ray astronomy. Astro E was the latest in the series in 2000 but was lost at launch

### astrolabe
An astronomical instrument in use until the Renaissance period, mainly for measuring celestial azimuths

### astrology
The ancient but still popular superstition for attempting to predict the future from celestial portents. Mocked by most (but not all) modern scientists, astrology separated from respectable astronomy in the 17th century as knowledge of the solar system grew, weakening the

argument that the positions of the planets in the sky could affect our fortunes. Astrology is apparently immune to extinction despite scientific advance and the spread of education

## astrometry
Branch of astronomy involving precise measurements of the positions of objects in the sky. Astrometry is done especially with the use of meridian telescopes, which can now record hundreds of observations per night onto computer discs. The **European Space Agency's Hipparcos telescope**, a success despite technical difficulties, was the first to be launched to perform astrometrical observations above the turbulence of the Earth's atmosphere

## Astron
Soviet orbiting telescope observing in ultraviolet wavelengths

## astronaut
Any human traveller in space

## Astronomical Unit
*See* AU

## Astronomical Netherlands Satellite (ANS)
One of the first ultraviolet astronomy satellites, launched in 1974

## astronomy
The study of objects in the heavens and of the Earth as an object in space, including their history and development and that of the universe as a whole. Astronomy is perhaps the most ancient of the sciences, since all known cultures have or have had ideas about the Cosmos. Modern astronomy is related closely to other sciences, especially physics, and has many subdivisions, most notably **cosmology** and **astrophysics**

## astrophysics
The branch of astronomy which examines astronomical phenomena in terms of the laws and principles of physics. One of the most fruitful branches of the science – and a science in its own right – astrophysics is especially powerful in areas like the properties of stars, interstellar gas clouds, and other large-scale objects, and in the study of the areas where modern nuclear and particle physics can be used to interpret astronomical objects, especially phenomena like pulsars and black holes where relativistic effects are important

## Aten
Asteroid which has given its name to a group with orbits of less than a year in duration. The 19th to be discovered, in 1995, had an orbit of only six and a half months, placing its mean position inside the orbit of Venus and far from the main asteroid orbits between Mars and Jupiter. *See* AMOR-APOLLO

## atmosphere
Any gaseous layer surrounding a solid object such as a planet, or a star.

Atmospheres in the solar system include the Earth's, which is the only one to include free oxygen and has been shaped by living matter, as well as that of Venus, which is massively corrosive and acidic, and those of the gas giants, whose atmospheres make up a large percentage of their total volume. The atmosphere of the Sun is highly active and energetic, with strong magnetic fields shaping its component parts. *See diagram below.*

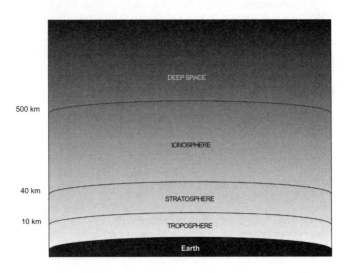

Earth's Atmosphere

### AU
Astronomical Unit, a measure of distance used in solar system studies equal to the average distance of the Earth from the Sun, 149.6 million km

### Auriga
Constellation of the northern hemisphere, covering a large area of sky. Brightest star is **Capella.**
*(Genitive is **Aurigae;** means the 'charioteer')*

### Aurora
Display of lights in the sky, usually best seen in polar areas and called Aurora Borealis in the northern hemisphere and Aurora Australis in the southern. The aurora is caused by the interaction between the solar wind and the upper atmosphere and is especially active when the Sun itself is.

The particles of the solar wind are funnelled into the polar regions by the Earth's magnetic field

## Australia Telescope
Situated in New South Wales, the Australia Telescope is the Southern Hemisphere's largest radio telescope, with six dishes over a 6km area

## australite
Type of **tektite** found in Australia and parts of Asia

## AXAF
*See* CHANDRA

## azimuth
The position of an astronomical object in the horizontal plane, usually measured in degrees clockwise from the north

# Bb

## B (Star classification)
Star type whose members have a surface temperature of
10,000–30,000°. Examples include the bright stars Rigel and Spica. The
hottest of stars apart from the O stars, the B type have neutral helium
rather than the O stars' ionised helium in their spectra

## Baade, Wilhelm (1893-1960)
German astronomer who worked on star types in galaxies, identifying
types **I and II stars**, and on the distances and structures of galaxies

## background radiation
Radiation observed from all directions in the universe and regarded by
astronomers as the fossil remnant of the 'big bang' at the birth of the
cosmos. The radiation is very faint and corresponds to a temperature of
only about 3 above absolute zero, because of the expansion of the
universe which has 'stretched' the radiation and reduced its apparent
temperature. The background radiation is one of the most powerful
pieces of evidence for our present view of the universe. The COBE
satellite and terrestrial observations have shown that it is highly
homogeneous, but contains enough fluctuation to be consistent with the
formation of structure in the universe itself, an elegant confirmation of
our main ideas about cosmology

## Baily's Beads
Points of light seen at the Moon's rim during a total eclipse of the Sun,
caused by sunlight coming through valleys and plains on the Moon's
surface

## balloons
Balloons have been used as platforms for astronomical instruments
since at least 1954, when French astronomers used one to place a
telescope above the bulk of the water vapour in the Earth's atmosphere
to allow the water vapour in the atmosphere of Mars to be observed.
Despite the advent of satellites, balloons continue to be used as a
comparatively cheap and rapid way of getting equipment above the bulk
of the Earth's atmosphere

## Balmer series
Set of spectral lines characterising hydrogen and seen in visible light.
The Balmer series is easily observable in the spectra of the Sun and
other stars and is caused by the movement of electrons to and from the
energy level possible in hydrogen above the normal ground state.

## Bamberga

One of the largest asteroids, some 200km across, and of low albedo

## bandwidth

The frequency spread of a signal in any part of the electromagnetic spectrum, expressed in units such as Hertz, either as observed in nature or as transmitted by a piece of equipment like a cable, an antenna or a length of optical fibre

## bar

Unit of pressure, approximately equal to the pressure of the Earth's atmosphere at sea level

## Barnard's Ring

A large ring of hydrogen-emitting gas some 300 light years across in the Orion region of the sky. Also known as Barnard's Loop, the Ring is in a region of the sky where new stars are forming. Some of the hydrogen not sucked into stars is set aglow by their early radiation

## Barnard's Star

The nearest star to the solar system after the **Alpha Centauri system**, 5.9 light years from the Sun. Barnard's star may have planets and has been proposed as a promising destination for the first interstellar flight from Earth. Barnard's star has the largest proper motion of any star in the sky, about 10 seconds per year. This motion was discovered by the US astronomer E E Barnard (1857-1923), also the discoverer of Barnard's Ring

## barred spiral

Type of spiral **galaxy** in which the spirals stem not from the centre of the galaxy but from a 'bar' of stars and other material. Since the bars in barred spirals can be either structurally dominant in the galaxy or almost invisible, barred and normal spirals seem to shade into each other rather than being two distinct species. Barred spirals are of type SBa, SBb or SBc according to the tightness of the spirals, 'a' being the tightest

## Barringer crater

Alternative name for the **Arizona Meteor Crater**, identified as a meteorite impact crater in 1905 by D M Barringer

## basalt

The commonest volcanic rock on Earth, also widespread on the Moon, Mars and Venus

## baseline

In interferometry, the distance between the farthest-separated points at which data is collected

## BATSE

The Burst and Transient Source Experiment, an instrument on the **Compton satellite** used to gather data on **Gamma Ray Bursters**

### BD
German star catalogue, the Bonner Durchmusterung, compiled in the mid-19th century and listing over 300,000 stars down to 2° south of the equator, later extended to 23° south

### Bellatrix
The 24th brightest star in the sky and the third brightest in Orion. Apparent magnitude 1.64, absolute magnitude -4.2, type B2, distance 470 light years

### BeppoSax
US-Italian space mission launched in 1996 to study **gamma-ray bursters**, named after Giuseppe "Beppo" Occhialini (1907-1993), one of the founders of gamma ray science. Sax was the name of its principal instrument.

### Bernal sphere
Hypothetical structure which might be manufactured around a star by an advanced civilisation capable of dismembering planets and redistributing their material in a sphere to catch all the star's radiation. A Bernal sphere would in principle be observable only by infrared radiation leaking away from it

### Bessel, Friedrich (1784-1864)
German astronomer who carried out work on star positions and movements. In 1834 he predicted that Sirius was a double star, and in 1838 discovered the first stellar **parallax**, of 61 Cygni

### BETA
The Billion-Channel Extraterrestrial Assay, a US project using a radio telescope in Massachusetts to search the sky for signals from extraterrestrial life.
*See* SETI; META

### Beta Crucis
19th brightest star in the sky, variable but with average apparent magnitude of 1.28 and absolute magnitude -4.6. Spectral type B0, distance 490 light years

### beta particle
An electron given off in radioactive decay or otherwise found outside an atom. Beta particles are among the commonest components of cosmic radiation

### Betelgeuse
The 9th brightest star in the sky and the brightest in the constellation Orion. A variable star with an average apparent magnitude of 0.41 and absolute magnitude of -5.6, Betelgeuse is a red giant of spectral type M2, and looks distinctly reddish-orange to the naked eye. Despite its distance of 520 light years it is one of the most distinctive stars in the sky

## big bang

The event which according to most modern cosmogony began the universe we now know, perhaps some 18 billion years ago. At that time, it seems, the whole of the matter now distributed throughout the universe was in a single compact mass whose properties can only be described in relativistic equations. Since then it has formed into galaxies, stars, planets and everything else we see, expanding constantly. From the point of view of the cosmologists, all these are details, and the basic shape of the universe in terms of the energy and matter it now contains was established in the big bang itself. It would be wrong to think of a small volume at the centre of the universe containing the whole of the mass we now see around us. Instead, the cosmos takes space with it as it expands. The problem of just what the initial fireball of material did before, during and immediately after the big bang is an elaborate one, touching on the nature of the subatomic particles and atomic forces now acting in the universe. However, there is powerful experimental proof that the big bang was a real event. The cosmic background radiation, which is made up of the heat left over from the big bang, is one proof, and its very homogeneous nature, allied to the shape of its spectrum, makes any other explanation of it implausible. In addition, the abundance of helium in the universe, making up about 23 per cent of its mass, with hydrogen making up almost all of the rest, is accounted for by the conditions of the big bang. The age of the universe is derived from measures of the **expansion** of the universe, which is determined by the measurement of galactic **redshifts**. These are now being revised because of the availability of data from the **Hubble Space Telescope** and there have been some indications of a much younger universe than had been thought

## big crunch

The possible end of our universe. If the universe is dense enough, it will eventually finish expanding and contract again under its own mass, eventually collapsing back into a single small volume in a reverse action replay of the big bang. This is the big crunch. The idea has gained credence in recent years with the growth of the idea that there is a large amount of 'missing mass,' material too dark to be observed, within the universe. If it is present in the amounts which now seem possible, the big crunch (during which there would be bizarre reversals of some of our present laws of physics) becomes more likely

## Big Dipper

The North American term for the prominent group of stars in Ursa Major known in the UK as the Plough and containing the Pointers, which allow the Pole Star to be found, as well as Alcor and Mizar, the noted double star

## binary star

A star system with two members. Most stars are doubles, and the different types include eclipsing, spectroscopic, visual and astrometric binaries according to the methods needed to separate them observationally

## bioshield

Protective cover used to keep terrestrial life forms, down to microbe size, from leaving the Earth on planetary landing spacecraft, for fear of biological effects if they get loose on another planet. Bioshields were used with the US Viking missions to Mars

## bipolar nebula

Nebula in Cygnus with bipolar appearance caused by heavy dust concentration, apparently a symptom of star formation

## BL Lacertae object

Type of quasar characterised by rapid fluctuation in brightness, also called Lacertid. Their light exhibits a very flat and featureless spectrum, is heavily polarised, and is accompanied by radio emissions.
*See also* BLAZAR

## black body

Any body which follows perfectly the physical laws on how matter should emit and absorb radiation. Black body radiation is almost never seen in practice but astronomers come closer than laboratory scientists to observing it, since the spectra of most stars correspond more closely than most artificial radiation. The hotter a body, the shorter the wavelength of the radiation it emits at its peak under the black body theory. Whatever the temperature, the shape of the curve showing how much radiation is emitted at varying frequencies has a steep limb towards shorter wavelengths and a shallower one to longer wavelengths. An electric fire, or Betelgeuse, emits its peak radiation in red light, while the Sun, which is hotter, has its peak in yellow light, while even hotter objects peak in ultraviolet light and beyond into X-rays, and cooler ones are at their brightest in infrared light

## black dwarf

The postulated final, dark form of a white dwarf star, reached when all its heat has been radiated away. The black dwarf stage would take so long to reach that, even if the theory is correct, none may yet exist anywhere in the Universe. But since every star weighing less than 1.4 times the Sun's mass is set to become one, there are going to be billions of them at some future point in the universe's development, unless they are all swept up by the contraction of an oscillatory universe. A black dwarf would contain no nuclear or other activity recognisable by outsiders and would be detectable mainly by its gravitation

## black hole

The zone from which no radiation can normally escape, formed in the collapse of a star of just over two solar masses or more. The theoretical description of a black hole, where time slows to a halt and other bizarre physical effects occur, was drawn up in 1916, and since then further complications (like the addition of rotation and electrical charge) have been added, as well as observational knowledge of objects like the Crab Nebula which seem to contain black holes. The cores of galaxies such as our own seem to contain massive black holes of millions of solar masses, which can be detected by measuring the orbital motion of stars near the centre of the galaxy. Their velocities betray the presence of an anomalously large mass at the core of the galaxy

## Blazar
*See* BL LACERTAE OBJECT

## Blue Book
Code name for a US Air Force investigation of the 1960s into the alleged phenomenon of unidentified flying objects (UFOs)

## Blue Haze
An obscuration seen in the atmosphere of Mars: sometimes disappears in an effect called the Blue Clearing Phenomenon

## blue sheet
Light captured by a black hole and collected at its event horizon. Such light must be highly blue-shifted, whence the name

## blueshift
Reduction in the wavelength of radiation caused by the observer and source approaching each other. This manifestation of the **Doppler effect** is seen far less often than the redshift in astronomy, since the latter is widely caused by the expansion of the universe. Blue and red shifts are used together in astronomy for measuring rotations of planets and stars, since the blueshift is observed at the limb approaching the observer and the redshift at the limb receding from it

## blue straggler
Member of a class of stars seen in globular clusters which are so massive that they should have become red giants, were they evolving normally, but have not, instead remaining blue. The cause may be that they have received a large, recent mass transfer from a companion star instead of evolving normally

## Bode's Law
Mathematical equation relating the distances between the distances of the planets from the Sun. More formally known as the Titius-Bode Law since Titius of Wittemberg published it in 1766 and Bode in Berlin made it widely known in 1782. Take the series 0, 3, 6...:add 4 to each number: divide by 10. In the Law this gives planetary distances in AU – 0.4 for Mercury, 0.7 for Venus, 1.0 for the Earth. Bode's Law breaks down later on and predicts a complete planet where there are only the asteroids. It is now regarded only as a fascinating coincidence

## Bok Globule
Globule of gas and dust undergoing the process of gravitational collapse en route to becoming a star. They were predicted by Bart Bok in 1947 and have since been observed

## Boltzmann Distribution
Law linking the temperature of a material such as a gas cloud with the number of molecules within it at different possible energy levels via Boltzmann's equation and Boltzmann's constant.

## bolide
Obsolete term for a large meteor, especially one giving rise to a meteorite fall

## Bondi, Hermann (born 1919)
British astronomer (born in Austria) who developed the steady state theory with **Gold** and **Hoyle** and has been active in science policy involving European space developments, including the foundation of the **European Space Agency**.

## bonding
The linking of atoms by bonds of electrons which gives rise to chemical compounds. Chemical bonds cannot exist at high temperatures, so that they are common in planets and other comparatively cool parts of the universe, including interstellar space, but only in the coolest stars, where chemical bonds produce distinctive spectra, especially in the infrared

## Boomerang
BALLOON OBSERVATIONS OF MILLIMETRIC EXTRAGALACTIC RADIATION AND GEOMAGNETICS
an Italian-led experiment with two balloon-borne telescope in 2000 designed to demonstrate the existence of the **inflation** period in the early universe and to test whether it is **flat** in the current era. It worked by examining the **Cosmic Background Radiation** for minute fluctuations in intensity.

## Bootes
Large constellation of the Northern hemisphere which contains the bright orange star Arcturus, and the radiant of the Quadrantid meteor shower.
*(Genitive is **Bootis**: name of a legendary herdsman)*

## bow shock
The front formed where the solar wind encounters the electromagnetic environment of another planet such as the Earth. The Earth's bow shock, the barrier between the Sun's influence and the Earth's, is at a distance of some eight Earth diameters from the Earth, whereas at the Moon the solar wind strikes the surface directly. Mars, Venus and Mercury are intermediate cases, since they have more magnetism than the Moon but less than the Earth, so that their bow shock is less than a

planetary diameter from the surface of the planet

## Brahe, Tycho de (1546-1601)

Danish astronomer whose observations allowed **Kepler** to discover his laws of planetary motion. An objectionable autocrat who kept his debtors in chains, maintained a pet dwarf and wore a metal nose – having lost the original in a duel – Tycho realised the importance of detailed positional astronomy, especially painstaking observations of the positions of the planets in the sky, without which the structure of the solar system could not be elucidated. He also supported his own model of the universe, with Mercury and Venus orbiting the Sun and the Sun and the other planets orbiting the Earth, and rationed Kepler's access to his data to try to gain his support for this model. Tycho was the last great observational astronomer of the pre-telescopic era, working on comets, which he proved to be at astronomical distances rather than in the atmosphere, and observing the supernova of 1572 in Cassiopeia as well as the Moon, about whose orbital motion he made significant discoveries

## Brans-Dicke Theory

A theory which attempts to explain effects (like the bending of light in gravitational fields) which are normally regarded as relativistic without reference to relativity. Proposed in the late 1960s by scientists at Princeton University, it essentially relies upon new notions about gravitation, with a varying gravitational constant, to explain effects usually ascribed to relativity. If true, the theory involves a steady decrease in gravitation as the universe has expanded **(Nortvedt effect)**

## breccia

Rock formed of fragments of an older rock type, sometimes produced under extreme force, for example in meteorite impacts and some very violent volcanic eruptions, and in other cases on Earth by gentler deposition of eroded fragments

## Bremsstrahlung

Radiation given out by fast-moving electrons or other particles encountering electromagnetic fields, observed especially in radio astronomy. Bremsstrahlung energy is released because of severe deceleration of electrons in a magnetic field and is observable in cosmic radiation

## Brown Dwarf

Object intermediate in mass between a star and a planet, giving out some radiation but not massive enough to allow full-scale **fusion**. Thought to be common in areas of star formation, they have proved elusive to observe but one, Gliese 229b, was definitively seen in 1995, 19 light years from Earth in the constellation Lepus. Other candidates for Brown Dwarf status have since been claimed.

## Bruno, Giordano

German philosopher and scientist burned at the stake in 1600 after a
confrontation with the Church of Rome over many theological issues,
including – but not centrally – the issue of whether the Earth is at the
centre of the Universe. He also taught that life is widespread in the
universe and held many other beliefs outwith those of the Church

## Bunsen, Robert (1811-1899)

German scientist who first identified chemical elements in the Sun from
its spectrum, in collaboration with **Kirchoff** – as well as inventing the
bunsen burner seen in all science laboratories. Their discovery consisted
of realising that the lines observed by Fraunhofer in the spectrum of the
Sun match others seen in the spectrum of gasses in the laboratory

## Burster

*See* X-RAY BURSTER

## bursters

Sources of intense blasts of celestial X-rays, also called X-ray bursters
and identified especially with multiple star systems. Bursts of X-rays
can be produced by effects such as the build-up of masses of gas on the
surface of a small star like a **neutron star** or in a **globular cluster**,
from which energy is released in a sudden pulse

## butterfly diagram

Chart of the latitude of **sunspots** against time. As the years pass through
different **sunspot** cycles it is seen that sunspots tend to start the cycle
near the poles and then appear in larger numbers nearer the Sun's
equator as the cycle proceeds. The diagram produced looks like a series
of pairs of butterfly wings. The spots tend to start at 30-40 latitude and
finish at about 5°. Spots in polar regions or at the equator are
comparatively rare. The first butterfly diagrams were drawn by E W
Maunder of the Royal Greenwich Observatory in England

## B-V

*See* COLOUR INDEX

# Cc

## 3C
*See* CAMBRIDGE THIRD CATALOGUE

## Caelum
Small constellation of the Southern hemisphere.
*(Genitive is **Caeli;** means the 'chisel')*

## calcium lines
Lines in the **spectra** of the Sun and other stars caused by the presence
of the metal calcium. There are many calcium lines of which two, H and
K, are the most conspicuous

## caldera
Crater formed by a volcanic explosion. Calderas are well-known from
terrestrial volcanic regions and have also been observed on the surface
of Mars

## calendar
Any device for keeping track of the passage of dates. Most calendars
are astronomical in basis, depending on the Sun and Moon. But they all
suffer from the problem that the day, month and year are slightly
variable and do not represent simple fractions or multiples of each
other. Much ingenuity has been exercised on this problem over many
millennia, giving rise, for example, to the Gregorian calendar now in
use in most of the world, which adds a leap day when the year number
is divisible by four, except in a century year, which has a leap day only
if divisible by 400. This system is accurate to one day in over 3000
years. Increased accuracy in measurement brings new complications.
Time is now measured by atomic clocks, which are more regular than
the Earth's rotation, which is gradually slowing. This necessitates the
insertion of 'leap seconds'.

## caliche
Salt deposit formed in deserts by percolating ground water, thought to
have been observed on the surface of Mars as well as on Earth

## Callisto
2410km radius satellite of Jupiter discovered by Galileo in 1610. A
favourite target for observation by amateur astronomers, it has been
viewed spectacularly by space probes in its 1.9 million km radius orbit.
Callisto has a low average density of 1.8 gm/cc and is thought to consist
of ice (and possibly water below the surface) surrounding a rocky core.
The surface of Callisto, the largest of the Galilean satellites, is marked

with bright impact craters, of which Valhalla is the most conspicuous

## Calypso
Tiny satellite of Saturn discovered by terrestrial telescope observation in 1980, sharing the same orbit as the larger satellite Tethys and Telesto, another small satellite

## Camelopardus
Large rambling constellation near the Northern celestial pole, distinguished by its lack of bright stars, its most impressive being of the 4th magnitude.
*(Genitive is **Camelopardi;** means the 'camel'; also known as **Camelopardalis**)*

## Cambridge Third Catalogue (3C)
Best-known catalogue of celestial objects at radio frequencies. Its designations begin with 3C, like 3C 273, the most notorious of the quasars

## camera
A device for producing photographic images. Most optical telescopes are used with a camera of some kind and many, like Schmidt telescopes, are cameras only. Photographic methods completely altered astronomy in the 19th and early 20th centuries, mainly because photographic exposures can be collected over many hours while the eye can only collect images over a very short period, allowing far more detail to be obtained. Film also provides a permanent record. The world of astronomical recording is now being revolutionised again by the move to digital data recording on tape and discs, and by **charge-coupled devices** (CCDs), which allows computer processing of data as received Cameras used in astronomy are at the edge of the technology, sharing with espionage the fastest films, the longest exposures and demands for information to be gathered in infrared as well as visible wavelengths

## Canada-France-Hawaii Telescope
3.6m telescope in Hawaii, completed in 1979

## canal
The canals of Mars were first described (as Canali, channels, originally without implying artificiality) by Giovanni Schiaparelli in 1877. They later became a cause celebre because they were taken up, mainly by US astronomer Percival Lowell, as a sign of life – and indeed large-scale civil engineering – on the surface of Mars. It turns out that they are optical illusions based on the tendency of the eye to make order out of random blotchy patterns like those seen on the surface of Mars. The laws of optics dictate that the canals as drawn by their supporters like Lowell were beyond the resolving power of the telescopes used

## Cancer
Constellation on the ecliptic in the northern hemisphere.
*(Genitive is **Cancri;** means the 'crab')*

## Canes Venatici
Small constellation of the northern hemisphere, containing few bright stars.
*(Genitive is **Canum Venaticorum:** means the 'Hunting Dogs')*

## Canis Major
Constellation of the southern hemisphere which contains Sirius, Alpha Canis Majoris, the brightest star in the night sky, as well as a portion of the Milky Way.
*(Genitive is **Canis Majoris;** means the 'greater dog')*

## Canis Minor
By contrast to Canis Major, the smaller dog. Small constellation near Canis Major and just inside the northern celestial hemisphere. Contains the bright star Procyon, Alpha Canis Minoris

## Canopus
Second brightest star in the night sky and the brightest in the constellation Carina. Apparent magnitude -0.72, absolute magnitude -3.1, type F0, distance 98 light years

## Capella
The 6th brightest star in the sky and the brightest in Auriga. Apparent magnitude 0.05, absolute magnitude -0.6, type G8, distance 45 light years

## Capricornus
Constellation on the ecliptic in the southern hemisphere.
*(Genitive is **Capricorni;** means the 'goat')*

## captured rotation
Dynamic condition whereby a body such as a satellite orbits another and rotates on its own axis in the same period, like the Moon in its orbit around the Earth. This means that (apart from areas visible because the Moon's orbit is not exactly circular) we only see one side of the Moon from the Earth. Space probes have shown that captured rotation is common in the solar system, and there are also less simple cases like that of Mercury, which turns on its axis three times in two Mercurian years

## capture theory
The now unfashionable notion that the Moon was formed separately from the Earth and 'captured' by its gravitation later. This capture seems difficult to justify mathematically and has been replaced by the idea of the Moon and Earth forming in something like their present combination, but with the Moon far closer to the Earth

## carbon
One of the commonest elements in the universe, carbon is found in stars, meteorites and planets as well as interstellar material. It is of special interest to us because its unusual chemistry, which allows it to

form very large complex molecules, is the basis of all Earthly biology

## carbonaceous chrondite
A rare class of meteorites containing carbon as well as chrondules, small round inclusions. Thought to be remnants of the primitive matter from which the solar system evolved, carbonaceous chrondites can contain up to 5 per cent of organic material

## carbon cycle
Process occurring in the cores of hot stars whereby hydrogen is fused into helium via carbon – and not to be confused with the terrestrial carbon cycle found in ecology. In the astrophysical version, a hydrogen nucleus fuses with one of carbon as the start of a complex process whereby nitrogen and oxygen nuclei are also produced en route. The final products are a helium nucleus and a carbon nucleus, so that the carbon is a catalyst in the reaction and is left over for recycling in another fusion

## carbon dioxide
Gas found in the atmospheres of the Earth, Venus and Mars. On Earth it is produced mainly by volcanoes and was the atmosphere's dominant active component (nitrogen, the main component of the atmosphere, is very inert chemically) until photosynthesis began and oxygen was produced

## carbon-nitrogen cycle
Same as the **carbon cycle** – also known as the CNO (Carbon-nitrogen-oxygen) cycle

## Carina
Constellation of the southern hemisphere which includes **Canopus**, the second brightest star in the sky. It is one of the constellations formed by the administrative division of the large and abandoned constellation **Argo Navis**, the ship Argo
*(Genitive is **Carinae**; means the 'ship's keel')*

## Carina arm
One of the spiral arms of our galaxy, seen at its best in the constellation Carina

## Carina nebula
A prominent nebula in Carina which in optical wavelengths is seen mainly as glowing gas. Orbiting X-ray observatories allow the bright young stars forming from the nebula to be seen, since the glow they produce in the surrounding nebula is mostly in visible wavelengths

## cartwheel galaxy
Peculiar galaxy which seems to have been produced by a collision between two spiral galaxies

## Cassegrain
Type of telescope which uses a small 'secondary' mirror to return light

reflected from the main 'primary' mirror back through a hole in the primary, where the image is formed. Large modern telescopes often use the Cassegrain principle, as do some pricier telephoto lenses. In both cases the fact of being able to make the instrument shorter for a given focal length is a useful feature of the Cassegrain

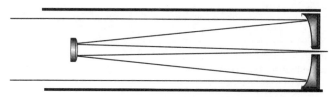

*Cassegrain telescope*

## Cassiopeia
Possibly the most distinctive constellation in the sky, Cassiopeia (called after a Queen of Greek mythology) is found near the north celestial pole and has a readily recognisable W shape. It is also crossed by the Milky Way and contains a wealth of interesting objects.
*(Genitive is **Cassiopeiae**)*

## Casimir
Proposed ESA mission designed to prove the nature of "empty" space, which according to **quantum theory** proposed by Danish physicist Hendrik Casimir is filled with short-lived particles. In space the minute forces generated by these particles would be far easier to measure than at the Earth's surface.

## Cassini, Jean-Dominique (1625-1712: baptised Giovanni Domenico)
Italian astronomer who lived in Paris, becoming a naturalised Frenchman, and made some of the earliest systematic telescopic examinations of the planets, especially the surface markings of Mars and Jupiter

## Cassini's Division
Discovered by **J-D Cassini**, Cassini's Division is the most significant gap in the rings of Saturn. Cassini's division is swept clear of material because anything there has about half the orbital period of the satellite Mimas, whose gravitational pull moves the object out of the gap

## Cassini
NASA/ESA mission to Saturn and its moons, especially Titan. Launched in 1997 it is due to arrive at Saturn in 2004 and will carry out experiments there including the release of the Huygens probe into the atmosphere of Titan.

## Castor
Fainter of the two bright stars of the constellation Gemini, the twins, the other being Pollux. Formally called Alpha Geminorum, despite the custom that Alpha is usually the brightest star in a constellation, Castor in fact consists of six stars. A telescope resolves three stars, Castor A, B and C, and spectroscopic examination shows that each in turn is double

## catalyst
Chemical term for an element or compound which speeds a reaction but is itself left unaltered when the process is complete. Catalysis is encountered – for example – in reactions in planetary atmospheres and in nucleosynthesis in stars, as in the carbon cycle

## catastrophe theory
Theory of planetary formation involving collision or near-collision between the Sun and another passing star. Such catastrophe theories now have few adherents. They should not be confused with a different catastrophe theory, related to concepts of chaos and non-linearity, which explains sudden events in geometrical terms

## causality
The traditional sequence of logic in which causes precede their effects. Causality seems obviously 'true' in the commonsense universe which we observe, but has limitations when applied to the whole of the cosmos. It is inherent in relativity that effects can sometimes precede their causes, in alternative universes and sometimes in our own. In addition, the Anthropic Principle involves reversing normal causality and has support from some scientists

## CCD
*See* CHARGE-COUPLED DEVICE

## celestial equator
The line running around the **celestial sphere** where it is cut by the outward extension of the plane of the Earth's equator, dividing the sky in two, symmetrically around the celestial poles

## celestial mechanics
The branch of astronomy which applies the laws of mechanics, especially the applied mathematics of motion, to celestial objects

## celestial pole
The points about which the celestial sphere appears to rotate, which are in the zenith for observers at the Earth's poles and are at an angle above the horizon equal to an observer's own latitude anywhere else on Earth. No bright star is very near the south celestial pole but the north celestial pole has the star **Polaris** nearby, a boon to nighttime travellers in the northern hemisphere

## celestial sphere
The sphere which seems to surround the Earth, and upon which

astronomical objects are seen. The night sky is in fact infinitely deep, but the celestial sphere is a powerful optical illusion of immense use. Treating it like the sphere of the Earth itself allows us to imagine lines of **right ascension** and **declination** upon it, analogous to longitude and latitude on the Earth, so that the positions of objects can be described

## cell

The mechanical housing used to hold a telescope mirror or lens. For cells in a different astronomical sense
*see* CONVECTION

## Celsius

Temperature scale (also called Centigrade) with 0°C at the freezing point of pure water and 100°C at its boiling point at standard atmospheric pressure at sea level on the Earth

## Centaur
*See* CHIRON

## Centaurus

Constellation of the southern hemisphere, best-known for including the **Alpha Centauri** star system, the solar system's nearest celestial neighbour.
*(Genitive is **Centauri;** means the 'Centaur')*

## Centaurus A

Unusual galaxy, probably formed by the collision of an elliptical and a spiral galaxy, and observed in both optical and radio wavelengths. It exhibits violent explosive activity and is expanding rapidly. The explosions have thrown off dust and gas in huge amounts, which are expanding apace around the galaxy itself

## centre of curvature

The point at the centre of the sphere formed by the surface of a mirror. Parallel light rays are brought to a focus at a distance of half the radius of curvature with a concave lens, and diverge away from a point half a radius behind a convex one

## centre of mass

The point at which the mass of a complex object appears to lie. For a simple object like the Earth the centre of mass is near its geometrical centre, but for a system like a multiple star the centre of mass is in constant motion and could lie in deep space rather than inside a particular object. Knowing the centre of mass of a system allows outside observers to simplify their calculations by pretending that a complex object is a point mass

## Cepheid Variable

Variable star type which in the early 20th century was used to determine the size of the universe, especially the distance of other galaxies from our own. Cepheids exhibit a constant relationship between their period of variation and their absolute magnitude. So finding them in other galaxies and observing their apparent magnitude and their period of variation allows their distances to be calculated. This method allowed the size of our own galaxy to be found as well as the distance to other nearby galaxies including the **Magellanic Clouds**. Fortunately Cepheids are inherently bright enough to be seen in other galaxies at a distance at which other types of star would not be discernible. Delta Cephei is the Cepheid from which the others take the name

## Cepheus
Constellation near the north celestial pole.
*(Genitive is **Cephei**. A proper name from mythology)*

## Cerenkov Radiation
Radiation, usually in visible wavelengths, produced when atomic particles at high speed meet a medium where the velocity of light is lower than their own velocity upon arrival. Nothing can travel through matter at more than the velocity of light, so the particles are forced to slow down, giving off energy in the process. The blue glow seen in pools in which nuclear reactions are occurring is Cerenkov radiation, which is practical evidence for relativity

## Ceres
The first asteroid to be discovered, and with a diameter of some 500km much the largest. Ceres was discovered by the monk **Giuseppe Piazzi** on New Year's Day 1801, as part of a search for the planet implied by Bode's Law: except that Bode had allowed for one planet, not the several thousand asteroids now known

## CETI
Communications with Extra-terrestrial Intelligence, usually meant to mean electromagnetic communications. CETI has been an empirical reality since 1960, when the first search for interstellar radio messages was made. In 1974, the **Arecibo** radio telescope was used to send the first message deliberately intended for alien intelligences. In addition, a US Voyager spacecraft leaving the solar system has been equipped with messages for any finders. But the most pervasive message humans are sending out from the Earth is a barrage of 'leaking' radio and TV broadcasts which, since they have been transmitted for several decades, are now tens of light years out. For more considered conversation, two large radio telescopes of the type used by earthly radio astronomers should suffice for conversations across much of a normal-sized galaxy like our own.
*See* SETI

## Cetus
Extremely large constellation – appropriately enough meaning the Whale – straddling the celestial equator.
*(Genitive is **Ceti**)*

## CFH
*See* CANADA-FRANCE-HAWAII TELESCOPE

## Chaldean astronomy
The astronomy of ancient Babylon, now remembered especially for its
accurate calendars and planetary observations. Although their universe
was a flat Earth in an outer sea, enclosed by a solid outer layer which
sometimes leaked, yielding rain, the Babylonians' observations were
astoundingly accurate and supported an astronomy which was an exact,
predictive science

## Chameleon
Small constellation near the south celestial pole.
*(Genitive is **Chameleontis**)*

## Chandra
NASA satellite for X-ray astronomy launched in 1999. Designed to
observe hot objects in the universe such as supernova remnants, it has
been placed in a high orbit which takes it over 100,000km from the
Earth at its most distant, to keep it away from the charged particle belts
around the Earth. Initially named the Advanced X-Ray Astronomy
Facility, it is now called after Subrahmanyan Chandrasekhar (*see next
entry*).

## Chandrasekhar Limit
The maximum size of a star above which it will not become a white
dwarf: about 1.4 solar masses. Below this mass, a dead star can be
supported by the force preventing more than one electron from
occupying the same position with the same amount of energy. Above
1.4 solar masses this force is overcome by gravitation and dead stars
can ultimately turn into black holes or neutron stars. Named for Indian
physicist Subrahmanyan Chandrasekhar (1910-1995) who worked
mainly in Chicago and worked on problems of stellar evolution

## chaotic terrain
Martian regions of irregular topography, possibly formed by the action
of large amounts of now-vanished water

## charge-coupled device (CCD)
Electronic device used in astronomy because it can register in digital
form the arrival of every photon striking it. CCDs can be used with
visible and ultraviolet light, whose photons cause charge to build up on
the CCD according to the amounts of radiation falling upon each small
area (pixel) of its surface

## Charon
Satellite of Pluto discovered in 1978. Its six-day, 17,000km orbit around
Pluto means that it was at first observed as a 'blob' distending images
of Pluto itself. Charon is about 800-1,000km across, which at about a
third the size of Pluto makes it much the biggest satellite in the solar

system relative to the planet it orbits. It has been shown to have a thin atmosphere

## chassignite
One of the three types of meteorite of Martian origin found on the Earth *See* SNC

## Chicxulub
Site in the Yucatan peninsula, Mexico, near the centre of an impact crater some hundreds of kilometres in diameter. The crater may be the remnant of an impact which 65 million years ago caused vast climatic change and thus triggered the end of many species including the dinosaurs

## Chinese astronomy
Chinese astronomers have been active for millennia, with their own constellations ('mansions') and star names, and their own careful observations – for example of comets and of the supernova of AD 1054 – which are still of use. The Purple Mountain Observatory, where the 1054 supernova was recorded, is probably the oldest observatory still active in the world. About AD 250 the Chinese astronomer Ch'i Meng was one of the first to propose a theory of the universe involving immense volumes of empty space, in contrast to the cramped, music-box universes of European culture

## Chiron
300km radius asteroid orbiting between 8.5 and 18.9AU from the Sun, from just within the orbit of Saturn to that of Uranus. This orbit is considered unstable and Chiron's future may involve either collision with a planet or gravitational ejection from the solar system. Asteroid 2060 in official nomenclature, Chiron is an escaped member of the **Kuiper belt** and is one of a group of six known 'Centaurs', small bodies beyond Saturn, which must be representatives of a far larger population. Despite its designation, Chiron is in fact a massive comet nucleus about 150km across, not an asteroid, and displays a coma

## chondrite
Meteorites containing chondrules, small grains, are called chrondrites and account for about 80% of all meteorites. They appear to consist of virtually unaltered material from the early days of the solar system, unlike the metallic meteorites or the achondritic stony ones, which have undergone later heating and other processes. About 2 per cent of meteorites are "carbonaceous chondrites," which seem to be unaltered material from the formation of the solar system, including volatile organic chemicals as well as water and interstellar dust.

## chromatic aberration
Spurious colouring of images by a lens. It is extremely difficult to produce optical components which treat each colour of light identically. Instead, light of different wavelengths is refracted differently, producing

a set of slightly separate images. Carefully designed systems, for
example using 'achromatic' lenses with elements made from different
types of glass, can cut the problem almost to zero

### chromosphere
Zone of the Sun's atmosphere visible at eclipses and with temperatures
varying from 4,500°C to over 1,000,000°C. The high temperatures
mean that its **spectrum** contains lines of highly ionised atoms unknown
on the Earth. The chromosphere has a depth of a few thousand
kilometres and is filled with rushing energy from the Sun's surface
below. This is expressed in sound waves and by other mechanisms. The
chromosphere has an emission spectrum consisting of bright lines on a
dark background

### chromospheric network
Pattern seen when the chromosphere is examined in visible light with
appropriate filters, and caused by magnetic fields and convection
patterns. Especially well seen in light matching calcium lines in the
spectrum

### Chryse
Plains area on the surface of Mars used for the touchdown of the **Viking
1 Lander** in 1976

### Circinus
Constellation near the south celestial pole.
*(Genitive is **Circini**; means the 'compass')*

### Circinus X-1
Prominent X-ray source in Circinus, apparently consisting of a black
hole and a normal star in orbit around each other, emitting X-rays as the
star's material is sucked into the black hole,

### circular light orbit
A possible orbit around a black hole in which light, instead of being
sucked into the hole, is trapped in a closed path around it. Such light
orbits are highly unstable, and energy in them, which forms a sphere
around the hole, is likely to be ejected from the system or sucked into
the hole

### circumpolar
Term for the part of the sky always above the horizon from the point of
view of an observer at a particular point on the Earth's surface. The area
of the sky from the pole down to the observer's own latitude is
circumpolar, never going below the horizon. At the equator there is no
circumpolar sky, while the poles have pure circumpolar sky, with the
same hemisphere of stars running round the sky parallel to the horizon

### Clementine
US mission to the Moon in 1994. Clementine was built and sent to the
Moon cheaply out of the US defence budget's funds for missile defence,

to prove technology for operations in high-radiation environments, and cost only $75 million. It mapped the whole of the Moon with a resolution of a few tens of metres, in visible and infrared light, allowing its surface composition to be determined, as well as sending back detailed altimetry data on lunar surface heights. It may also have observed ice in polar craters of the Moon. But it failed in its planned second mission, a flyby of the asteroid 1620 Geographos. Despite this, small missions like Clementine may be the future of solar system exploration.

## clock

Device for keeping time. Clocks and astronomy have influenced each other profoundly for centuries. Sundials were the first clocks, and their relation to the sky is obvious and direct. They have been supplanted by clockwork and electronics, which are more precise, and by atomic clocks, which depend upon the vibrations of atoms themselves and are the most precise timekeepers known. The historic quest of clockmakers is to find a clock which is as accurate as the Earth's own rotation, the Moon's journey around the Earth, and the Earth's around the Sun, which are basis of all clocks and calendars. But atomic clocks are more steady and predictable than the Earth itself, making them powerful tools for scientific investigation

## closed universe

A possible condition of our universe in which its density is great enough to make it collapse under its own weight, reversing its present expansion. The question of whether the universe is closed is difficult to resolve, depending upon the amount of invisible dark matter between the stars

## cluster[1]

A region of space with a high density of stars or galaxies. Clusters of galaxies are often grouped in **superclusters** which are the largest organised objects known. Types of star cluster include **open** and the more tight-packed **globular clusters**. Open or galactic clusters – like the **Pleiades** in Taurus, which are visible to the naked eye – contain a few hundred stars in a space of a few hundred cubic parsecs. Globular clusters can include up to a million stars in a somewhat larger volume

## Cluster[2]

Array of four satellites launched in 2000 by the European Space Agency after a first set were destroyed on launch in 1997. Named Rumba, Salsa, Samba and Tango, the four are designed to provide a three-dimensional view of the interactions between the Earth and the Sun, especially the way the solar wind interacts with the Earth's **magnetosphere.** The satellites carry large amounts of fuel to allow them to fly in formation over the Earth's poles to make observations which will coordinate with ground-based measurements and observations made with the **Soho** satellite.

### Coalsack
Dark interstellar cloud seen against the Milky Way in the southern sky, mostly in the constellation Crux, and covering an area of over 20 square degrees

### Coast
The Cambridge Optical Aperture Synthesis Telescope, a telescope opened in Cambridge, England, in 1996 which uses **aperture synthesis** to allow four 40cm telescopes to imitate a single much larger telescope

### COBE
*See* COSMIC BACKGROUND EXPLORER

### collimator
Lens or mirror used in an optical system to produce light in a parallel beam for further processing, for example in a spectrograph

### colour
Property of light caused by the mix of different wavelengths it contains. Light of a single wavelength is called monochromatic, one-colour. The colours of the rainbow show the spectrum from which the other visual colours are made by mixing. In addition, astronomers apply the term colour to radiation in non-visible wavelengths and use terms derived from visual observation to describe it. Thus they call radio signals with a wide range of energy 'white' since white light contains all the spectrum colours in balanced amounts, and talk about redshifts in invisible frequencies

### colour index
A quantitative measure of the colour of astronomical objects. Colour indices are arrived at by comparing the strength of light at different wavelengths from an object. B-V (blue minus visual, the straw colour which marks the peak acuity of the human eye) is the most commonly used colour index

### Columba
Constellation adjacent to Canis Major in the southern hemisphere.
*(Genitive is **Columbae;** means the 'dove')*

### coma
The mass of dust and gas surrounding the nucleus of a comet. Coma plus **nucleus** make up the head of a comet

### Coma Berenices
Constellation of the northern hemisphere containing many visible nebulae. These may have helped it be named after the hair of the mythical Berenice.
*(Genitive is **Comae Berenices**)*

## Coma Cluster
Cluster of some 5,000 galaxies in Coma Berenices. The cluster is dominated by large galaxies which seem to have grown by swallowing smaller ones

## Coma (optics)
*See* ABERRATION

## comet
Mass of dust, gas and solid matter in orbit around the Sun. Comets contain very little mass but are of interest to astronomers for several reasons. One is that they can be highly spectacular. More significantly, they are remnants of very early matter within the solar system. They also tie into other small objects in the solar system, like meteoroids, many of whose orbits resemble those of comets, and the asteroids, which in some cases seem to be comets attracted into the asteroid belt by Jupiter's gravitation and stripped of their gaseous matter by solar radiation. Beyond the planets there may lie billions of comets in a zone called **Oort's cloud**, occasionally tipped into the inner solar system by random gravitational effects or visiting it in long orbits which send the comets into deep space most of the time. If other stars have also formed like the Sun, leaving material not swept up around them into planets or the stars themselves, there must be incalculably large numbers of comets in the apparently bare space between stars.

*Comet*

## cometary masers
Radio astronomers have observed masers acting in the tails of comets and broadcasting with a strength of a few tens of watts

### compound lens
A lens which contains more than one glass element, to reduce the
**chromatic aberration**, astigmatism and other inaccuracies associated
with single-element lenses

### compression wave
A wave which travels through a body in the form of a compression of
matter. Compression waves are known from earthquakes and seem to
form the spiral arms of galaxies

### Compton
17-tonne US spacecraft also called the Gamma Ray Observatory and
used to observe the gamma-ray sky. Launched in 1991, it housed
several instruments including BATSE, the Burst and Transient Source
Experiment, for looking at short-lived gamma-ray events, the Imaging
Compton Telescope, EGRET, the Energetic Gamma Ray Experiment
Telescope, and OSSE, the Oriented Scintillation Spectrometer
Experiment. Arthur Compton (1892-1962) was the US physicist who
discovered the Compton Effect of the scattering of X and Gamma
radiation by matter, the fundamental scientific finding in the field. It
was destroyed in 2000 by being brought into the Earth's atmosphere
over the Pacific, to avoid the danger of damage from fragments
resulting from an uncontrolled re-entry.

### condensation theory
The now widely accepted theory that the Moon formed in the same
manner as the Earth – from small particles aggregating into a single
body – and at about the same time

### conformal map
A drawing showing different regions of space-time, drawn up according
to relativistic rules. Conformal maps are single diagrams on which time
and space appear on different axes of the same map, which can also
include alternative universes in the same picture. They were developed
by the British scientist Roger Penrose (born 1931), and allow imaginary
universes to be displayed simply

### conic sections
Shapes including the circle, the ellipse, the parabola and the hyperbola,
which are produced by cutting a cone with a plane at varying angles

### conjunction
Close apparent approach of two objects in the sky as seen from the
Earth, usually the Sun and a planet. With Venus and Mercury the
convention is that inferior conjunction has the inner planet between
Earth and Sun and superior conjunction has it on the far side of the Sun

### Conservation Laws
Laws of Physics providing that energy, mass, angular momentum and
other physical properties of systems are unvarying. Thus energy is not

destroyed by use – merely degraded into useless forms – and a car which wears out weighs as much as a new one until pieces start to fall off. Alterations in the amount of mass, energy or angular momentum in a system show that the system itself is not fully closed, as when atmospheric drag slows a satellite and causes it to reenter the Earth's atmosphere. In relativistic systems, like a star or a nuclear power station, matter can be changed into energy, but even then the total amount of both resources is conserved

## constellation

Area of the sky accepted by astronomers as a unit of the celestial sphere. Many constellations are still called after the familiar objects or mythological figures picked out by ancient astronomers in the patterns made by their prominent stars, an exception being the constellations of the extreme southern hemisphere, which were named in the last few hundred years. 88 constellations are now recognised by the **International Astronomical Union.** This dictionary gives the names of the constellations and their genitives – the reason is explained under **Star Classification.**

## continental drift

The relative motion of large areas of the Earth's surface. Similar effects have been hypothesised for other terrestrial planets, notably Venus. On the Earth, continental drift is driven by convection movements deep within the Earth and involves volcanic and earthquake activity along the lines where matter is pushed to the surface or sucked beneath it. This way of looking at the Earth has in recent years established itself as a powerful scientific technique but its application to other planets remains uncertain

## continuous spectrum

Spectrum seen as a band of light of differing wavelengths against which dark absorption lines are seen. Stars exhibiting a continuous spectrum are those, like the Sun, where we observe mainly the surface of the star rather than its atmosphere, with the absorption lines providing information about the atoms present in the atmosphere rather than the surface

## convection zone

Area within the Sun where heat is convected to the surface from about 150,000km deep. The heat is carried through convection cells, of which the largest are the deepest. The smallest are at the surface and are only a few hundred km across. With good seeing and the best telescopes they can be distinguished as a fine speckle pattern at the Sun's surface

## coordinates

The position of an object – like a star in the sky – is established with reference to coordinate systems, like those of right ascension (east to west) and declination (north to south), matching the ideas of longitude and latitude on the Earth. Similar coordinate systems to terrestrial longitude and latitude have been established on other planets, especially in recent years as reliable maps have become available The term is also used in relativistic contexts. In relativity space itself ceases to be 'flat' in the commonsense way we appreciate it, making a choice of coordinate systems necessary for the drawing of maps, with polar, elliptic and other types of coordinate being chosen for tasks such as the mapping of a black hole

## coordinate time

Time as measured by an observer far from a source of strong gravitation such as a black hole, providing a framework against which the relativistic effects encountered in such an object can be measured

## Copernicus, Nicholas (1473-1543)

Polish astronomer who established the idea that the Earth moves through space while the Sun stands still at the centre of a solar system of planets. This scheme, now accepted almost universally, is known as the Copernican system. His great book **'De Revolutionibus Orbium Coelestium'** used his own and others' observations to demonstrate that this logic – using a circular orbit for the Earth rather than the elliptical ones introduced by Kepler – was a simpler way of explaining the apparent movement of the planets. At the time he first published these thoughts the Catholic church, of which he was a Canon, was more amenable to the idea than it later became in its dealings with Galileo and others. But Copernicus's ideas – developed at a time of great upheaval, with Copernicus himself caught up in the warfare of the reformation – did not catch on in his own lifetime, and the first copy of **'De Revolutionibus'** was brought to Copernicus on his deathbed. The Copernican principle is the idea that the Earth's position in the universe is not special, one of the most powerful ideas in science. The astronomical observatory Copernicus was launched in 1972 for ultraviolet astronomy

## core

The central region of a star, planet or other body. In stars the core is the region where temperature and pressure are high enough to support fusion, containing half or more of its mass in a few per cent of the volume. The Earth's core is a molten zone containing large amounts of iron, whose convection is the cause of the Earth's magnetism, although there seems to be a small solid inner core at the very centre

## Coriolis Force

Force which appears to operate on anything travelling from the pole of a rotating object, like the Earth, towards its equator. The Coriolis Force results from the rotation itself, which moves the Earth under the body as it is in motion. On the Earth, Coriolis Forces affect missiles, ocean currents and airliners in flight. The idea of Coriolis Forces illustrates relative frames of reference – the force seems to act on the smaller object, although an outside observer would be more likely to see it in terms of the large object moving relative the smaller one, and to see the latter as being in a state of straight line motion

## corona

The outermost portion of the Sun's atmosphere, extending more than 10 solar radii and maintaining a temperature of 1,000,000° or more. The material of the corona is not very dense and acts mainly as a medium through which solar energy passes almost unaltered. The corona gives out some radiation of its own at X-ray and other wavelengths but is best seen during eclipses. Patterns within the corona vary with the stage of the sunspot cycle, which dictates the shape of the Sun's magnetic field and the distribution of the charged particles affected by it. Because of their high temperatures, coronas of stars other than the Sun can be observed in X-rays

## Corona Australis

Small constellation of the southern hemisphere, meaning the Southern Crown.
*(Genitive is **Coronae Australis**)*

## Corona Borealis

The Northern Crown, a small constellation of the northern hemisphere.
*(Genitive is **Coronae Borealis**)*

## coronagraph

Device for viewing the Sun's corona without an eclipse. Consists essentially of a telescope with a disc to blank out the body of the Sun, and sited somewhere at high altitude with good seeing or on a satellite

## coronal clouds

Short-lived type of prominence observed in the corona a few tens of thousands of kilometres above the surface of the Sun. Prominences in the corona can be larger than the Earth, and last a few days, showering material back into the lower reaches of the Sun's atmosphere as they hang in the corona. They are distinct from the curved **prominences** which are joined at each end to the Sun's surface

## coronal holes

Gaps in the corona observed at X-ray wavelengths and apparently associated with the Sun's magnetic field

## coronal plumes

Glowing matter suspended in the corona above the Sun's poles

## coronal prominences

Prominences seen in the corona rather than the Sun's lower atmosphere.

## coronal rain

Material falling back from the corona – often from coronal prominences – along routes usually dictated by the Sun's magnetic field. Coronal rain can fall at up to 100km per second

## coronal streamers
Long bright features in the Sun's atmosphere in the solar equatorial region

## correction plate
The thin lens at the skyward end of a **Schmidt Camera** and some other types of telescope such as the Maksutov, which allows a large area of the sky to be photographed accurately. The correction plate has to match the optical characteristics of the camera's main mirror, the two being made as a pair, for wide areas of the sky to be recorded faithfully

## Corvus
Constellation of the southern hemisphere near Virgo.
*(Genitive is **Corvi;** means the 'Crow')*

## Cos-B
European gamma ray astronomy satellite launched in 1975

## cosmic background radiation
*See* BACKGROUND RADIATION

## Cosmic Background Explorer (COBE)
US satellite launched in November 1989, and operational until 1993. It was equipped for only one, very important, experiment, to study the structure of the cosmic background radiation. It turns out that the radiation is homogeneous enough to be unmistakably associated with the origin of the universe, but varies slightly according to the direction from which it is being received, an observation which accords with theory by allowing for enough inhomogeneity in the early universe for structure – including galaxies – to form

## cosmic censorship
The principle that a singularity such as a black hole is never directly visible. Black holes, for example, are obscured by the material falling into them or by radiation or matter trapped around them. Singularities are a problem area for science, and the need to explain the fact that none are seen has produced two schools of thought – censorship and the rival opinion that 'naked' singularities might sometimes be visible in the universe, when unusual physical effects would become apparent

## cosmic fireball
The mass of hot, dense material present in the universe at the time of the big bang and containing all the material now observed. The temperature of the fireball shortly into the big bang would have been many billions of degrees, according to the evidence of the background radiation now observed

## cosmic rays
Subatomic particles entering the Earth's atmosphere from above. Most cosmic rays are of solar origin and their composition reflects the Sun's

own, consisting mainly of **neutrons** and **alpha particles**, since the Sun consists mainly of hydrogen and helium. But other cosmic rays appear to come from deep space, especially from supernovae, which accounts for the appearance of heavier nuclei among cosmic rays

## cosmochronology
The science of putting dates to events in the history of the universe. The term is applied especially to the radioisotope dating of the development of the solar system by tests on moonrock and meteorites. These allow timescales for the major events of solar system history, such as the formation of the planets, to be built up

## cosmogony
The study of the origin of the universe and the larger-scale objects within it; a subdivision of the science of cosmology

## cosmological principle
The idea that on a very large scale all the matter in the universe is distributed evenly, so that hypothetical astronomers a long way from the Earth would see the same universe, on the biggest scale, as we do. The problem with testing the cosmological principle is that it operates on a scale so vast that even galaxies and clusters of galaxies are merely local clumps of material by its standards. This means that observational tests of the principle are difficult to carry out and are vexed by the fact that looking into the universe different distances also involves looking back over different time periods. The Cosmological Principle can be viewed as a modern restatement of the Copernican Principle on a bigger stage. Patterns seen in the universe on a massive scale, such as 'bubbles' of galaxy clusters, could be regarded as arguments against the principle

## cosmology
The study of the universe as a whole, including its structure and long-term development as well as its origins. Cosmologists leave to lesser breeds like astronomers and astrophysicists the detail of how particular objects in the universe behave

## Cosmos
In astronomy, the Cosmos is effectively synonymous with the Universe, and takes in the whole of the matter and energy in existence. Also the term used by the former Soviet Union for the series under which almost all its spacecraft were classified, both military and civilian

## covariance
The principle that the laws of the universe are everywhere the same. The idea is implicit in most astronomy, but there are schools of thought which consider, for example, that gravitation may not operate over large distances according to the same inverse square law seen in action over the scale of the solar system

## Coudé focus

The point at which light can be turned into an image in some modern large telescopes. Located at the polar axis of the telescope, the Coudé focus does not move as the telescope tracks objects in the sky, making it the place to site heavy instruments which cannot readily be pivoted as a telescope turns

## Crab Nebula

The remnant of the supernova of AD 1054 in Taurus. The Crab Nebula is one of the most interesting objects in the sky for modern astronomers because it contains one of the most rapid pulsars known, which operates in optical as well as radio wavelengths, and is thought to indicate the presence of a neutron star

## Crater

Constellation of the Southern hemisphere.
*(Genitive is **Crateris;** means the 'cup')*

## crater

Depression, normally surrounded by a ridge, on the surface of a planet or satellite, and usually caused by meteorite impact. Water action and volcanic activity can also cause craters to form. A long controversy about the origin of the craters of the Moon was settled in the 1960s and early 1970s by evidence that most are meteoritic in origin but some are volcanic. Meteorite craters have been used to date the surfaces of the Moon, Mars and Mercury, because the number of craters per unit area increases with the time the surface has been exposed to impacts, especially if the surface was exposed during the early history of the solar system when there were more impacting objects than now. Large meteorites produce explosion craters with such violence that it can be impossible to find meteorite fragments nearby. In moonrock – which has effectively no atmospheric protection from outer space – there are meteorite craters all the way down to micrometeorite pits visible only with the aid of a microscope

## crust

The outermost solid layer of the Earth, or of similar solid planets

## Crux

Diminutive constellation of the southern hemisphere through which the Milky Way passes. Also known as Crux Australis, Crux consists almost entirely of the well-known cross of five stars which features in the flags of Brazil, Australia and other nations of the southern hemisphere
*(Genitive is **Crucis;** means the 'Cross')*

## curvature of space

The property of space whereby, over large distances, it appears to obey the laws of spherical rather than plane geometry in terms of gravitation, the transmission of radiation, and other effects. The curvature of space is predicted by the General Theory of Relativity, and it implies, for example, that two lines cannot be parallel over cosmically large distances – or precisely parallel over shorter ones. Under relativity, it is not merely space but space-time which is curved. But space-time curves so gradually that experiments to discover the size and direction of the curvature are almost impossible to devise

## cusp
Angular horn-like point on the visible, lit face of the Moon, or of Mercury or Venus. They are also seen on space probe photographs of the other major planets, but not from Earth because the other planets are seen virtually fully lit by observers on the Earth

## Cutlass
Ground-based radar for work on the interaction between solar radiation and the Earth's atmosphere, sited in Finland. Means the Cooperative UK Twin Located Auroral Sounding System

## Cyclical Climate Theory
*See* SAGAN-WARD THEORY

## Cyclops
Plan – not now close to being carried out – to build a massive array of radio telescopes on the Earth's surface to detect and communicate with extraterrestrial life

## Cygnus
Impressive constellation of the northern hemisphere including the bright star Deneb and many fine nebulae and other features. In radio wavelengths it contains Cygnus A, one of the most prominent radio galaxies. Its stars even manage to form a realistic outline of the Swan, after which it is named
*(Genitive is **Cygni**)*

## Cygnus Loop
Supernova remnant in Cygnus, seen as a loop because Earthly observers view the thickest part of the three-dimensional gas bubble speeding away from the supernova

## Cygnus Superbubble
1000 light year diameter bubble of gas discovered in 1979 in Cygnus and with a temperature of up to 2,000,000°C. The superbubble contains prodigious amounts of both energy and material and is thought to be powered by radiation from large numbers of bright young stars.

## Cygnus X-1
X-ray source in Cygnus which is probably the site of the first black hole to be discovered. The X-rays are emitted by a disc of material around the black hole, orbiting just a few hundred miles above the hole itself. The material is being sucked from a companion star whose outer layers are gradually vanishing into the black hole

## Cytherian

Adjective to describe anything associated with the planet Venus.
'Venusian' is just as acceptable

# Dd

## D lines
Pattern of lines seen in stellar **spectra**, including the spectrum of the Sun, due to the presence of sodium. The two D lines are very close together in the spectrum and account for the characteristic orange colour of sodium lights. There is also a much fainter sodium line in the green part of the spectrum

## Daedalus
Plan produced in the 1970s by members of the British Interplanetary Society for an unmanned rocket mission to Barnard's Star, powered by fusion motors. Project Daedalus is unlikely to be carried out in the near future, not least because it would require huge amounts of Helium 3 as fuel, 'mined' from the atmosphere of Jupiter or Saturn. But Barnard's Star remains a tantalising target because unlike nearer star systems like the Alpha Centauri group it seems to have at least one planet

## Dall-Kirkham Cassegrain
Type of telescope based on **Cassegrain** geometry, but rendered cheaper and easier to manufacture at the expense of optical accuracy

## dark matter
Material in the universe which cannot be observed directly. The rotational velocity of stars around the centres of galaxies reveals that they contain more material than can be observed directly. Many types of material, including small planet-sized objects of normal matter as well as concentrations of exotic 'non-baryonic' material unknown on Earth, have been proposed as possible solutions to the missing mass problem, whose solution is vital to such large problems as working out whether the universe will continue to expand indefinitely.

## dark nebula
Several thousand dark nebulae cover about 2 per cent of the sky. They include large features like the **Coalsack** and smaller nebulae within our own galaxy. Some other galaxies seem to contain far more dark material than our own, in some cases accounting for a significant quantity of their mass

## Dawes' Limit
The theoretical limit to the resolving power of a telescope, equal to 2/1000 times the wavelength of light in Ångstroms divided by the telescope aperture in centimetres, for a result in arc seconds

## deceleration parameter
The possible slowing down of the expansion of the universe, which may lead to a reversal of the expansion at some future time

## declination
The angular distance of a body in the sky north or south of the celestial equator, which along with Right Ascension gives its position in the sky. Declination is the celestial equivalent of latitude on the Earth

## deferent
In ancient astronomy, the large circles on which the Sun, Moon and planets were thought to orbit the Earth

## deflection of light
Light is deflected from straight lines by mass, although the effect can only be observed for very large objects such as stars. The deflection is strong evidence of the special theory of relativity. It was first observed in 1919 by recording the positions of stars during a total solar eclipse. This revealed that the Sun's mass drew passing starlight towards it

## degeneracy
The collapse of matter under very intense gravitation. The two main types are neutron and electron degeneracy. Electron degeneracy is the condition found in white dwarf stars of less than 1.4 solar masses. Their material collapses so completely that only the repulsion pressures which prevent two electrons from occupying the same niche in the material holds it up at all. Neutron degeneracy applies for larger masses where the electrons are crushed into the nuclei of atoms, turning virtually the whole star into a mass of neutrons. Then the same pressure, this time acting upon the neutrons, allows the material to become stable as a neutron star of immense density

## degree of arc
Standard measure of angle, equal to a 360th part of a circle, itself divided into 60 minutes, each of 60 seconds

## Deimos
One of the two satellites of Mars, just 16km across and irregularly shaped, showing signs of heavy meteorite impact. Orbits Mars in 1.3 days in a 23,500km orbit. Discovered by **Hall** in 1877

## Delphinus
Small constellation of the northern hemisphere.
*(Genitive is **Delphini**; means the 'Dolphin')*

## Delta Aquarids
Meteor shower occurring in July, with radiant near delta aquarii

## Deneb
Brightest star in Cygnus and the 18th brightest in the sky. Type A2, distance 1,600 light years, apparent magnitude 1.26, absolute magnitude -7.1

### Denebola
The star Beta Leonis

### density
The amount of matter in a unit volume of material. Density is usually measured in grams per millilitre (or cubic centimetre, almost the same thing), a scale on which water has a density of one. On this scale the Earth's average density is 5.52gm/cc and that of the Moon 3.34, while the Sun is at 1.41 and a white dwarf in the region of 100,000 gm/cc

### density wave theory
Theory, now widely supported, that the arms of spiral galaxies are caused by compression waves moving in a circular plane about the galaxy's centre through the disc containing most of its mass

### Descartes, René (1596-1650)
French scientist and philosopher whose astronomical thought – a small part of his life's work – included developing coherent theories of the origin of the planets. His view that planets are expired stars was proven wrong later but his view of an infinite universe capable of logical explanation was original and far-sighted. He also worked on optics, including improved telescope manufacture, and the nature of light

### deuterium
Isotope of hydrogen with a neutron as well as a proton in its nucleus, discovered by Harold Urey (1893-1981) and of importance to both nuclear technology and astrophysics

### deuteron
The nucleus of a deuterium atom, consisting of a neutron and a proton

### diameter
The full width of a celestial object, measured either in units of distance or of angular measure as seen from the Earth or some other point

### diamond ring effect
Dazzling exhibition of the last few **Baily's Beads** at a solar eclipse

### differential rotation
Phenomenon of varying orbital periods of different parts of a celestial object. Many non-solid objects can show differential rotation. In the gas giant planets it can be observed by timing the rotation of spots and other surface features. Also seen on the Sun, and in whole galaxies, as well as objects like planetary rings which are made up of large numbers of smaller bodies

### differentiation
The process whereby materials of lower melting and boiling points migrate to the outside of a planet, as in the case of the Earth which has seas and an atmosphere on the outside and metal at its core. On the Earth differentiation has been driven by mechanisms including plate tectonic action and vulcanism. Other planets also seem to be

differentiated, possibly to a lesser degree, which suggests that they too
have had a geologically active past

## diffraction

The spreading of light or other wave energy around obstacles. The
longer the wave, the more the diffraction. Thus sound diffracts so easily
that we are not surprised to hear noise from around a corner. Light,
including starlight, also diffracts, especially around corners and edges
of solid objects. The different rates of diffraction of light of different
wavelengths is the principle behind the diffraction grating, which has
replaced the glass prism for most spectrum-gathering. A diffraction
grating consists of an array of fine lines ruled parallel to each other on a
flat surface which can either reflect or transmit the light falling on it (to
give a transmission or reflection grating). The diffraction of light
around the edges of the lines on the grating produces the spectrum

## diffuse interstellar bands

Broad absorption lines seen in spectra of objects beyond our galaxy,
now thought to be due to large organic molecules in deep space

## diffuse nebula

Nebula of non-compact type such as the **Coalsack**. Many are seen in
our own and other galaxies

## Dione

Satellite of Saturn some 800km across and in a 377,000km, 2.7 day
orbit. Discovered by **Cassini** in 1684 and well seen by Voyager 1 in
1980. Dione appears to consist of a mixture of rock and ice and has a
heavily cratered and fractured surface consistent with past internal
geological activity as well as cratering from meteorite impact

## disc

Discs of matter are found around stars including our own Sun, whose
attendant gas and dust disc gives rise to the **zodiacal light**. Denser
disks, like the one from which the solar system condensed, are seen
around younger stars. The disc around the star **Beta Pictoris** is one of
the best-observed. Other stars accumulate disc-shaped masses of
material, typically by gravitational attraction removing it from
companion stars. These are called **accretion discs** and are seen on a
larger scale around some galaxies

## diurnal

Occurring in a daily cycle, like the rising and setting of the Sun and stars

## Dobsonian

Telescope type using Newtonian optics with an especially cheap, simple
and steady mounting, allowing large telescopes to be built
unprecedentedly cheaply. They have been responsible for a revolution
in amateur astronomy by making previously unaffordable telescopes
available.

## Doppler effect

The shifting of the wavelength of wave energy caused by relative motion between source and observer. Observed on the largest possible scale in the expansion of the universe, the Doppler effect lengthens the wavelength of light if source and observer are moving away from each other and shortens it if they are approaching. Astronomers call this a redshift for recession and a blueshift for approach, since red light has the longest wavelengths in the visible wavebands and blue light the shortest. The Doppler effect can be used to unravel many astronomical problems, for example to measure the rotation of stars and planets where it is possible to observe one limb approaching the Earth and another receding from it, and to sort out the orbits of multiple star systems

## Dorado

Small constellation of the southern hemisphere containing most of the Greater Magellanic Cloud
*(Genitive is **Doradus;** means the 'swordfish')*

## double cluster

Pair of galactic clusters in Perseus, a noted sight for observers using small telescopes

## double star

Pair of stars seen in the sky where the stars are in orbit about each other rather than being simply aligned by chance as seen from Earth. Most stars are in double, or even more complex, systems, reflecting the conditions under which they formed from dust and gas. Such pairs can include widely differing star types. The Sun is atypical in having no companion

## Draco

Large constellation near the north celestial pole which contains the north pole of the ecliptic
*(Genitive is **Draconis;** means the 'Dragon')*

## Draconitic Month

The month measured from node to node of the Moon's orbit, equal to 27.21 days
*See* MONTH

## Drake Equation

Postulated means of calculating the number of civilisations in the galaxy by multiplying up variables like the number of stars, the percentage of these likely to have planets, the likelihood of life arising and continuing, etc. Thought up by US astronomer Frank Drake, the Drake Equation might be regarded as a triumph of mathematics over sanity, since most of the figures injected into it contain vast amounts of uncertainty and value judgment. If the assumptions on which it is based are sound the number of civilisations in our galaxy could be a few dozen. The Drake logic defines a civilisation as a planetary life form with the ability to communicate with others by radio – whales or dinosaurs would not qualify, but we would

## Draper Catalogue
Listing of almost 300,000 stars, in wide use by professional astronomers. Draper entries have the prefix HD or HDE. Named after Henry Draper (1837-1882), also a pioneer of astronomical photography, like his father John Draper (1811-1882)

## Dresden Codex
Astronomical text produced some 1000 years ago by Mayan people of what are now Mexico and Guatemala, containing a wealth of numerical data on eclipses, the motion of Venus, and other topics

## Dumbbell Nebula
Planetary nebula in Vulpecula, M27 in the Messier catalogue

## dust
Dusty material is common throughout the observable universe. It is present in our immediate astronomical area, accounting for much of the mass of comets and producing meteor showers. On a larger scale are dust clouds in galaxies with masses many hundreds of times that of the Sun, either dark, or glowing from stellar radiation. Dusty areas of galaxies also seem to be the seats of star and planet formation, so that dusty material may be the original form of most of the matter around us

## dust lanes
Broad, dark bands of dust seen obscuring the starlight of some galaxies. A dust cloud is classed as a lane only if it is of significant size compared to the galaxy as a whole

## dust tail
One of the two types of comet tail – the other being the **gas tail**.

## dwarf Cepheids
A mysterious class of variable star which may consist of a binary star in a small nebula which conceals the star itself

## dwarf Novae
Very faint stars which are prone to episodes of extreme brightening at more or less regular intervals. Their light output can increase more than tenfold in a few hours before diminishing to its normal level over a period of a few weeks. The brightening seems to be caused by material sucked from a red giant companion star flaring up near the surface of a white dwarf which traps material from the expanding red giant

## dwarf spiral
Category of galaxy of far less mass than most seen in the **Hubble** classification. They can exhibit the same characteristics including spiral structure and central bulges

## dwarf star

Any star which is not a giant. The term thus includes most stars in the sky, including the Sun, as well as tiny stars like the white dwarfs

## Dynamic Explorer

Pair of US satellites launched in 1981 to investigate the processes in the Earth's upper atmosphere, and placed in an orbit designed especially to give useful observations of the north pole area including the Aurora Borealis

## Dyson Sphere

Sphere postulated by US physicist Freeman Dyson (born 1923 in England) which would be made by dismembering planets and reassembling their material in a sphere around a star to capture all its radiation output. A Dyson Sphere would be the ultimate in energy conservation. From the outside an observer would see only a weak **infra-red emission** as a sign of the presence of a star and a surface-dwelling civilisation on the interior of the sphere

# Ee

## Earth
The third planet of the solar system and the only one known to house life, the Earth is also remarkable for its seas of liquid water and its oxygen-bearing atmosphere and for being geologically very active. The Earth's equatorial radius is 6 378km, about a third of a percent more than its polar radius because of the Earth's rotation. About 4 500 million years old, like the other planets, the Earth rotates on its axis in a day, orbits the Sun in a year and has a satellite, the Moon, which orbits it once per lunar month

## Earth chauvinism
The idea that life can only arise on planets, especially those with similar temperature, chemistry, gravitation and other characteristics to the Earth

## earthquake
Release of energy within the Earth due to chemical phase changes, the relief of stress built up along faults, and possibly other causes. 'Marsquakes' and 'Moonquakes' have been detected on other planets and space technology – the use of satellites for precise measurements of small movements of the Earth's crust – is helping to revolutionise the study and possible prediction of earthquakes

## earthshine
Light illuminating the part of the face of the Moon not lit by sunlight, which it reaches by being reflected from the clouds and surface of the Earth

## eccentricity
The amount by which an ellipse, such as an orbit, differs from an exact circle. Eccentricity is measured as the difference between the large and

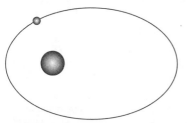 

*Orbital eccentricity*

small radii (the semi-major and semi-minor axes) divided by the semi-major axis. Some Earth satellites are placed in virtually circular orbits, and the orbital eccentricities of most major solar system objects are less than 0.1, but Nereid, a satellite of Neptune, has an orbit with an eccentricity of 0.75 !

## eclipse

The cutting off of the illumination of an astronomical object, as in an eclipse of the Moon, when the Earth comes between the Moon and Sun, so that its shadow crosses the Moon's surface. The term is also used universally but in fact wrongly for occasions when the Sun's disc is blotted out by the Moon from the point of view of Earthly observers. These events are in fact occultations of the Moon, or eclipses of the Earth. The Moon and the Sun are almost exactly the same size – about half a degree – in the Earth's sky, making it possible, by coincidence, to observe the eclipsed Sun. This provides a powerful experimental tool for examining the Sun's atmosphere. The Moon's shadow at the Earth is so narrow that any given solar eclipse is visible only from a narrow line on the Earth's surface. If the Moon is too far away in its orbit the full eclipse effect is not seen, but an **annular eclipse** is observed instead

## eclipse year

The year measured in terms of the time taken for the Sun to return to the Moon's orbital node, equal to 346.62 days
*See* YEAR

## eclipsing binary

**Variable star** whose changes in magnitude are caused by the partners in a binary star periodically blocking one another's light from the observer. The best-known eclipsing binary is Algol in Perseus. Algol has eclipses every 69 hours, when its magnitude falls from 2.3 to 3.5. There is also a third member of the Algol group which does not get involved in the eclipses as seen from Earth. Observing eclipsing binaries allows us to discover the orbital characteristics of the stars involved and so to measure their mass

## ecliptic

The path of the Sun in the sky, tilted at about 23° to the celestial equator. Because the other planets orbit the Sun in about the same plane as the Earth, they also stick close to the ecliptic from the point of view of Earthly observers. The plane of the ecliptic is the imaginary flat surface in space made by the Earth's orbit, and the points geometrically north and south of it on the celestial sphere are the poles of the ecliptic – the northern is in Draco and the southern in Dorado

## E-Corona

Component of the Sun's corona seen close to the Sun's limb during eclipses, and consisting of emission lines. The E-corona is exceptionally faint and hard to observe

## ecosphere
The inhabited part of the Earth, or other possible inhabited planets, and its inhabitants. In the Earth's case the ecosphere includes most of the atmosphere and oceans and a thin smear of the crust

## Eddington, Arthur (1882-1944)
British astronomer whose observations included the key eclipse data which confirmed the special theory of relativity. An expert on stellar interiors, he was an early convert to the idea that the stars are driven by nuclear energy, until when the source of power of the stars had been a mystery

## Einstein, Albert (1879-1955)
Physicist of Swiss birth who lived most of his life in the US. His work on relativity altered the face of modern physics and produced many insights of value to astronomy. His work altered many fields of science but Einstein is now recalled mainly for proving that matter and energy are interlinked and that time itself can vary with velocity and the presence of fields such as gravitation. In astronomy, his work illuminates everything from the behaviour of dust in the solar system to the origin of the universe itself. The bending of starlight by the gravitational field of the Sun, observed at the solar eclipse of 1919 was one of the key proofs of relativity, which also accounts for previously unexplained precession of the orbit of Mercury. A US X-ray astronomy satellite, Einstein, was launched in 1978. His name has attached itself to many other objects and phenomena, for example Einstein rings, the arcs of light or other radiation formed by **gravitational lensing**.

## Eiscat
The European Incoherent Scatter Facility, a radar system based in northern Europe and used for investigating solar effects on the Earth's upper atmosphere

## Elara
Satellite of Jupiter some 40km across and discovered in 1905. Orbits Jupiter in about 260 days in an 11.7 million km orbit

## electromagnetic force
The force which acts between charged particles in chemical reactions and elsewhere

## electromagnetic spectrum
The range of energy capable of being transmitted through the universe by the propagation of electrical and magnetic fields, of which the visible spectrum which we experience as light is only a minute fraction. The full electromagnetic spectrum starts with radio waves, which run the gamut from very low frequency to extra high frequency across a range of about 100,000m wavelength to about 1mm. Below this come infrared wavelengths until the longest visible light, the red, is encountered with a wavelength of some 780 nanometres. The visible runs from here to the

end of the violet at 380nm, after which the ultraviolet runs up to about
0.01nm. After this come the gamma rays up to about a thousand
trillionth of a metre wavelength. X-rays overlap the boundary between
ultraviolet and gamma rays. Objects at different temperatures emit
radiation preferentially at different wavelengths, getting shorter as the
object gets hotter. This forces astronomers wanting to see the whole
variety of objects in the universe to look at the whole electromagnetic
spectrum. They can now do this with satellites, to allow wavelengths
cut out by the Earth's atmosphere to be observed, and with new tools
like radio and infrared telescopes. The radiation reaching the Earth in
non-light frequencies is very weak compared to that in visible
wavelengths, which is why our eyes have evolved to operate in what we
think of as visible light, the band of frequencies in which most radiation
from the Sun arrives

## electron
Negatively charged atomic particle of small mass. Normal atoms consist
of a positively-charged nucleus of protons and neutrons and an
electrically balancing cloud of electrons in orbit around it

## electron volt
A measure of energy used in physics, equal to the energy accumulated
by an electron passing through a one-volt electric potential. Symbol is
eV

## element
The elements are the chemically discrete types of atom which make up
the universe and of which chemical compounds are composed. Atoms
of a particular element can vary in the number of neutrons in their
nucleus, with the variants being called isotopes, but must always have
the same number of positively-charged protons, and an equivalent
number of electrons in orbit around the nucleus. The simplest example
is the three isotopes of hydrogen, normal hydrogen, deuterium and
tritium, which have no neutrons, one neutron and two neutrons
respectively. Each has one proton, with one electron in orbit around the
nucleus

## elements of orbit
The elements of an orbit are the numbers which define its size, shape
and disposition relative to known reference points. Artificial satellites,
planetary satellites and stars in multiple systems can all have the
elements of their orbits defined, but they are best explained with
reference to solar system objects. Here the elements include the size of
the semi-major axis and the orbit's eccentricity, which give its overall
dimensions. Also specified are the orbit's inclination to the ecliptic,
which along with the angle along the ecliptic at which the object crosses
it heading north and the longitude of its perihelion, locate the orbit in
three-dimensional space. The other elements of the orbit are its 'period,'

or the time taken for an orbit in relation to the Earth or the stars, and the location of the object along its orbit at a given time, usually the start of a particular year, to allow its location along the orbit to be fixed in time and space. These elements allow the planet or other object to be located on its orbit indefinitely into the past or future providing the orbit does not vary

### elemental abundances
*See* ABUNDANCE

### ellipse
One of the **conic sections**, of special importance in astronomy because most orbits are elliptical. Instead of having a single centre, like a circle, an ellipse has two foci and the object being orbited – like the Sun in the solar system – lies at one of them

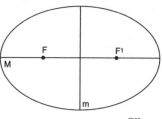

*Ellipse*

### elliptical galaxy
Elliptical galaxies are the commonest type in the **Hubble classification** of the galaxies. Most are smaller than the spiral galaxies like our own, and they run from type E0, virtually circular, to E7, which are extended types of high eccentricity

### Elnath
The 25th brightest star in the sky and the second brightest in Taurus, with apparent magnitude 1.65 and absolute magnitude -3.2. Distance 300 light years, type B7

### embedding diagram
Drawing showing the curvature of spacetime, for example the 'well' formed by the strong gravity of a large star or a black hole. Embedding diagrams allow the effects of strong gravitational fields, like the bending of light rays as they pass by, to be mapped

### emission line
Bright line seen in an **emission spectrum**. Usually caused by radiation from a hot gas superimposing its spectrum on the radiation from a cooler object, as with the Sun's outer atmosphere modifying radiation from the Sun's surface. If emission processes in the gas are using all the energy passing through it, a spectrum can consist entirely of bright lines on a dark background. Otherwise the observer sees bright lines on a background which also contains radiation, but at a lower level of energy

### emission spectrum
**Spectrum** consisting wholly or mainly of emission lines

## emulsion
The part of a photographic film which responds chemically to incident light to produce an image

## Enceladus
Satellite of Saturn discovered by **William Herschel** in 1789. 600km across, it has a 1.37 day, 238,000km orbit precisely in the plane of Saturn's orbit. Enceladus has a surface which is apparently almost free of craters, implying that some process is sweeping it clean of them. It is also very white, with the highest **albedo** of any object in the solar system

## Encke's Comet
Small comet orbiting in the asteroid belt of the solar system, important because of the increasingly clear connections between comets and asteroids. It has been regularly visible in the solar system for two hundred years, at up to about magnitude 20, rather than appearing only for fleeting visits. Formally Comet P/Encke 1786 I

## Encke Gap
One of the gaps in the rings of Saturn, and the widest gap in Saturn's A ring, 133,500km from the centre of Saturn. Discovered (as was the periodicity of **Encke's Comet**) by the German astronomer Johann Franz Encke (1791-1865)

## energy level
A possible state at which an electron can exist in an atom. The fact that any particular atom can house electrons only at specific energy levels gives rise to the lines in spectra, which exist as sharp features because they reflect the difference in energy between two energy levels. They are produced as bright features when electrons go from higher levels to lower, or as dark ones when electrons are raised from lower levels to higher, absorbing energy rather than emitting it

## energy of mass
The amount of energy which can be released by converting a given amount of matter entirely to energy, given by the amount of matter multiplied by the velocity of light squared, in Einstein's famous equation $e = mc^2$. The huge amount of energy obtainable from tiny amounts of matter accounts for the long lives of the stars – and for the portable size of highly destructive nuclear weapons

## energy transport
The processes whereby energy is shifted about within and between celestial objects. The term encompasses energy movement within atmospheres (meteorology is more or less a subsidiary problem within energy transport), oceans, and in astronomy, gas and dust clouds as well as stars. Within stars it attains its greatest complexity. Thus the energy produced in the Sun appears at its core in the form of energetic gamma rays. It travels outwards by means of radiation, interacting with atomic

particles on the way in a journey which takes many weeks, losing energy as it goes and being shifted mainly into the visible wavelengths which dominate the solar spectrum. Only in the outer layers does convection seem to take over as the dominant mechanism, by means of convection cells which bring the energy to the surface

## eolian
Deposited by the wind – a term used of desert deposits on the surface of the Earth and Mars. Aeolian is an alternative

## Eotvos experiment
Experiment carried out by Hungarian physicist Roland von Eotvos (1848-1914) using the torsion balance, which he invented, showing that gravitational forces affect all forms of matter equally spelling

## ephemeris
A table showing the expected position of a planet, comet or other astronomical object in time. An ephemeris for an object like a newly-discovered comet is a vital tool for astronomers wanting to follow it, and is constructed from an orbit, derived from early observations, plus calculations of other factors like the gravitational attraction of planets (usually Jupiter) near enough or massive enough to perturb it from its orbit significantly.
*(Plural is **ephemerides**)*

## ephemeris time
Clock time corrected to allow for small irregularities in the Earth's rotation, and differing from clock time by under a minute

## epicycle
The smaller of the two types of circle in which the planets, the Sun and the Moon were thought to move around the Earth in the universe according to **Ptolemy**, being lesser circles with their centres on the rim of the larger, called the **deferent**.

## Epimetheus
Small satellite of Saturn orbiting just beyond its ring system, and one of a number whose gravitation influences the location of the gaps in the rings

## Epsilon Eridani
Star which is a near neighbour of the Sun, at about 10.5 light years, and which seems to be accompanied by a planet several times as large as Jupiter. A K2 type star, smaller and cooler than the Sun. Epsilon Eridani's possible planet was surmised from an apparent gravitational 'wobble' in Epsilon Eridani's proper motion, but remains contentious, like the possible planet of **Barnard's Star**.

## equant
The point about which the **epicycle** moved uniformly in the universe postulated by **Ptolemy**

## equation of time
The difference, of a few minutes at most, between noon and the time at which the Sun reaches the meridian on a particular day. The difference is a consequence of the eccentricity of the Earth's orbit, which prevents the Earth's rotation and its orbital motion from remaining in perfect step

## equator
The imaginary line half-way between the poles of the Earth, the celestial poles, or the poles of other celestial objects exhibiting reasonably uniform rotation.

## equatorial mount
Telescope mount with an axis pointing to the **celestial pole** from its site on the Earth. This means that the telescope can track a star by being moved on only one axis

## equinox
Day on which the Sun is at the **celestial equator**, so that night and day are of 12 hours each. Due to northern hemisphere chauvinism they are called the spring or vernal equinox (around March 21) and the autumn equinox (around September 23)

## equivalence principle
The idea that the forces resulting from gravitation and acceleration are indistinguishable except over large distances. Equivalence is a means within relativity of removing the idea that there is anything special about gravitation – it is just another accelerating force, no different from the perceived pull of a train leaving the station

## Equuleus
Small constellation – means the little horse – near its larger equine neighbour Pegasus in the northern hemisphere.
*(Genitive is **Equulei**)*

## Eratosthenes (c.273BC – c.192BC)
Astronomer born in north Africa, who lived mainly in Egypt where he produced a fairly accurate estimate of the Earth's diameter, accurate to within about 20 per cent. He did this by noticing that the Sun is exactly overhead at Aswan (Syene) in Egypt at the summer solstice, but at a measurable angle from the vertical at Alexandria, due north. The known distance between the two allows the total size of the Earth to be determined provided Eratosthenes assumed that the Sun is infinitely distant and the Earth round, both assumptions being correct for this purpose. He also measured the obliquity of the ecliptic to the equator

## ergosphere
The region surrounding a black hole where matter cannot remain at rest or in orbit but must fall into the hole

## Eridanus
Constellation covering a huge area of the southern hemisphere and

called after the mythical river Eridanus.
*(Genitive is **Eridani**)*

## Eros

Small, stony asteroid capable of coming close to the Earth, and possibly of hitting it. One of the **Apollo-Amor** asteroids with Earth-crossing orbits. On February 14, 2000, the **NEAR** space mission entered orbit around Eros after a 4-year journey and revealed that it has a cratered and rocky surface. Near's one-year mission will allow Eros to be probed with spectrometers and other instruments. Previous space missions had only flown by asteroids rather than orbiting them for long periods.

   Objects on the surface of Eros have been named after the great real and fictional lovers of history.

## erosion

The wearing down of landforms by natural processes. On the Earth's surface, water, wind and ice are the main elements of erosion, but on other planets slower agencies like micrometeorite impact and solar radiation are likely to be of more importance, as in the case of Mercury and the Moon. Earth-type erosion due to water and wind seems to be important on Mars, and the atmosphere of Venus is so dense and fast-moving that it must also cause severe erosion

## ESA

The European Space Agency, a Paris-based organisation set up in 1975 to organise European civilian space efforts. Among its successes have been the Ariane launcher and the Giotto mission to Halley's Comet

## escape velocity

The velocity needed to escape completely from the gravitational field of a planet or other object, 11km per second in the case of the Earth

## ESO

*See* EUROPEAN SOUTHERN OBSERVATORY

## Eta Aquarids

Meteor shower seen in early May

## Eta Carinae

Star in **Carina** which is a highly visible feature of the infrared sky. The star seen in visible light brightened by many magnitudes in the 1840s and has now faded to telescope visibility. It seems to be surrounded by a dust cloud several times the size of the solar system, which is maintained by the star's radiation at a temperature of about 250K and suggests severe mass loss from the star. The star is seen at visible wavelengths and the cloud at infrared. The cloud is sometimes called the Homunculus because of its supposed human appearance

## Eudoxus (c.408BC – c.355BC)

Astronomer born in Asia Minor who produced an early model of the solar system based on concentric spheres, using a complex model devised to preserve the structure of the universe in terms of circular rather than asymmetrical shapes. **Ptolemy** took this scheme to a higher level of development

## Europa

One of the four large satellites of Jupiter discovered by **Galileo** in 1610. Travelling in a 671,000km, 3 day orbit, Europa is 3,100km in diameter and seems to have an icy crust and a rocky interior. Its surface is blotchy and covered in a system of long fracture lines, but Europa's density, slightly greater than that of the Moon, indicates that this icy surface must have rock beneath it, making up most of the satellite's body. There may be liquid water below tens of kilometres of ice. The ice seems to be able to flow and generate new surface material, since the surface has few impact craters, indicating a young average age. In 1995 its extremely thin atmosphere, with a pressure of about one hundred thousandth that of the Earth's atmosphere, was shown to consist of oxygen

## European Southern Observatory

Consortium organisation of European nations which runs the **Very Large Telescope** and **ALMA** in Chile. At the time of writing in 2000 it was planning future projects including OWL, the Overwhelmingly Large Telescope, a possible 100m telescope. At the same time the United Kingdom was considering joining.

## European Space Agency
*See* ESA

## EUV
*See* XUV

## EUVE
*See* EXTREME ULTRA-VIOLET EXPLORER

## eV
*See* ELECTRON VOLT

## evaporation

The process by which molecules of a liquid turn into a gas, the vapour, below the liquid's boiling point, when they acquire enough energy to leave the body of the liquid. The term is also used by analogy to describe the process by which matter and energy can leak out of a black hole, leaving nothing behind. In the case of small black holes this process can be so rapid that they explode, because their temperature rises rapidly as more material is removed

## event horizon

The surface of a black hole, at which a distant observer sees time stop and below which he or she can see nothing. From the point of view of an observer travelling into a black hole, the event horizon is the point beyond which it is not possible to escape the hole, however powerful a rocket is used. Black holes are small – even one of 100 solar masses has an event horizon with a radius of just under 300km. This is the **Schwarzschild** radius

## exclusion principle
The rule that not more than one particle can have the same quantum conditions in the same atom. They must differ in energy level, spin or some other characteristic. Also called the Pauli Exclusion Principle after Swiss physicist Wolfgang Pauli (1900-1958) this rule is fundamental to nuclear structure and in astrophysics is vital to understanding how white dwarfs and neutron stars are formed

## exit cone
The cone-shaped volume in which radiation can escape from a strong gravitational field. A black hole occurs when the exit cone becomes vanishingly small

## exit pupil
The area near the eyepiece of a telescope (or microscope) which contains the smallest, brightest image of the object being viewed, and therefore the place to put the eye for viewing

## exobiology
The study of possible life in the universe other than on the Earth. Considering that it is a science with absolutely no data, exobiology is given a lot of thought by scientists, who have produced figures on the number of habitable planets **(Drake Equation)** , speculations on the limits of our type of carbon-based biology and theories on alternative ways of organising life. There is also a less popular school of thought to the effect that the Earth is the only inhabited planet in the galaxy – otherwise the aliens would be here by now – a simple case of the fallacy of anthropomorphism

## Exosat
ESA satellite for **X-ray astronomy**, launched in 1983 and used until 1986 with great success. Its payload included two telescopes, a counter for incoming X-rays and a spectrometer

## expansion of the universe
The universe is expanding from the Big Bang which marked its birth, perhaps some 20 billion years ago. The expansion is seen by terrestrial observers in the form of the **redshift** in the radiation from distant galaxies. The **Hubble Constant** which tells us how fast objects recede for their distance is today put at 55 kilometres per second per million parsecs of distance. Distance has been determined from looking at Cepheid variables in nearby galaxies and by other means for more distant ones, while the velocities are found from redshifts in optical or other wavelengths

## external tank

The fuel tank of the US **Space Shuttle**, consisting of tanks for liquid oxygen and hydrogen in an external body. The external tank is designed for one shuttle flight only, although it could in principle be carried into orbit as a way of providing a large volume of usable space in orbit

## extinction

In biology, the annihilation of an entire species. In astronomy, the dimming and reddening of starlight by interstellar dust, which in free space in our part of the galaxy seems to happen at a rate of about one **magnitude** per 1000 **parsecs**, away from major dust clouds. The dimming of starlight by the Earth's atmosphere before it reaches ground-based telescopes is also termed extinction

## Extrasolar planet

Planet of a star other than the Sun.
*See* PLANET

## Extreme Ultra-Violet Explorer (EUVE)

US spacecraft launched in 1992 to produce the first full-scale survey of the extreme **ultra-violet** sky in the 100-1000 Ångstrom wavelength range. It has been used to catalogue the sky and to examine spectra of UV-emitting objects including **active galactic nuclei and quasars, planetary nebulae, flare stars** and **white dwarfs**

## eyepiece

The small lens of a telescope (or microscope) at which the image is viewed

# Ff

### F Corona
**Corona** seen around the Sun during eclipses or with a coronagraph for a distance of several solar radii from the Sun. The F Corona is large because it consists of light which has set out from the Sun's photosphere and been scattered to the Earth by dust, which is distributed throughout the inner solar system, unlike the electrons which cause the K Corona and are found in high densities mainly near the Sun

### F Stars
Stars with a surface temperature of 6000-7500° and strong calcium and hydrogen lines. Examples include **Canopus** and **Polaris**. The **H** and **K** **lines** due to singly ionised calcium are the most distinctive feature of their spectra

### facula
Bright burst of gas given off from the Sun's surface, usually associated with sunspots and having a lifetime of a few hours. Faculae are bright, white features which ascend high into the Sun's atmosphere, and can be seen outlined against the dark of space when at the Sun's limb

### fairy castle structure
The fine structure of meteoritic and interstellar dust, which has little mechanical strength and therefore little ability to survive impact with the Earth's atmosphere or collisions with other objects

### FAME
FULL-SKY ASTROMETRIC MAPPING EXPLORER
a NASA mission designed to give precise position measurements for 40 million stars, due for launch in 2004. It will allow distances in the universe to be known with much greater precision

### FAUST
The Far Ultraviolet Shuttle Telescope, a French-built telescope flown several times on the Space Shuttle and used to make observations in the 1400-1800 Ångstrom range

### featherweight star
Star of less than seven percent of the Sun's mass, which collapses into a black dwarf without ever shining like a true star. The term is therefore something of a misnomer

### fibril
Fine, dark line seen on the Sun's **photosphere** with the aid of filters in patterns which reflect the granular structure of the Sun's surface

## field

The main types of field encountered in astronomy are gravitational, magnetic and electric. Any mass has a gravitational field, which like electric and magnetic fields are subject to an inverse square law. Electric fields are found surrounding electric charges, and can involve objects being attracted (if they have a charge opposite to that of the object whose field they are in), repelled (if they bear the same charge) or not affected at all if they are electrically neutral. An electric field can be produced by flowing electric current or by a static electric charge. Electric and magnetic fields are essentially manifestations of the same effect, and electricity is generated by movement in magnetic fields. Magnetic fields affect mainly iron, nickel and similar magnetic materials as well as ionised materials like charged particles in the Sun or the Earth's outer atmosphere

## field of view

The area of sky visible in a telescope with a particular power and type of eyepiece in use

## filament

Dark, sinuous feature seen against the Sun's surface: when seen at the Sun's limb the same structures are seen as prominences. The prominences stand out bright against the dark of space but are cooler than the Sun's photosphere, against which they look dark

## filter

In optical astronomy, a device for selecting a wavelength of radiation, for example to allow only yellow light or only light of a particular spectral line to be observed. Optical filters can be made to allow light from a range of just a few Ångstroms to be passed, although this means losing almost all the light received, so that solar astronomers, who have lots of energy to play with, are the main users of these very narrow filters. In radio astronomy, filter effects are obtained by tuning receivers to record a wider or narrower range of radiation

## fireball

Bright meteor, usually of magnitude -6 or brighter, especially one which gives rise to a fall of meteorites

## Firewheel

Space experiment carried out in 1980, involving a release of barium into the upper atmosphere to trace the Earth's magnetic and electrical fields by tracing the progress of the ionised metal

## FIRST

Proposed ESA space observatory, the Far Infrared Submillimetre Space Telescope, scheduled for launch in about 2007. Designed to observe the universe in the 0.1-1mm wavelength range, it is intended to view objects cooler than those seen by existing infrared telescopes such as **ISO**, such as areas in which stars are forming.

## fission

Process of decomposition of unstable atomic nuclei, and the basis of atom bombs and nuclear reactors. Nuclear fission in nature happens at a known rate for particular isotopes **(half-life)** which allows the age of meteorites and other rocks to be determined. It is also the source of heat within the bodies of planets, including the Earth, allowing the Earth to have a molten, metallic core which drives its magnetic field. Stars are driven by fusion rather than fission but the fusion process **(carbon cycle)** involves both fission and fusion to reach its end result of producing helium from hydrogen

## fission theory

Now-abandoned theory that the Moon is a broken-off fragment of the Earth. At one time the Pacific Ocean was thought of as the scar created by the Moon's breakaway, although it is now known to have been formed by plate **tectonic forces**

## Fitzgerald Contraction

Effect whereby a stationary observer sees objects moving at velocities near that of light shrink along their line of motion. The Fitzgerald Contraction becomes significant only near the velocity of light, like other relativistic effects. Bodies shrink to half their rest length at about 50percent the velocity of light. The contraction can be observed experimentally in particle accelerators where matter is brought to relativistic velocities

## fixed stars

Archaic term for the stars rather than the planets, since the former stay largely in the same relative positions while the latter move through the constellations. We now know that the 'fixed' stars move too, but the discovery of difference between the two types was one of the most fundamental in ancient astronomy

## Flamsteed, John (1646-1719)

First of England's Astronomers Royal (Scotland has its own) and the first head of the English national observatory in Greenwich, a suburb of London. (The Royal Greenwich Observatory has now merged with its counterpart in Edinburgh to form the Astronomy Technology Centre, based in Edinburgh.) Flamsteed produced one of the first modern star catalogues and positional observations of the Moon and planets

## flare

Short, brilliant flash of light at the Sun's surface in which huge amounts of charged particles are ejected into space. Flares are of intense practical interest because the particles which they eject cause brilliant aurorae but also interfere with radio communications

## flare star

Low-mass type of variable star prone to intense flaring which can more than double the star's overall light output

## flash spectrum
Spectrum of the Sun's **chromosphere** obtainable at the beginning and end of a solar eclipse. The flash spectrum consists of **emission lines** superimposed on a faint continuum

## flatness
Feature of the universe whereby it seems to contain almost exactly enough mass to continue expanding without gravitation causing it to collapse, without expanding so much that gravitation has become insignificant because of the dispersion of its mass. Numerous experiments including **Boomerang** and **Cobe** at the end of the 20th century confirmed the probable flatness of the universe by measuring its density and the uniformity of the **Cosmic Background Radiation**.

## fluorescence
Emission of light from material capable of storing received energy and retransmitting it after a time delay

## fly-by
Close approach of a spacecraft to a celestial object without landing

## focal length
The distance at which a converging mirror or lens will bring parallel light to a point, or the distance from which a parallel beam will appear to diverge after passing through a diverging lens or mirror. For a simple mirror with a surface which is part of a sphere, the focal length is half of the radius of curvature. Since astronomical objects are in effect infinitely far away, a mirror or lens will focus light from them at its own focal length, near which an eyepiece can form a visible image

## Foucault Pendulum
A long pendulum set to swing with a heavy weight at its extreme end. If set up with adequate care, a Foucault Pendulum can be seen to rotate once a day through a full circle as the Earth turns beneath it, providing simple and powerful proof of the Earth's rotation. Invented by Leon Foucault (1819-1868), French physicist

## Fomalhaut
16th brightest star in the sky, and the brightest in the constellation Piscis Austrinus. Type A3, 22.6 light years from Earth, apparent magnitude 1.15, absolute magnitude 2.0. Fomalhaut is surrounded by a **circumstellar disc** like that around **Beta Pictoris**

## forbidden lines
Lines in stellar spectra which were thought to be impossible but which turn out to be due to atoms in a far higher state of **ionisation** than can be produced in terrestrial conditions

## force
Four types of force are encountered in the universe. The strong force which binds atomic nuclei together and the weak force, encountered in

particle physics, are the least familiar, while the other two, electromagnetic and gravitational forces, are also encountered in everyday life. These four forces appear to account for all the interactions of matter which we know about. A force was defined by **Newton** as anything which alters a body's state of rest or uniform motion, a definition which he used mainly to describe the operation of gravitation in the solar system. The strong force is expressed by a variety of particles called Quarks and is some hundred times as powerful as the electromagnetic forces, which govern chemical reactions and the emission of electromagnetic radiation. They in turn are some 100 billion times as strong as the weak force, which is itself 100 trillion trillion times as strong as gravitation. This is why a minute pocket magnet can hold a lump of iron in mid-air, defying the whole of the Earth's gravitation

## Fornax
Constellation of the Southern hemisphere, meaning the Furnace. *(Genitive is **Fornacis**)*

## Fortuna
Asteroid which is probably the ninth largest in the solar system, some 200km across and with a dark surface

## Fraunhofer Lines
Absorption lines in the spectrum of the Sun's photosphere, first observed by the Englishman William Wollaston (1766-1828) in 1802 and later mapped in detail by Joseph von Fraunhofer, (1887-1826), a German physicist. The lines are caused by the removal of energy from the Sun's radiation by a layer of the Sun's atmosphere a few hundred kilometres deep above the photosphere. Analysis of the strength of some of the many thousands of Fraunhofer lines has given detailed data about the elements present there and their abundances as well as data about temperatures and magnetic fields

## frequency
The number of waves of radiation of a particular wavelength passing a fixed point per second. The unit of frequency is the Hertz, one per second. The frequency of a signal multiplied by its wavelength equals its velocity, so that electromagnetic radiation of one metre wavelength must have a frequency of 300,000,000 hertz, or 300MHz, since all electromagnetic radiation has a velocity of 300,000 km per second in empty space. The same principle applies to other forms of wave energy like seismic waves and vibrations in interstellar gas clouds

## frost
Thin frost has been observed by **Viking** spacecraft on the surface of Mars, and ambiguous observations from lunar orbit by **Clementine** suggest that it might also be found in sheltered areas near the Moon's poles

## FUSE
### FAR ULTRAVIOLET SPECTROSCOPIC EXPLORER
NASA's Far Ultraviolet Spectroscopic Explorer, launched in 1999 to observe the sky in the 90-120nm waveband. It has been used to observe hot gases and cold hydrogen in our galaxy

## fusion
The energy-producing process encountered in stars as well as in hydrogen bombs, and involving the production of heavier nuclei from lighter ones. The small difference in mass between the starting and final nuclei is converted to energy, which makes the stars shine. Most stellar energy production takes place by the conversion of hydrogen to helium, and these elements account for the bulk of the mass of most stars. This fusion process involves converting just 0.7percent of the material involved into energy, but this is enough to keep stars shining for billions of years. The realisation in 1920 that fusion powers the stars ended millennia of speculation about how the stars keep shining, in which every idea was pursued from making them out of burning coal to powering them by kinetic energy released from matter falling into the stars from space. Many of these ideas would have worked but none would allow the stars to shine for millions of years, as the Sun is known to have done from the evidence of geology. Kinetic energy, however, is still regarded as important in the early life of stars, while enough material builds up to produce the high temperatures and pressures needed for fusion.

# Gg

### G Star
Type of star, including conspicuously the Sun, with surface
temperatures in the 5000-6000° range, yellow surfaces and strong **H**
and **K** lines in their spectra, due to calcium and potassium

### Gagarin, Yuri
Soviet fighter pilot who in 1961 became the first person to fly in space.
Born in 1934, he was killed in an air crash in 1968

### galactic centre
The centres of galaxies are often highly disturbed and energetic. The
core of our own galaxy, which lies in Sagittarius, cannot be observed in
visible light because of the dense dust and gas clouds obscuring it. But
it is highly active in X and gamma ray frequencies, which has given rise
to theories that it contains a massive black hole. The galactic core is
seen in radio wavelengths – radio astronomers call it Sagittarius A – and
at these frequencies it resembles a quieter version of the active nuclei of
Seyfert galaxies and quasars. The galactic centre seems to give off
about 0.1 per cent of the radiation of the whole galaxy – about 80
million times as much as the Sun – in a tiny fraction of the overall
volume of the galaxy

### galactic cluster
Type of star cluster found in the arms of spiral galaxies, containing
between a few dozen and a few hundred stars. The Pleiades, a galactic
cluster of several hundred stars, visible to the naked eye in Taurus, are
the best-known example. (Only a few stars are visible to the naked eye.)
The stars of galactic clusters appear to have the same composition as
other stars in spiral arms and are less tightly packed than those in the
**globular clusters**

### galactic network
Postulated galaxy-wide civilisation, consisting of a number of cultures
of differing types, which may exist on the basis of radio communication
in this or other galaxies

### galactic year
Period taken by the Sun for an orbit around the centre of the galaxy,
about 250 million Earth years

### Galatea
150-km diameter satellite of Neptune which orbits just inside the main
ring of Neptune's ring system and keeps the matter there in a narrow

orbit by resonance effects

## galaxy

Galaxies are massive assemblies of stars, dust, gas and other components, and appear to be the main building blocks of the universe. Galaxies gather in clusters of dozens of galaxies and superclusters with hundreds of members, and interact with each other by colliding and in other ways, but are usually autonomous groupings of stars and other material. The main types (**Hubble Classification**) are spiral galaxies, barred spirals, elliptical, irregular and peculiar, a portmanteau term whose members account for only a few percent of the total. It appears from the velocities at which stars orbit the galactic centre that astronomers are observing only a small fraction – perhaps about 10 per cent – of the mass of galaxies in the form of visible matter, and that they contain a much larger amount of **dark matter** in and around the visible disc of an average galaxy. However, it was also suggested in 1995 that part of the missing mass might be present in the form of small galaxies which have been missed by previous sky surveys. Little is known about the relationship between the different types of galaxy, or about the mechanism whereby contrasting types can appear near each other in a single cluster. The rare distorted types seem to be produced by the gravitational effects of near-collisions between galaxies. Our own galaxy is known as the **Milky Way** galaxy because the path of the Milky Way across the sky marks the main mass of the galaxy, whose centre is in the constellation **Scorpius.**

## Galilean Satellites

The four large satellites of Jupiter discovered in 1610 by **Galileo – Io, Europa, Ganymede** and **Callisto**

## Galileo Galilei (1564-1642)

Italian astronomer who was one of the first people to look at the sky through a telescope. He concluded from sights like the craters of the Moon, the satellites of Jupiter and the phases of Venus that the heavens contain as much imperfection and movement as the Earth and that the Earth moves like other astronomical objects, a conclusion which led him to a showdown with the Church of Rome in which he was forced to retract. His last book was published in the protestant Netherlands, away from the influence of Rome, in 1638. He also applied mathematical analysis to movement of bodies in a way which was a precursor to **Newton's** work on motion, and was an inventor whose devices ranged from clocks to artillery. He observed Neptune without recognising it as an unknown planet

## Galileo

US spacecraft launched in 1989 which has done large amounts of first-rate science despite the failure of its main communications antenna designed to keep it in touch with Earth. It flew by Venus in 1990 and the Earth/Moon system twice, in 1990 and 1992, to gather energy for a trip deep into the solar system. These visits also generated useful images of the Earth's and Venus's atmosphere and of the Moon's North Pole. Thereafter it flew close to the asteroids 951 **Gaspra** and 243 **Ida** en route to an arrival at Jupiter in December 1995. Its observations have allowed the complex interactions of the atmosphere of Jupiter to be analysed fully for the first time and have also shown us the volcanoes of Io, the ice-pack of Europa and the surfaces of the other satellites of Jupiter in unprecedented detail. In January 1996 it sent a parachute probe into the massive atmosphere of Jupiter to provide the first data on its composition, temperature and pressure. It detected winds of up to 500kph and severe turbulence in Jupiter's atmosphere along with a surprising dearth of water, during a descent 150km into Jupiter's clouds. At this depth, an hour after beginning its descent into the clouds, the probe encountered pressures 22 times those of the Earth's atmosphere at sea level and temperatures of 150°C. Galileo began its Jupiter researches in 1994 by making observations of the impact of comet **Shoemaker-Levy 9** with the planet.

## gamma rays

The shortest-wavelength form of electromagnetic radiation, with a wavelength of 0.1nm or less. Because gamma rays are the most energetic radiation observable, they yield information about the most energetic events. This means that astronomers can get information about objects like gamma ray bursters only by observing in gamma ray frequencies. This can be done in space – gamma rays were first observed from space by accident by satellites intended to spot nuclear weapons tests – or by setting up detectors on the Earth's surface to spot the bursts of visible **Cerenkov** radiation produced by gamma rays striking the top of the Earth's atmosphere

## Gamma Ray Observatory
*See* COMPTON

## gamma ray burster

Type of celestial object which emits bursts of gamma rays lasting from less than a second to several tens of minutes. Little is known about the nature of gamma ray bursters, although it is clear that they give out thousands of times as much energy as the Sun when the burst is occurring. They seem to be associated with neutron stars and pulsars, and may have to do with material being sucked into the objects or with pulsar material rearranging itself energetically. Detectors on the **Compton** and **Ulysses** spacecraft have provided most of our information on bursters. Over 2,400,300 GRBs are known and their redshifts and distribution in the sky implies that they lie well beyond our own galaxy.

## Ganymede

One of the four satellites of Jupiter discovered by **Galileo** in 1610.
2640km in diameter, it has a 1.07 million km, 7.2 day orbit. Ganymede
is the largest of the Galilean satellites and of low density. Its surface is
cratered and crossed by tectonic features like long, deep grooves. The
appearance of Ganymede is thought to imply the presence of both ice
and rocky material in the satellite's interior, possibly with layers of dirty
ice overlying a rocky core. The **Galileo** spacecraft discovered a
magnetic field at Ganymede in 1996. Galileo also revealed aurorae and
snowy polar caps on Ganymede.

## Gas Chromatograph Mass Spectrometer

Experiment run on Viking landers on the surface of Mars to look for
organic material in Martian soil. It found no definite evidence of
biological processes active there

## gas cloud

Clouds of gas are a common component of galaxies including our own.
They can become visible when they shine with light produced under the
influence of intense radiation from nearby stars. Gas clouds can be
observed by radio astronomers by the radiation they emit at a
wavelength of 21cm. The Doppler effects observed in 21cm radiation
from gas clouds at different parts of the galaxy are a powerful means of
determining the distribution of material in the galaxy and the orbital
paths it pursues around the galactic centre. Gas clouds are classified into
**HI** and **HII** types

## Gas Exchange Experiment

Experiment run on the martian surface by Viking landers to look for
signs of Earth-type life, without positive results

## gas giant

Term for the large, gassy planets of the outer solar system, Jupiter,
Saturn, Uranus and Neptune

## gas tail

One of the two types of comet tail, the other being the **dust tail**

## Gaspra

Asteroid 951, visited by the **Galileo** space probe in 1991. Heavily
cratered like other asteroids, Gaspra, about 19km long, has a magnetic
field and appears to be metal-rich

## Gauss, Karl Friederich (1777-1855)

German astronomer who was director of the Gottingen observatory for
most of his career and did original work in mathematics and surveying
and on solar system orbits

## Gegenschein

The 'counter-glow' – the literal meaning of its German name –
sometimes seen in the sky opposite the Sun at dawn or dusk. This

extremely faint light is caused by sunlight being scattered back to the Earth from dust in interplanetary space. The Gegenschein can only be seen from sites with very good viewing conditions

### Geiger-Muller Counter
Standard device for detecting radiation, used on spacecraft as well as for a wide variety of Earthly applications

### gelifluction
Process of downhill flow of frozen material in cold regions, apparently observed on Mars as well as on the Earth

### Geminga
The pulsar 2CG 195 +04, which appears to be only about just over 500 light years from Earth and therefore the closest highly condensed matter object (neutron star or black hole) to us. Geminga is a supernova remnant and is observable optically and in gamma radiation and X-rays. Its nearness is indicated by its brightness in both types of radiation as well as by its large proper motion of about 0.4 arc seconds per year. The supernova explosion occurred about 300,000 years ago and would have appeared as bright as the full Moon from Earth

### Gemini[1]
Constellation of the Zodiac in the northern hemisphere. Meaning the twins, Gemini is best known for the bright stars Castor and Pollux, representing the mythical twins.
*(Genitive is **Geminorum**)*

### Gemini[2]
US two-man spacecraft programme, carried out between 1961 and 1963

### Gemini[3]
A pair of 8.1m telescopes on Mauna Kea, Hawaii (Gemini North) and Cerro Pachon in Chile (Gemini South), built by a multinational consortium and nearing completion at the time of writing.

### Geminids
Meteor shower with radiant near Castor, observed in December and noted for containing a large number of bright meteors and fireballs. They share an orbit with the asteroid 3200 Phaethon, which may be an extinct comet

### General Catalogue
Listing of several thousand nebulae, including galaxies, published in 1864 by **John Herschel**. Superseded by the **New General Catalogue**

### geodesic
In relativistic physics, a geodesic is the shortest path in spacetime between two points

### GEODSS
The Ground-Based Electro-Optical Deep Space Surveillance System, a

US system of telescopes for keeping track of space objects for mainly military purposes from sites scattered around the equator. The GEODSS system produces masses of optical data about the Earth's space environment which is also of astronomical value

## Geographos
Small stony asteroid, in an orbit capable of bringing it very close to the Earth

## geomagnetic storm
Disturbance of the Earth's magnetic field by the arrival of charged particles from the Sun during periods of exceptional solar activity. Geomagnetic storms can seriously disrupt radio communications

## geomagnetic tail
The extension of the Earth's magnetosphere away from the Earth, stretching many Earth radii into space

## George Ellery Hale telescope
200-inch telescope on Palomar Mountain, California, US, completed in 1948. It was the biggest telescope in the world for 25 years

## giant planets
The large planets of the outer solar system, also called the gas giants; Jupiter (318 Earth masses), Saturn (95 Earth masses), Uranus (15 Earth masses) and Neptune (17 Earth masses), but not the tiny Pluto. As well as being large, the giant planets are of low density and their composition includes much volatile material like water, ammonia and methane. The giants are obviously members of a single class of planet – although they vary in size and density markedly, with a density of 0.7 for Saturn and 1.77 for Neptune. They all have ring systems and large collections of satellites

## giant stars
Stars much larger in size than the Sun, including both those which are of large mass and others of about the same mass as the Sun which have expanded as a result of being in a later stage of development

## Gibbous
Phase of the Moon (or Venus or Mercury) between half and full, with the disc more than 50% lit as seen from Earth

## Giotto
**ESA** mission to **Halley's Comet** which in March 1986 flew close to the nucleus of the Comet and provided the first-ever detailed information about the nucleus of a comet. Called after the Italian painter whose **'Adoration of the Magi'** may depict the 1301 appearance of Halley's Comet

## GLAST
The Gamma-ray Large Area Space Telescope, a NASA mission planned for launch in 2005 and intended as a successor to **Compton**

**Global Oscillation Network Group**
*see* GONG

**globular cluster**
Tight-packed type of star cluster – in contrast to the galactic clusters – which can contain 10,000 to over a million stars and which are found above and below the plane of the galaxy, but rarely near to it. Globular clusters are ancient objects at whose heart there may often lie a black hole (a thesis put forward because of X-rays observed coming from globular clusters). Their great age is shown by the spectra of globular cluster stars, which are poor in heavy elements, indicating that they formed when there were lower abundances of such elements than now. M3 in Canes Venatici is a well-known globular cluster. The stars in a globular cluster concentrate near its centre, where an observer would see a sky which was massively brighter than our own night sky

**GMT**
*See* GREENWICH MEAN TIME

**gnomon**
Upright stick or stone used for projecting shadows and for other purposes in ancient astronomy: eg the upright used to cast the shadow on a sundial

**Gold, Thomas (born 1920)**
Astronomer born in Austria, now a US citizen, who developed the steady state theory with **Hoyle** and **Bondi**. More recently he has been pursuing the idea that natural gas from within the earth is not of vegetable origin but dates back to the Earth's formation and is present at depth in huge amounts

**GONG**
Global Oscillation Network Group, an organisation which uses sites around the world to observe small fluctuations in the diameter of the Sun

**Gould's Belt**
Zone of stars in the Southern hemisphere which are systematically whiter or yellower than the average, making them stand out preferentially on photographs by comparison with their naked eye appearance

**granulation**
Fine structure of the solar surface, which appears grainy because of convection in the upper layers of the Sun. The granules are typically a few hundred kilometres across and are best seen with specialised solar telescopes on high mountains or sent aloft on balloons or into space. Granules come and go on a timescale of just a few minutes

**Gran Telescopio Canarias**
Spanish telescope with a 10.4m main mirror, due to enter service in 2002 on La Palma, Canary Islands.

### graphite
The most common crystalline form of carbon, found in pencils and interstellar gas clouds

### gravitation
The apparently universal attractive force between matter, increasing according to the two masses multiplied together and decreasing with the square of their distance apart, according to the law of gravitation set out by **Isaac Newton**. The size of the force for any particular combination of distance and mass is given by the Gravitational Constant. Newton's theory of gravitation allowed him to prove **Kepler's Laws** describing the orbits of the planets and is in use today to describe orbital motion on every scale from Earth satellites to galaxies. In addition, gravitation as Newton understood it is now incorporated within the larger body of physical theory known as **Relativity**, in which it is viewed as a form of acceleration rather than as a force, and regarded as an effect of the curvature of spacetime

### gravitational contraction
The collapse of gas and dust to form stars, planets and other objects, under gravitational attraction. The process leads to the release of potential energy as the mass becomes more closely packed. This process may, along with radioactive decay, account for the internal heat within the planets, and power the early 'protostar' phase of stellar evolution

### gravitational lens
Concentration of matter dense enough to refract light into an image. The idea of gravitational lensing arises from general **Relativity**, with its proof that the straight-line paths of light can be bent by gravitation *(see* **Einstein***)*. Many cases of small galaxies and other objects performing gravitational lensing have been observed by astronomers and the method has been used as a technique for hunting missing mass in the universe. If such mass is in compact form, it will lens the light from distant galaxies. Lenses form elaborate images of distant objects in the universe, sometimes forming several images of the same object and

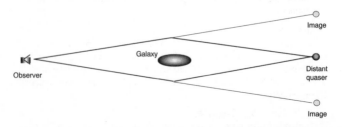

*Gravitational Lens*

generating distorted, arc-shaped images of distant galaxies called
Einstein Rings. Many have now been observed

### gravitational radiation
Form of energy whose existence is predicted by general **Relativity**. It
has been looked for by physicists and astronomers using instruments
such as large metal cylinders carefully suspended in caverns below the
Earth's surface. Gravitational Radiation would be observed, if at all, in
the form of gravity waves, very long waves of fluctuating gravitational
attraction. Gravity waves are extremely weak – the orbital movement of
Jupiter about the Sun produces about 5kW of gravitational radiation,
about as much as the electricity consumption of a small house. Binaries
with massive, close components contain more gravitational energy and
seem likelier candidates to emit detectable gravity waves. Construction
of a German/UK detector for such waves began in 1996

### gravitational radius
The radius for a collapsing star at which light can no longer escape:
synonym is the **Schwarzschild Radius**. Equal to the radius of the
**Event Horizon**.

### gravitational redshift
**Redshift** of light or other electromagnetic radiation caused by its
passing through a strong gravitational field, rather than being due to a
Doppler effect

### gravitino
Proposed particle which carries gravitational energy in unified field
theory physics, much as neutrinos are the carriers of angular momentum

### graviton
Proposed subatomic particle which carries gravitational forces between
massive particles as photons carry electromagnetic energy. Gravitons
and gravitinos are brought to bear in some solutions to the **dark matter**
or **missing mass problem**

### gravity assist
Technique for giving interplanetary space probes acceleration by flying
them close to large planets from which they can acquire small amounts
of energy as they fly by

### Gravity Probe B
US space probe proposed to test **special relativity** by looking for an
effect called Frame Dragging, the pulling of **spacetime** by the Earth's
rotation. The project had not been approved at the time of writing but
had a tentative launch date of 1999

### Gravity Wave
*See* GRAVITATIONAL RADIATION

### grazing incidence
Technique whereby radiation is reflected from a surface on which it

falls at a tiny angle. X-ray telescopes have usually been built on a grazing incidence principle since X-rays cannot easily be focused by conventional optics

## great annihilator
Source of gamma radiation near the centre of our galaxy, so-called because it seems to work by producing protons which annihilate electrons in surrounding space to produce the gamma rays. It may consist of a small, dense plasma cloud

## Great attractor
Hundreds of galaxies appear to be affected by the attractor's gravitation. With a mass about 100,000 times that of our galaxy and a distance of about 200 million light years, it has been tentatively identified with a galaxy cluster called Abell 3627

## Great Dark Spot
*See* NEPTUNE

## Great Red Spot
Huge reddish oval storm structure, 14,000 by 30,000km, which has been observed in the atmosphere of Jupiter since telescopes were first turned on it in the 17th century. The Spot is an anticyclone whose boundary with the rest of the Jovian atmosphere is the site of immense activity, with other spots being swept past the Spot and sometimes merging with it. For the last 40 years three companion white spots have also been visible near the Great Red Spot. Numerous theoretical models exist of possible structures for the Great Red Spot, although the need to account for its longevity is a severe constraint on possible explanations

## Greek Alphabet
The Greek Alphabet is widely used by astronomers to provide symbols for a wide variety of purposes, especially for classifying the brighter stars in constellations, generally with Alpha as the brightest and so on. The full Greek Alphabet runs Alpha ( ), Beta ( ), Gamma ( ), Delta ( )

## Greenwich Mean Time (GMT)
local time on the 0 meridian where it passes through Greenwich, England; used to calculate international time zones

## Grey Hole
Object which might be formed by the collapse of a massive star too small to form a black hole but too large to form a neutron star. Such an object would have a central black hole with material lying outside it and a sphere of photons outside the material layer. It would be possible for photons to escape from this sphere, making the Grey Hole visible – grey rather than black

## GRO
*See* COMPTON

# Hh

### H
*See* HYDROGEN ALPHA

### H Lines
Lines due to calcium seen in the spectra of the Sun and other stars, especially **G type** stars of which the Sun is one

### HI
Neutral hydrogen in interstellar gas clouds. HI regions are those where most of the hydrogen present is un-ionised. It can be present either as hydrogen atoms or as molecules of two hydrogen atoms

### HII
Ionised hydrogen in interstellar gas clouds. HII regions generally arise where stars are present and emit enough energy to remove electrons from hydrogen atoms

### Hadar
Second brightest star in Taurus and the 11th brightest in the night sky. Apparent magnitude -0.63, absolute magnitude -5.2 (both averages since Hadar is a variable star), type B1, 490 light years from Earth

### Hale-Bopp, Comet
Comet Hale-Bopp was seen in March and April 1997 as one of the most spectacular naked-eye comets of the century. It was clearly visible even from brightly-lit city centres. It was discovered by two US astronomers, Alan Hale in New Mexico and Thomas Bopp in Arizona, who saw it within 20 minutes of each other in 1995. At its closest approach to the Sun, the comet was shedding over two million tonnes of water per day into space as solar heat evaporated its icy nucleus. Observations of the comet with the ISO satellite showed that it contained the complex mineral olivine which is found deep within the Earth, showing the connection between comets and the formation of planets. Hale-Bopp has now retreated to the outer solar system. Our descendants will see its next visit to the Sun in about 4,000 years.
*See also* ISO, COMET

### half-life
The time taken for half of the atoms of an unstable isotope to decay. Half-lives can be under a second (0.3 seconds for Sodium 20) or millions of years (about 4.5 billion years for Uranium 238)

### Hall, Asaph (1829-1907)
US astronomer best remembered for discovering **Deimos** and **Phobos**,

the satellites of Mars, in 1877 while he was working at the US Naval Observatory

## Halley, Edmond (1656-1742)

English astronomer best remembered for the realisation that the great comet of 1682 was in fact a periodic comet identical to others seen at 76-year intervals throughout history. Halley later became Astronomer Royal and was one of the circle including Newton, Hooke and others which produced many discoveries in mathematics, physics and astronomy. He carried out researches into gravitation and produced a large number of theories about the catastrophic effects of comet collisions with the Earth (thinking amongst other things that one had caused Noah's flood). But he did not live to see his reputation established for ever by the return of his comet, formally called Comet Halley or Comet P/Halley, as predicted, in 1758

## Halley's Comet

This best-known comet, publicly notorious because it reappears predictably and is bright enough to be seen with the naked eye. These factors also make it fascinating to astronomers: its brightness and the fact that it spends almost all of its 76 year orbit in deep space mean that Halley's Comet is an almost unaltered chunk of material from the earliest days of the solar system, which presents itself for observation at predictable intervals. The comet's 1986 appearance was greeted by a shoal of spacecraft from Europe, Japan and the USSR (especially ESA's **Giotto**, which flew closest to the Comet's nucleus), and was viewed by thousands of terrestrial observers

## halo[1]

In a galaxy, the volume of space above and below the plane of its main structure. The halo contains old stars and globular clusters as well as gas clouds consisting mainly of neutral hydrogen. The halo contains a far lower density of matter than the main body of the galaxy, which is crammed with stars and other material

## halo[2]

Atmospheric phenomenon consisting of a circular ring of light around the Sun, caused by refraction of sunlight by ice crystals high in the Earth's atmosphere. These crystals can also form a faint second image of the Sun.

## Hawking, Stephen (born 1942)

British cosmologist based in Cambridge, best known for work on relativistic phenomena such as black holes and as the author of **'A Brief History of Time'**, a popular-science best-seller

## head

The small central part of a comet from which the tail or tails of the comet emerge under the heating influence of solar radiation as it approaches the Sun. The head consists of the nucleus, apparently only a

few kilometres across, as well as the **coma**, a mass of material
surrounding the nucleus and originating from it

## HEAO
*See* HIGH ENERGY ASTRONOMY OBSERVATORIES

## heavy elements
Elements with nuclei heavier than that of iron. These elements cannot
be produced in normal stars and are instead produced from iron cores
built up at the centre of heavy stars before or during **supernova
explosions**. The **fusion** process which builds up the lighter elements
stops at iron because beyond it fusion uses up energy rather than
releasing it. The small abundance of heavier elements by comparison
with the lighter ones is due to the small amount of the universe's total
matter which has to date been reprocessed through supernovae

## heavyweight stars
Stars of more than eight solar masses, which can turn into **supernovae
and eventually black holes**

## heliopause
The outer boundary of the solar system, where the solar wind matches
in pressure the incoming charged material of interstellar space. Data
from **Voyagers 1** and **2** and **Pioneer 11** suggest that the heliopause is
80-180 astronomical units from the Sun

## Helios
Space probe placed in orbit around the Sun in 1974 by the former West
Germany

## helium
The second most abundant element in the universe after hydrogen, and
the lightest element apart from hydrogen. Helium was discovered in the
laboratory after being suspected (by **Norman Lockyer**) from the
existence of unexplained lines in the spectrum of the Sun. Most stars
shine with the energy produced by fusing hydrogen into helium **(carbon
cycle)**. This means that the abundance of helium in the universe is
constantly increasing. But this process is so slow that most of the
helium we observe is that created in the **big bang** itself. This may
amount to 20-30% of the total mass of the universe, although the exact
figure is difficult to determine. Within the solar system, helium is
present in the Sun and in the **gas giants** but is only a trace element in
the Earth's atmosphere. The helium used by astronomers to hoist
telescopes into the atmosphere in balloons is extracted from natural gas

## helium flash
Brief but energetic period of a few years in stellar evolution when stars
fuse helium into carbon

## helmet streamer
Plasma columns, of a size of up to two solar radii, which stream from

active areas of the Sun's surface

## Heraclides (c.388BC-c.315BC)

Pupil of Plato who developed the idea of the Earth's rotation and the notion, usually associated with Tycho Brahe, that Venus and Mercury orbit the Sun but the other planets known in ancient times orbit the Earth

## Herbig-Haro Objects

Bright dust and gas regions which seem to be associated with star formation. Over 100 are known in our galaxy, and they are thought to be shock fronts driven by celestial masers and other powerful energy sources active in gas cloud regions where stars are forming

## Hercules

Extremely large constellation of the northern hemisphere, called after the classical hero of the same name. The north pole of the **ecliptic** is found within its boundaries, so that it is the centre of rotation of the **precession** of the equinoxes
*(Genitive is **Herculis**)*

## Hercules Supercluster

Large array of clusters of galaxies in Hercules, containing a wide variety of types of galaxy, and thought to be the largest agglomeration of material known. It consists of about 150 galaxies whose redshifts have been determined and many other smaller ones

## Herschel, John (1792-1871)

Son of William Herschel and a distinguished astronomer in his own right. He produced the General Catalogue, made some of the first systematic observations of the southern sky with telescopes in South Africa and pioneered astrophotography and astronomical spectroscopy

## Herschel, William (1738-1822)

Astronomer born in Hanover, Germany but who lived most of his adult life in England. He worked as a musician until his discovery of Uranus in 1781 assured his fame and allowed him to take up astronomy full-time. He and his sister Caroline built the world's largest telescopes. Herschel was one of history's most prodigious observers of the skies, producing a listing of nebulae which dwarfs Messier's, mapping out the broad outlines of the galaxy and establishing the Solar System's direction of motion through space. He also discovered the two largest satellites of Uranus and observed infrared radiation in sunlight. His survey of the heavens was the most systematic undertaken up to that date. When congratulated on his luck in finding Uranus, he upbraided the speaker by saying that if he had not spotted it when he did because of other engagements, he would simply have found it the following evening.

## William Herschel Telescope

4.2m telescope on a mountaintop on Palma in the Canaries, Spain, and used by UK, Dutch and Spanish astronomers

## Herschelian

Type of reflecting telescope in which the main mirror is tilted to take the light into an eyepiece at the side of the telescope tube. This type of telescope is not in general use because of problems with image distortion

## hertz

Unit of frequency, signifying one cycle (such as a complete wave of electromagnetic radiation) per second

## Hertzsprung, Ejnar (1873-1967)

Danish astrophysicist who was one of the developers of the **Hertzsprung-Russell Diagram**, first drawn in 1910

## Hertzsprung Gap

Region of the **Hertzsprung-Russell Diagram** in which few stars are found, indicating a phase of stellar evolution through which they pass rapidly

## Hertzsprung-Russell Diagram *or* H-R Diagram

Graph showing the relationship between the surface temperature and brightness of stars, first drawn in 1910 independently by **Ejnar Hertzsprung** and Henry Norris **Russell**. The H-R Diagram is a fundamental underpinning of modern astronomy and astrophysics. Far from showing a uniform or random distribution of stars, the diagram shows that most stars lie on a single band called the main sequence, with white dwarfs below and giant and supergiant stars above. It is also possible to produce more detailed H-R diagrams for particular groups of stars, such as all those in a specific cluster – this is particularly simple because they can be assumed to be at essentially the same distance from the observer. This yields information about the distinguishing characteristics of particular clusters. In addition, the information on the H-R diagram is now so well established that it can with confidence be used 'backwards,' to yield the distance of a star of known type from its apparent magnitude, since the relationship between brightness (absolute magnitude) and spectral type is fixed on the H-R diagram

## HETE

High Energy Transient Experiment, a NASA mission to examine gamma-ray **bursters** in X-ray, gamma ray and ultraviolet wavelengths. The first HETE was lost on launching in 1996 and a second launched in 2000.

## Hevelius, Johannes (1611-1687)

Polish astronomer now best remembered for his sky atlas published in 1690. He also named many features on the Moon and produced an early

Moon atlas, and had a noted observatory in his birthplace of Gdansk

## High Energy Astronomy Observatories
Series of three US satellites launched between 1979 and 1981 to observe radiation too energetic to reach the Earth's surface. HEAO2's X-ray telescope and HEAO3's gamma ray telescope were two of the outstanding instruments flown on the HEAO series, along with cosmic ray detectors and other devices

## Highlands
The mountainous areas of the Moon, which are lighter-coloured, more heavily cratered and older than the lower Mare regions. The Highland rocks resemble Earthly ones called gabbros, and are rich in the mineral plagioclase

## Hilda
Asteroid which has given its name to a group whose orbital periods are two-thirds that of Jupiter

## Hipparchus (Hipparchos)
Greek astronomer (about 180BC-125BC) who carried out early systematic work on the stars, including developing the **magnitude system** which astronomers still use and producing the first major star catalogue. He discovered the precession of the equinoxes and probably observed a bright nova. He came from the island of Rhodes

## Hipparcos
**ESA** satellite designed to produce very precise astrometric measurements and launched in 1989. The spacecraft went into the wrong orbit and suffered major mechanical problems but still fulfilled its mission of providing precise positions for over 100,000 stars, along with magnitude and colour data and parallaxes, in a programme which ended in August 1993

## Hiten
Japanese Moon probe launched in 1990 which was placed in a very eccentric Earth orbit before being captured (intentionally) by the Moon's gravity in 1992. It was used until 1993 for experiments in micrometeorite detection and also placed a smaller satellite, Hagoromo, in lunar orbit

## Hobby-Eberly Telescope
9.1m telescope in Texas, US, completed in 1997. Its main mirror consists of 91 small mirrors. It is used mainly for spectroscopy

## horizon
The plane mid-way between the zenith and the nadir which in a flat landscape divides earth from sky. Not to be confused with the **event horizon**, as found in black holes

## Horizontal Branch
Zone of the **Hertzsprung-Russell Diagram** in which stars of **globular**

clusters are found. The stars here are of about zero **absolute magnitude** but have **spectral types** from about A to G, including some **main sequence stars** and some which have left the main sequence

### Horologium
Large constellation of the southern hemisphere, meaning the clock. *(Genitive is **Horologii**)*

### Horrocks, Jeremiah (1619-1641)
British astronomer born in Liverpool, and who died at the age of 22. At Much Hoole in Lancashire he observed part of the transit of Venus of November 24, 1639, and used it to measure the orbital velocity of Venus. His reputation as one of the founders of our understanding of the solar system became established only after his death

### Horsehead nebula
Dark nebula in Orion, seen by contrast with glowing material behind it, and having a distinctive horsehead shape

### Hoyle, Fred (born 1915)
British astronomer and cosmologist best-known as one of the founders of the steady-state theory of the universe, with **Bondi** and **Gold**. Has also proselytised the view that an influx of biological material from space is significant in terrestrial evolution and the spread of infectious disease, and written science fiction

### H-R Diagram
*See* HERTZSPRUNG-RUSSELL DIAGRAM

### HST
*See* HUBBLE SPACE TELESCOPE

### Hubble, Edwin P (1889-1953)
Possibly the most distinguished astronomer of the 20th century, Hubble – who trained as a lawyer – revolutionised all thinking about the large-scale structure of the universe by methodical study of the galaxies. He discovered that they are receding at a rate dependent on their distance from us, which led to the idea of the expansion of the universe. He also developed the now standard classification of galactic types

### Hubble Classification
The generally-used classification of the galaxies into elliptical, spiral and barred spiral types, which is used to describe all but the most unusual types of galaxy. Within these overall headings are subdivisions. The ellipticals are classed as E0 to E7, becoming steadily more elongated as the number increases. Spirals are classed as Sa, Sb or Sc, with the spirals less tightly wound for the later letters, and the same system is adopted for the barred spirals, which are classed as SBa, SBb and SBc. Type S0 indicates a regular ellipse apparently intermediate between the three categories. Galaxies which fall between the categories are sometimes classed as Sbc or some similar hybrid. It is important to

note that the actual relation between the different types of galaxy may well be less neat than this family tree implies

## Hubble Constant

The number linking the rate of recession of the galaxies with their distance from us, now thought to be between 50 and 100km/sec of recession velocity per megaparsec of distance. The actual value of the constant has been the subject of strong disagreement, and **Hubble** himself thought that it must be far larger than the figure now accepted. There is also speculation among cosmologists that it may vary with time. Deep space analysis with the **Hubble Space Telescope** seemed in 1996 to support a figure of about 80km/sec per megaparsec

## Hubble Diagram

Graph showing distance of galaxies against their velocity of recession from the Earth. The steepness of the graph gives the **Hubble Constant**

## Hubble Space Telescope

One of the most successful instruments in the history of science, the HST was placed into orbit in 1990 after many years of planning and delay, especially caused by the 1986 Challenger space shuttle disaster. The 12 tonne spacecraft has a telescope with a 2.4m main mirror, which by being placed above the Earth's atmosphere can be used to see objects as faint as the 31st magnitude. After launch the telescope, a joint project between **NASA** and **ESA**, has been serviced by visiting astronauts whose missions have included replacing its solar arrays, which were causing the spacecraft to shake as they expanded and contracted upon entering and leaving sunlight, and supplemented its optics to compensate for a slight miscalculation in the shape of its main mirror surface. The HST's instruments include faint-object and wide-field cameras and photometers and spectrographs. It is used mainly to examine objects in deep space, including distant galaxies and parts of our own galaxy where activities such as star formation are going on, but has also produced startling images of solar system objects such as Mars, and Jupiter during the 1994 impact of Comet Shoemaker Levy 9. The determination of the distance scale of the universe – in other words of the **Hubble Constant** – is, appropriately, its most significant mission. It is likely to last 15-20 years in orbit

## Humason, Milton L (1891-1972)

US astronomer who collaborated with Hubble in the establishment of Hubble's Law

## Hungaria

Asteroid which has given its name to a small group lying just beyond the orbit of Mars in almost circular orbits

## Huygenian

Type of telescope eyepiece invented by Huygens

## Huygens, Christiaan (1629-1693)

Dutch astronomer who lived mainly in Paris. He was a very able builder of telescopes, and contributed much to the theory of optics. He also made some of the first telescopic observations of Mars, discovered Titan, the largest satellite of Saturn, and solved the mystery of Saturn's strange appearance. Galileo's telescope had shown that Saturn has an odd and variable triform appearance, but Huygens was able to show that this is due to the presence of its ring system

## Huygens

NASA/ESA plan for a probe of the atmosphere of **Titan.** Huygens would be flown to the Saturn system with the **Cassini** orbiter and descend through the Titanian atmosphere measuring its composition, temperature and pressure winds. It will also have a camera to return pictures of the surface of Titan

## Huygens Gap

Gap in Saturn's rings at 117,500km from the planet's centre, at the inner edge of the **Cassini Division**

## Hyades

**Galactic cluster** in Taurus, known for thousands of years because it is a naked-eye object near the bright star Aldebaran

## Hydra

Extensive constellation of the southern hemisphere. Means the Water Monster.
*(Genitive is **Hydrae**)*

## hydrogen

Much the most common element in the universe, hydrogen accounts for most known matter and has given rise to all the rest by means of **fusion**. A hydrogen atom is the simplest imaginable, consisting of a proton (containing almost all the mass) and an electron in orbit around it. Hydrogen at reasonably low temperatures and where it is in sufficient concentration will form a stable molecule of two atoms. Hydrogen in deep space can be mapped by radio emissions at a wavelength of 21cm. This is the frequency of the energy absorbed or emitted when the electron shifts orbit from moving in the same direction as the proton's own rotation to moving in the opposite direction, which involves slightly less energy. Hydrogen has two isotopes, deuterium and tritium

## hydrogen alpha

Wavelength of red light corresponding to the energy emitted or absorbed by hydrogen when its electron shifts from its third possible energy level to the second, or back, in one of the Balmer series of hydrogen transitions **(hydrogen lines)**. Light at this wavelength is emitted abundantly by the Sun, and filters to select it are used for examining energetic areas of the Sun's surface

## hydrogen burning
The normal process of stellar energy production, in which hydrogen is fused to yield helium

## hydrogen lines
Lines in the spectrum caused by transitions between the various possible locations for the electron of a hydrogen atom. There are several series of hydrogen lines, each known by the name of a scientist involved in their elucidation. The first is the Lyman series, which involves transitions between the ground state and the five excited states above it, and which are observed in the ultraviolet. The Balmer series involves transitions between the first excited level and the four above it and is observable in visible light (**hydrogen alpha**). In the infrared come the Paschen and Brackett series, which are produced by transitions to and from the second and third excitement states from above

## Hydrus
Constellation of the southern hemisphere.
*(Genitive is **Hydri**; means the 'sea serpent')*

## Hygeia
Fourth largest of the asteroids, some 300km across

## hyperfine structure
Detailed energy level structure of the electrons of an atom. The hyperfine structure of hydrogen, for example, includes the slight difference in energy level between the two possible directions of the electron's orbit (see hydrogen), rather than the gross difference between the different energy levels which the electron can occupy

## Hyperion
Satellite of Saturn discovered by Bond in 1848. It orbits Saturn in a 21 day, 1.48 million km orbit of high eccentricity (0.104), and appears to have an icy surface. The **Voyager 2** encounter with Saturn reveals Hyperion as a distorted sphere which measures about 410 by 210km and which has been severely deformed, possibly by impact. It turns on its short axis, parallel to Saturn, every 13 days, with the long axis pointing towards Saturn, a pattern which may be unstable over long periods and may be caused by a gravitational interaction between Hyperion, Saturn and **Titan**

## hypersphere
Sphere whose surface is curved in four or more dimensions: a construct encountered in some relativistic physics. If the universe is finite in spacetime its overall shape could be a hypersphere

## hypersurface
A flat surface showing a section through **spacetime**. Hypersurfaces can be used like contours on a conventional map to illustrate the topography of spacetime, for example in the region of a gravitational singularity

# Ii

### Iapetus
Satellite of Saturn some 1500km in diameter, in a 3.56 million km, 79 day orbit. Iapetus was discovered by **Cassini** in 1671 and is one of the oddest worlds in the solar system. Its magnitude as seen from the Earth varies drastically because one hemisphere, that facing backwards in Iapetus's orbit, is icy and of high albedo while the other side is very much darker, possibly because of material thrown out from another of Saturn's satellites by impact

### IAU
*See* INTERNATIONAL ASTRONOMICAL UNION

### Icarus
2km diameter asteroid in a 1.08AU orbit which allows it to approach the Earth very closely. A rocky body, Icarus could cause catastrophic tidal, seismic and other effects if it hit the Earth – a possibility which has given rise to a disaster movie and studies of the possibility of using nuclear weapons to prevent the collision. In the early 1990s a US lobby for world preparations against such a disaster was active, although its real target may have been the unemployment and budget cuts faced by military scientists in need of new projects after the end of the Cold War

### ICE
*See* INTERNATIONAL COMETARY EXPLORER

### Ida
Asteroid 243 Ida, visited by the **Galileo** space probe in 1993, when it turned out to have a small companion asteroid, named **Dactyl**. Ida is an **S-type** asteroid with a heavily cratered and therefore ancient surface

### IGM
*See* INTERGALACTIC MEDIUM

### image
The rendition of an object under examination by an instrument (a telescope operating in any wavelength, a camera, a microscope, etc.), or by a particular subsystem within it like a specific lens or mirror

### image intensifier
Opto-electronic device using materials which emit large numbers of photons in response to the arrival of a single photon. This allows image intensifiers to produce increased light fluxes from weak sources under observation

**image plane**

Plane at right angles to the optical axis of a telescope at which the image is produced

**IMAGE**

Imager for Magnetopause-to-Aurora Global Exploration, NASA spacecraft launched in 2000 to use six instruments to examine the structure of the Earth's **magnetosphere**.

**images, primary and secondary**

In relativistic cosmology, the primary image is the main image of a star orbiting a black hole. Because of gravitational attraction pulling the star's light towards the hole, this image traces out a complex path during the course of a single orbit of the star around the black hole. The secondary image, however, traces out a yet more complex pattern in the sky. It is made up of light which has made a single orbit of the black hole before escaping to be observed, so that the geometry governing the route taken by the light on the way to the observer is complex. There are also tertiary and higher images, of even more complexity. In these cases the light has had a more lengthy entanglement in the gravitational field of the hole before escaping to the observer. These higher order images contain steadily less and less energy, making them ever less likely to be observed. They would exhibit a single point of light moving according to the inclination of the black hole's rotation to the Earth and other factors

**image processing**

The use of computer-based techniques to distinguish data about astronomical objects from its surroundings. Astronomers use image processing methods of great power, related to those used by geophysicists, telecommunications engineers, spies and others

**image stabilisation**

Method by which binoculars with microprocessor-controlled motors (or gimbals in lower-tech versions) can produce shake-free images, in contrast to the visible motion of the image usually seen with hand-held binoculars. Amateur astronomers, sailors and others have taken up the technology.

**imaging system**

Space technologist's term for a complete camera system including optics along with the computers, data storage equipment and other accompanying hardware and software used with them on spacecraft

**IMAX**

Type of wide-field camera used on space shuttle missions

**inclination**

The angle at which an orbit is tilted to some given plane – in the solar system, usually that of the ecliptic. One of the **elements** of an orbit which define its size, shape and disposition in space

### Indus
Constellation of the southern hemisphere.
*(Genitive is **Indi;** means 'Indian')*

### inertial upper stage
Type of rocket motors developed to carry loads from the cargo bay of
the Space Shuttle to high orbits, including geostationary ones, and to
permit interplanetary probes to be launched out of Earth gravity

### inferior conjunction
The closest approach of Mercury or Venus to the Earth, when it is in a
straight line (except for the inclination of its orbit to the ecliptic)
between Sun and Earth. Despite its closeness, a planet at inferior
conjunction is hard to observe because it is near the Sun in the sky and
because its unlit face is turned to the Earth

### inferior planets
Little-used term for Mercury and Venus, the planets closer to the Sun
than Earth

### inflation
A feature of some proposed models of the early universe. These involve
a history of the first second of the universe in which it underwent
accelerated expansion from a size of only a few centimetres. The
expansion allows for the homogeneity of the universe we observe
despite its immense size, which means that it is not possible for
information to be exchanged across the universe

### infrared astronomy
Infrared light has wavelengths between those of visible light and
microwaves. Nearest to light is the near infrared (wavelengths
0.75-2.5 microns), followed by the middle (2.5-30 microns) and far
(30-1000 microns) infrared. Infrared light is associated especially with
emissions from warm objects, of which astronomers have detected
some thousands with ground-based telescopes (which can observe
some celestial infrared light) and from space. Gas and dust clouds in
space heated by nearby stars are especially readily observed in
infrared light, and includes material which may be associated with
planetary systems of other stars. In the future, large infra-red
telescopes in space such as **ISO** will yield new information on
star-forming areas, interstellar molecules, and the condition of very
distant (and therefore old) galaxies, as well as solar system objects.
Distant galaxies are so redshifted that we observe the light from them
mostly in infrared rather than visible wavelengths. Large
ground-based optical telescopes are typically configured to allow
them to make infra-red observations as well. Water vapour in the
Earth's atmosphere cuts out much infrared light but mountaintop
observatories are sited above most of the water in the atmosphere. In

addition, high-flying aircraft can be used for infrared astronomy, as can infrared telescopes in orbit. The first infrared observatory in space was **IRAS**

## Infrared Astronomy Satellite (IRAS)
Joint US/British/Dutch satellite, launched in 1983, which provided several years of highly fruitful infrared observations from space with a 60cm telescope

## Infrared Space Observatory (ISO)
Satellite launched in 1995 by ESA to observe both solar system and deep space objects in the infra-red and join the search for dark matter in the universe. ISO uses detectors to form true images of infrared-emitting objects in the sky, using a 60cm telescope with a gold-plated mirror. Its use of infrared light means it can view parts of the sky obscured by dust for optical observing. For example it has been used to view stars near the centre of our galaxy which have never been observable before.

## inner planets
Mercury, Venus, the Earth and Mars, the four rocky planets orbiting nearer to the Sun than the gas giants. More usually termed the terrestrial planets

## Integral
The International Gamma-Ray Physics Observatory, an **ESA** mission planned for a launch in 2001 designed as the next step beyond the **Compton** satellite in X-ray and Gamma Ray astronomy

## intensity interferometer
Device using two sets of telescope mirrors spaced many metres apart, which can be used to give a direct measure of the size of nearby stars from the interference pattern set up when the light from the two mirror systems is combined

## Inter-Crater Plains
Areas of the surface of Mercury which are free of large craters. The Plains abound with small craters but lack the large ones which cover most of Mercury. They may be areas of great antiquity which have avoided being modified by large impacts, or more recent areas formed after the solar system was swept free of large bodies which could produce major impacts

## interference
Interaction of radiation from more than one source, but of a single wavelength, to produce a stationary wave pattern called an interference pattern. The pattern is bright where the waves add and dark where they subtract. Interference patterns contain information about the detailed structure of emissions in visible or other wavelengths of electromagnetic radiation and can be used to provide details of the

structure of materials on the scale of the wavelength of light, for example the optical accuracy of a telescope mirror. A familiar example is a Moiré pattern

### interferometer
Device using the principle of interference to produce details of stellar surfaces or other astronomical objects which cannot be observed directly

### interferometry
Technique in which interferometers are used for astronomical observation. Radio and optical astronomy both make use of interferometry. In radio astronomy, interferometry can be practised on a massive scale by combining the signals from radio telescopes hundreds or even thousands of kilometres apart. This is known as Very Long Baseline Interferometry or **VLBI**. It has even been tried with one antenna in orbit, on the former Soviet Union's Salyut space station. The Very Large Array **(VLA)** in the US is the world's largest purpose-built VLBI system

### intergalactic medium (IGM)
The space between the galaxies. The IGM is thought to have a very low density, on the evidence of the effects it seems to have on light from distant galaxies

### International Astronomical Union (IAU)
International body with membership drawn from professional astronomers throughout the world. It promotes cooperation via conferences, standing committees and other means

### International Cometary Explorer (ICE)
US spacecraft launched as one of three International Sun-Earth Explorers in 1977 to look at the solar wind. It was later renamed and diverted to observe Comet Giacobini-Zinner in 1985 and to pass over 30 million Km from Halley's Comet in 1986

### International Date Line
Line running at or near 180° of longitude, mainly through the Pacific Ocean, where the date is changed back one day for eastbound travellers

### International Sun-Earth Explorer (ISEE)
Group of three satellites launched in 1977 carrying solar wind experiments from ten countries. ISEE 1 later became the **International Cometary Explorer**

### International Ultraviolet Explorer
Very successful astronomy satellite run by NASA, ESA and the UK's Particle Physics and Astronomy Research Council. Launched in 1978 and remaining in use until 1996, IUE examined a wide range of hot stars and other objects in our own galaxy, as well as distant active galaxies and other objects such as Halley's Comet during its 1986 visit

## interplanetary magnetic field
The magnetic field of the solar system, arising from the magnetic activity of the Sun and strongly affecting the flow of particles in the solar wind. For many years most knowledge of this magnetic field came from observations made in the plane of the Earth's orbit, from satellites in Earth orbit. But in the 1990s the **Ulysses** mission provided detailed measurements of the solar wind and solar magnetism deep into the solar system and high above the plane of the ecliptic. Here the main influence is the field around the Sun's polar region rather than that at its equator

## interplanetary medium
The dust and gas found between the planets, which is responsible for the **Zodiacal light** and is concentrated mainly near the plane of the ecliptic. The material there is highly divided and dispersed, although it can be studied by means such as measuring the polarising effects it has on incoming starlight

## interplanetary scintillation
Fluctuation in brightness of celestial radio sources caused by the effects of the solar wind

## interpulse
Small secondary signal sometimes received between the main signals from a pulsar

## interstellar cloud
Little-used synonym for nebula – any mass of dust or gas within a galaxy

## interstellar dust
Dusty material is a common component of nebulae and probably accounts typically for a few percent of their mass, including most of their heavy metal content

## interstellar medium
The gas and dust spread through the galaxy, observable by means including its reddening effect on starlight, its infrared emissions and the 21cm absorption and emission lines which it shows in radio frequencies. The interstellar medium is at its most visible where it is gathered into dense nebulae which emit visible light, which can also be the seats of star formation. It consists mainly of hydrogen and helium atoms dating back to the formation of the universe, plus heavier atoms formed inside stars and emitted from them during their normal lifetimes or by nova and supernova explosions

## interstellar molecules
Since 1937, over 100 molecules have been identified in deep space, almost all from spectral lines in radio wavelengths. Most are carbon-containing molecules ranging in complexity from carbon

monoxide (CO) up to such species as methylacetylene, $CH_3C_2H$. The presence of these molecules is a strong indicator of active organic chemistry in space. Inorganic molecules detected include water, sulphur dioxide, common salt (sodium chloride NaCl) and ammonia, $NH_3$. The list grows longer each year and the National Radio Astronomy Observatory in the US is the champion interstellar molecule finder

### inter-universe tunnel
Possible route from a black hole in one universe into a white hole in another time and universe

### inverse square law
Law whereby field effects originating from a central point, especially magnetic, electric and gravitational fields or the incidence of electromagnetic radiation, decrease with the square of distance from their source

### Io
One of the satellites of Jupiter discovered in 1610 by **Galileo**. 3,660km across and an average of 422,000km from Jupiter's centre, Io has an orbit taking 1.8 days to complete. Space probes have shown Io as a world whose yellow-red surface is made up of vast sulphur deposits, and Io's surface is marked by huge sulphur volcanoes. This vulcanism, which may also involve silicate material like those found in terrestrial rocks, is still active, and is driven by energy transferred from Jupiter by tidal effects. Io also interacts with Jupiter's magnetic field and affects its radio emissions

### ion
Atom which has an electric charge by virtue of receiving more electrons than usual, making it a negative ion, or losing one or more to give it a positive charge. Material in strong electric fields or at high temperatures is especially likely to be ionised, as in the Earth's outer atmosphere or the insides of stars, where neutral atoms tend to be the exception rather than the rule

### ion drive
Type of rocket motor which drives spacecraft with a stream of ions instead of a jet of hot gas in normal rockets. Ion drives are powered by electricity and have been tested in orbit

### ionisation temperature
Temperature at which a particular type of atom can be expected to shed a particular electron. Knowledge of ionisation temperatures allows stellar temperatures to be deduced from star spectra

### ionosphere
The uppermost layer of the Earth's atmosphere, where most of the atoms are ionised. Some 350km above sea level, the ionosphere has high temperatures of up to 1500° because high-energy solar photons are

captured there, including those in X-ray wavelengths. This prevents radiation which would otherwise be fatal to human and other life from reaching sea level, so that without the ionosphere any life on Earth would have evolved very differently. The ionosphere is also useful for communications and radar, since it is possible to bounce radio signals off it for transmission beyond the visible horizon

### ion tail
Ionised portion of the tail of a comet. Almost synonymous with the gas tail since most gas in comet tails is ionised near the Sun where comet tails are observed

### IRAS
*See* INFRARED ASTRONOMY SATELLITE

### irghizite
Type of tektite found in southern Russia

### irregular galaxy
Type of galaxy which is neither spiral nor elliptical, but excluding the peculiar galaxies. The Irregulars include types classed as Irr I, capable of being resolved into stars, clusters, nebulae, etc, and Irr II, which remain unresolved. The **Magellanic Clouds** are the nearest examples. Apart from displaying no regular form, the irregulars are a disparate group, with some showing some trace of form while others are amorphous. They account for a few percent of all galaxies.
*See also* HUBBLE CLASSIFICATION

### ISEE
*See* INTERNATIONAL SUN-EARTH EXPLORER

### island universe
Obsolete term used for the galaxies when it was first realised that they exist separately from our own galaxy and at great distances from each other

### ISO
*See* INFRARED SPACE OBSERVATORY

### isotopes
Stable or unstable atoms of the same chemical element having different atomic weights. Thus there are three isotopes of hydrogen – normal hydrogen, deuterium and tritium, each with one proton in its nucleus but with no, one and two neutrons respectively. Some heavier elements such as lead have over 10 isotopes

### isotropy
Property of a material whereby it has the same properties from different directions. Some crystals, for example, are anisotropic rather than isotropic because they refract light differently depending on which face the light falls upon. Isotropy is significant in optics and on a larger scale as a property of the universe in general

# IUE
*See* INTERNATIONAL ULTRAVIOLET EXPLORER

# Jj

### Jansky, Karl (1905-1950)
US scientist who began radio astronomy in 1931 when he detected what turned out to be radio emissions from the centre of our galaxy. He is commemorated by the Jansky, the unit of radio emission strength

### Janus
Minute satellite of Saturn, orbiting just beyond its rings and discovered in 1966. Janus and the four other satellites with similar orbits are thought to have very low densities, consistent with porous, icy compositions

### JD
*See* JULIAN DATE

### Jeans, James (1877-1946)
British astronomer and populariser of science, known for fundamental work on cosmology and stellar evolution

### jet
Outward projection observed springing from some active galaxies and quasars. Jets are thought to be crucial to the processes by which **active galactic nuclei** emit large amounts of radiation in many wavelengths, and to **quasar energy production**. They are especially conspicuous in radio galaxies

### Jet Propulsion Laboratory (JPL)
Research centre in Pasadena, California, managed by the University of California for **NASA**. Best-known as the centre from which NASA's major space probes are operated after launch. JPL is a world centre for solar system science, especially that making use of space data, and for the computational and other skills needed to carry out space missions. It also carries out research in other areas – even jet propulsion

### Jones-Bird Telescope
Compact version of a Newtonian telescope which uses a lens between the primary and secondary mirror to bring the light to a focus in less distance than would otherwise be necessary. Jones-Bird telescopes are rare because Newtonian designs are uncommon when short length is a principal consideration, and because a lens of sufficient optical quality is expensive by comparison with the rest of the optics, putting up the price

### Jovian
*referring to* JUPITER

## JPL
*See* JET PROPULSION LABORATORY

## Julian Calendar
Calendar system with a leap year every four years, so-called because it was introduced during Julius Caesar's period as ruler of Rome in 46BC. The Julian Calendar ceased to be used between the 16th and 20th centuries as the more accurate **Gregorian calendar** entered use

## Julian Date
Date in years, days and decimals of a day, taken from the arbitrary start date of 465BC and with the days counted from noon rather than midnight. Julian dates figure in much astronomical calculation and reckoning, with the abbreviation JD. They are unrelated to the Julian calendar

## Juno
The third asteroid discovered – under 200km across but with a high albedo (by asteroid standards) which makes it comparatively bright and easy to observe

## Jupiter
The largest planet of the solar system, 318 times as massive as the Earth and eleven times as large, with an equatorial radius of 72,000km. Jupiter has a mean distance of 778 million km from the Sun, which it takes 12 years to orbit. Jupiter is accompanied by a thin ring system and a huge array of satellites. Jupiter has long been a favourite object for terrestrial observers of the planets, who mapped its cloud belts and the spots and features on them, especially the **Great Red Spot**, as well as tracking its larger satellites, especially the **Galilean group**. Jupiter is also active in radio wavelengths with emissions like those from terrestrial lightning. The **Voyager 1** and **2** probes generated a wealth of detailed information about Jupiter and its satellites, and allowed some of the mysteries of its cloud system to be resolved. The dominant colour of Jupiter, yellow, seems to be due mainly to the presence of sulphur. Jupiter's overall meteorology appears stable, on the evidence of centuries of telescopic observation. Jupiter's rings were discovered during the 1979 flyby by Voyager 1. Less prominent than the Saturnian ring system, Jupiter's differs from Saturn's by having no defined inner edge – instead it fades away towards the cloud tops of the planet proper. But it has the same pattern of gaps influenced by outer satellites as the Saturnian ring system. Jupiter is massively the most influential object in the solar system after the Sun itself, accounting for 71% of the mass of the solar system outside the Sun. Its gravitation greatly influences the orbits of asteroids and of comets entering the inner solar system. In 1994 Jupiter's cloud system was rocked by the impact of Comet Shoemaker-Levy 9, spectacularly recorded by the Hubble Space Telescope and observers on Earth. It is possible that such impacts are also the explanation of short-lived spots in the Jupiter cloud system seen by earlier observers

# Kk

### K
*See* KELVIN

### K (Star Type)
Category of red/orange stars including Arcturus and Aldebaran, which have a surface temperature in the 3500-5000K region and spectra with large numbers of metal lines. K stars are the coolest apart from the M class

### K-Ar Dating
*See* POTASSIUM-ARGON DATING

### K Corona
Part of the Sun's corona seen by sunlight scattered towards the Earth from electrons in the Sun's atmosphere, and visible only near the limb of the Sun

### K line
Line seen in stellar **spectra** which indicates the presence of singly ionised calcium. K lines are among the most prominent features of the solar spectrum and those of other types of star

### Kant, Immanuel (1724-1804)
German philosopher remembered in astronomy mainly for the suggestion, made in 1775, that the Sun and the planets formed from a single source of material, as is now thought. He proposed that a disc-shaped nebula had produced both the Sun and the planets, a speculation which is now generally accepted. The idea produced by Kant has now been developed into a detailed model of the aggregation of the Sun and planets – although there is still disagreement between scientists about the exact mechanics. Small solar system objects like comets are regarded as pieces not swept up – at least yet – into bigger bodies

### Keck Telescope
10m optical telescope at Mauna Kea on Hawaii, run by the California Institute of Technology and the University of California. The telescope has a mosaic of 36 hexagonal mirrors each just under 2m across

### Keeler Gap
Narrow gap in the A ring, one of the rings of Saturn, 136-500km from the planet's centre

## Kelvin (K)
Scale of temperature using degrees of the same size as those in the Celsius scale – whereby each degree is a hundredth of the range between melting and boiling water at atmospheric pressure – but starting not at freezing point but at absolute zero, 273° below zero Celsius

## Kepler, Johannes (1571-1630)
German astronomer who used Tycho Brahe's data to produce the three laws describing the motion of the planets around the Sun, demolishing the ancient view that all celestial motion had to be circular and uniform. He arrived at this solution after numerous false starts, including the idea that the orbits of the planets could be described by shapes within the perfect geometric solids like the sphere and the cube. He finally produced the laws of planetary motion after a lengthy fight with Brahe to get access to his best data on Mars – the inner planet with the most eccentric orbit – which was found to be eight minutes of arc from its theoretical position under the old cosmology. He was also a pioneer of optics and of the calculus, and like many astronomers of his era cast horoscopes, both because he believed in astrology and for money

## Kepler's Laws of Planetary Motion
The first law states that the orbit of a planet is an **ellipse**, with the Sun at one focus. The second states that a line between the Sun and a particular planet sweeps out equal areas in equal times. The line is termed the radius vector. This law means that the nearer a planet is to the Sun, the faster it moves. The third law states that the square of the orbital period of a planet is proportional to the cube of its distance from the Sun. Neptune is on average thirty times as far from the Sun as the Earth, but takes 165 times as long to orbit the Sun, since $30^3$ is 27,000, as is $165^2$. This law means that more distant planets have much longer years. Kepler's laws also apply to the orbits of artificial and natural satellites, binary stars, and other celestial objects including comets and asteroids

## Kerr Black Hole
Black Hole with rotation but no electric charge

## Kerr's Solution
Solution to the equations governing general relativity for a **Kerr Black Hole**. For holes with an electric charge the Kerr-Newman solution is used instead

## kinetic energy
Energy which a body possesses because of its motion

## kinetic temperature
Temperature of a material (usually a gas) due to the motion of its particles

## Kirchoff, Gustav (1824-1887)

German chemist who in 1859 recognised that the presence of the D line in the spectrum of the Sun must mean sodium in the Sun's atmosphere and who went on with **Bunsen** to map the important lines in the solar spectrum and lay the foundations of astronomical and laboratory spectroscopy

## Kirkwood Gaps

Gaps in the asteroid belt where few if any asteroids are found. The gaps are caused by resonances with the orbital period of Jupiter. Asteroids in the gaps would have periods of a third, two fifths, three sevenths, a half or three fifths of one Jovian year, subjecting them to severe gravitational disturbance by Jupiter at regular intervals. This means that the gaps are swept clear of asteroids. The same resonance effects are responsible for sweeping clear the gaps in planetary rings, which are also sometimes called Kirkwood Gaps. US astronomer Daniel Kirkwood (1814-1895) investigated both types of solar system resonance in the 1860s

## Kitt Peak National Observatory

The USA's main optical astronomy observatory, located in Arizona. The Kitt Peak site houses 11 major telescopes and forms part of the **National Optical Astronomy Observatories**

## KREEP

Type of lunar basalt containing potassium (K), rare earth elements (REE) and phosphorus (P). KREEP rocks seem to be over 4 billion years old, almost as ancient as the Moon itself

## Kreutz Group

Family of 'Sungrazer' comets capable of coming very close to the Sun, perhaps within 1-2 million km. In recent years our knowledge of the Kreutz Group has been expanded by observations made by US Air Force satellites used for solar observation, which show that encounters between Kreutz comets and the Sun can lead to the comet colliding with the Sun or being destroyed by the intense radiation encountered near it. The known Kreutz Group members have similar retrograde orbits about the Sun

## Kruskal-Szekeres Diagram

Graphical representation of the whole of spacetime for a Schwarzschild black hole

## Kuiper, Gerald (1905-1973)

US astronomer born in the Netherlands who worked in all aspects of planetary astronomy, especially the study of Mars and the Moon. A flying observatory used by US astronomers is called the Kuiper Airborne Observatory and was used for the observations which led to the discovery of the rings of Uranus. Kuiper is regarded by many as the founder of the present-day scientific study of the solar system

## Kuiper Belt

Zone beyond the orbits of Neptune and Pluto, some 30-60AU and
mainly in the plane of the ecliptic, in which many millions of comets
are postulated to exist. Some possible Kuiper Belt comets have been
observed. The short-period comets that enter the inner solar system may
be Kuiper Belt members whose orbits have been perturbed. The Kuiper
Belt would form an intermediate comet group between the Oort Cloud
and the Sun

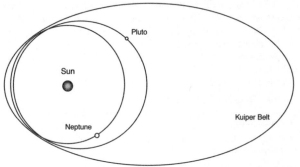

*Kuiper Belt*

# LI

## L4, L5
**Lagrangian points** in the Earth-Moon. The L4 and L5 Lagrangian points lie 60° ahead of and behind the Moon in the same orbit around the Earth and are two of five stable points in the Earth-Moon system where bodies can in principle remain in stable positions for long periods. It has been proposed that they would be possible sites for human space colonies, but this plan has the drawback that dust tends to gather there, which could damage spacecraft in the same location. Small 'cloud satellites' have been tentatively observed at L5

## Labelled Release Experiment
Carried out on the Martian surface by US **Viking Landers**, the Labelled Release Experiment was designed to detect life by feeding a nutrient including radioactive carbon to Martian surface material and see whether any radioactive carbon could be detected in the waste gas it they might produce. Any Martians present didn't have earth-type digestion or did not like American cooking – no positive results ensued

## Lacerta
Constellation of the Northern hemisphere crossed by the Milky Way, and the site of bright novae in 1910 and 1936.
*(Genitive is **Lacertae**; means the 'Lizard')*

## Lacertids
Unusual type of quasar of which the first example known was **BL Lacertae**, apparently involving activity in giant elliptical galaxies

## Lageos
US satellite launched in 1976, consisting of a brass core covered in mirrors to reflect laser light directed at it from the Earth, allowing precise distances between points on the Earth's surface to be determined with an accuracy of centimetres

## lagging core
Possible remnant of the big bang which does not share in the general expansion of the universe. Such a laggard fragment could turn into a white hole from which matter from other universes emerges into our own. The gravitation around such a white hole could be so immense that a black hole would form around it

## Lagoon Nebula
The beautiful nebula M8 in Sagittarius

## Lagrangian Point

Points in a two-body orbital system (like the Earth and the Moon, or the Sun and Jupiter), where matter can be placed stably without being pulled towards either object. The Earth-Moon system has five Lagrangian points, L 1, 2, 3, 4 and 5, at which dust appears to accumulate. Two of the points are ahead of and behind the Moon in the same orbit **(L4, L5)** and the other three are opposite the Moon in the same orbit (L3) and on the Earth-Moon line just this side of (L1) and beyond (L2) the Moon. Other cases of matter accumulating at Lagrangian points are also known in the solar system, notably the Trojan asteroids in Jupiter's orbit, 60° ahead of or behind it. Another case is 1980 S6, a tiny satellite of Saturn in the same orbit as Saturn's satellite Dione and 60° ahead of it. Joseph Louis Lagrange (1736-1813) originally developed the idea of Lagrangian points in the context of the Jupiter/Sun system

## L'Aigle Event

Meteorite fall, accompanied by a bright fireball, which in 1808 forced scientists to concede that meteorites fall from the sky

## Landsat

US series of remote sensing satellites, originally called the Earth Resources Technology Satellites, which established remote sensing as a serious industry in the US and elsewhere. The latest Landsats – now run by the private sector rather than the US government – have instruments capable of showing the Earth's surface with a resolution of about 30m, but new satellite technology is now making Earth images with 1m resolution generally available.

## Laplace, Pierre Simon de (1749-1827)

French mathematician who in 1796 first proposed that the solar system had formed from a spinning gas cloud, the solar nebula, as is now generally believed. He also wrote a massive text, **'Celestial Mechanics'**, covering every aspect of the use of mathematics in astronomy as then known, especially gravitational theory and its astronomical applications, including the orbits of the Moon and of Jupiter and Saturn

## Large Binocular Telescope

Pair of 8.4m telescopes on a single mount, under construction on Mount Graham, Arizona, US and scheduled for completion in 2004, by a US-European consortium.

## laser

(Light Amplification by Simulated Emission of Radiation) Lasers are made by gathering light energy in a special 'cavity' and releasing it in bursts of the same wavelength and with every wave in phase, in other words in step rather than randomly distributed. Laser light has many uses – for example, it can pack enough power to be used to reflect from

mirrors in orbit or on the surface of the Moon **(Laser Ranging)**. In
addition, astronomers have found weak natural lasers acting in space
where gas clouds can form a natural cavity. The atmospheres of Jupiter
and Mars are known to house such lasers as are the gasses surrounding
new stars in Orion and Cygnus

## Laser Interferometer Gravitational Wave Observatory (LIGO)
Proposed instrument for observing gravitational waves by detecting the
change in the interference pattern produced by interacting laser beams.
Two sets of equipment would be used to allow spurious events observed
at only one to be eliminated. Work on LIGO was due to start in 1995
but the project, involving identical instruments at sites in Washington
State and Louisiana in the United States, had many technical, financial
and political problems

## laser ranging
Use of lasers for precise distance finding. On Earth, surveyors and
others use lasers as accurate, rapid tape measures which need not be
stretched between the points whose separation is being measured. In
astronomy they are used by reflecting light from special mirrors on
satellites and on the Moon. Laser methods have allowed the Moon's
orbit and rotation to be determined a hundred times more accurately
than before and have provided evidence suggesting that the Moon may
still be vibrating from a major meteorite impact a few centuries ago

## Late Medieval Minimum
Period of low sunspot activity between about AD1400 and 1600, also
called the Sporer Minimum. The evidence for the Late Medieval
Minimum comes mainly from Far Eastern observations **Medieval
Minor Minimum** and **Maunder Minimum**

## latitude
Position of an object on the Earth's surface relative to the equator,
measured in degrees so that the poles are at 90°. Latitude in the sky,
measured from the **celestial equator**, is called **declination**. The
mapping of celestial bodies like Mercury, Mars, Venus and many
planetary satellites has allowed latitudes and longitudes there to be
defined accurately

## launcher
Rocket used to put spacecraft into orbit or deep space. Launcher types
include expendables – one-shot rockets mostly related to military
missiles – and reusable types of which only the **Space Shuttle** has so
far entered service.

## launch window
The time period during which a particular space launch must occur for a
mission to be possible, dictated, for example, by the relative positions of
the Earth and the planet which is the mission's target

### lava

Geologists' term for molten rock emitted on the surface of a planet and also for the rock formed when it solidifies. Lavas are cooled more rapidly than rocks which solidify at depth in a planet, so that they have crystals of smaller average size. The commonest type of lava is basalt

### LDEF
*See* LONG DURATION EXPOSURE FACILITY

### Leap Day
*See* LEAP YEAR

### Leap Second

Extra second inserted into clock time to allow for the fact that the Earth's rotation is less regular than the atomic clocks by which it is measured. Leap seconds have to be placed into clock time rather than being taken out of it because the Earth's rotation is gradually slowing

### Leap Year

Year in which an extra day has to be added because of the fact that there are about 365.25 days in a year. An extra day, the leap day, every four years keeps the calendar almost correct, although it is omitted when the year is a round century not divisible by 400, for extra accuracy.

### Leavitt, Henrietta (1868-1921)

US astronomer known best as the discoverer of the **Cepheid variables**, which allowed the distances of galaxies to be determined

### Leda

Satellite of Jupiter, discovered in 1974 by telescopic observation from Earth, and the 13th to be named. A few kilometres across, Leda has a 240 day orbit an average of 11.1 million km from Jupiter

### lens

Any object which alters the behaviour of light passing through it by making it converge towards a focal point or diverge away from one. Lenses are usually made of glass or plastic. They work because light crossing the surface of the lens moves from a medium with one velocity of light to one where it has a different velocity, and alters direction as it does so. Accurate lenses for astronomical telescopes use 'elements' of different types of glass, mainly in an attempt to eliminate **chromatic aberration**. Lenses of unusual materials can be used to focus infrared and other types of radiation. Lenses are avoided for large telescopes, which tend to be reflectors, using mirrors, rather than refractors, with lenses, because they cannot be supported from behind and tend to sag under gravity, and because they are more costly to produce. With a mirror the image is formed by one surface, not several, so there is less expense and less scope for light to be absorbed, which happens each time light is reflected or refracted. For natural lenses in space *see* GRAVITATIONAL LENS

## Lens-Thirring Effect
Dragging of spacetime by rotating objects. Trivial for, say, the Earth, but of importance in calculations on relativistic objects like black holes

## Leo
Constellation of the Zodiac in the northern hemisphere. Contains the bright star Regulus, Alpha Leonis
*(Genitive is **Leonis;** means (and even looks like) a 'Lion')*

## Leo Minor
Constellation adjacent to Leo and meaning the lesser lion.
*(Genitive is **Leonis Minoris**)*

## Leonids
Meteor shower seen in November with radiant in Leo. The Leonids have their origin in Comet Tempel-Tuttle, and at 33 year intervals, matching the orbit of the comet, can give rise to thousands of meteors per hour. The 1833 display seems to have been the first time meteors were noticed as coming from a particular radiant in the sky. They were seen spectacularly in 1998 and 1999.

## Lepus
Small constellation of the southern hemisphere.
*(Genitive is **Leporis;** means the 'Hare')*

## Leverrier, Urbain Jean Joseph (1811-1877)
French mathematician and astronomer whose calculations led to the discovery of Neptune. He also worked on cometary orbits and other problems of celestial mechanics. Was sufficiently egotistical to mount a campaign to have the name Neptune abandoned in favour of Leverrier

## Libra
Constellation of the southern hemisphere crossed by the Zodiac, meaning the scales.
*(Genitive is **Librae**)*

## libration
Effect whereby more than half of the Moon's surface can be seen from the Earth despite its **captured rotation**. The slight 'nodding' and 'rocking' effects are caused by the fact that the Moon's orbit is slightly tilted to the ecliptic and is eccentric, so that the Earth and the Moon alter their relative positions with time. Libration in longitude allows us to see around the eastern and western limbs of the Moon and libration in latitude shows us the regions beyond the Moon's north and south poles

## life
The ability to erect barriers and organise within them material and information in a way which the laws of thermodynamics would otherwise prevent. Definitions of life are chronically complex and controversial, and are biassed hopelessly by the fact that we base them solely on our experience of life on Earth

## light
Electromagnetic radiation in the wavelengths perceived by human eyes, generally taken as being from 400 to 800 nanometres from violet to red. This is the part of the spectrum in which most solar energy is received on Earth, making it the best choice for animals needing to operate on the Earth's surface, although animals other than man have eyes which respond to light in somewhat different wavelength bands from ours, and not all people respond to exactly the same light wavelengths

## light cone
The imaginary cone shape in time and space on whose surface we can observe objects elsewhere in the universe. Since light travels at about 300,000km/sec, we can see things that happened in the last second at that distance. For a time ten billion years ago, a significant fraction of the age of the universe, we can see events ten billion light years away, defining the size of the light cone we see at that depth in time

## light curve
Graph showing the variation in magnitude of a variable star over time

## Lighthouse Model
Model of a pulsar whereby the pulses are caused by a thin beam of radiation – like the beam from a lighthouse – sweeping over the observer at fixed intervals. If the Lighthouse Model is correct, the pulsars we see are only a fraction of the total population in the sky – the others have beams which do not sweep across the Earth for astronomers to detect

## lightlike path
Path through spacetime at the velocity of light. In practice, our present ideas about the universe debar travel at the velocity of light, so that lightlike paths are an unreachable limiting case rather than reality

## light pollution
Effect whereby light from industrial or builtup areas makes astronomy difficult by brightening the night sky. Some US cities have altered their lighting patterns to help astronomy continue, but the usual answer to light pollution is to do astronomy in more remote places. Unlike pollution due to radiation or chemicals, pollution of the electromagnetic spectrum has the pleasing property that a throw of a switch can stop it at once. This means that campaigns against light pollution can succeed rapidly. Low-energy lighting which minimises light sent upwards and places more on the ground where it is needed can allow astronomers to see the stars while people who need light stay happy and lighting bills fall

## light year
Astronomical unit of distance equal to the space covered by light in a year in a vacuum. Equal to 9.3 billion km or 0.3 **parsec**. Light years are frowned upon by serious astronomers, who like to work in parsecs, even

though parallaxes cannot be detected for any but the nearest astronomical objects while the time taken for light to reach the observer from distant parts of the universe is of direct interest in astronomy and cosmology

## LIGO
*See* LASER INTERFEROMETER GRAVITATIONAL WAVE OBSERVATORY

## limb brightening
Brightening of stars towards their edges, seen because some stars have outer layers which are hotter than the layers immediately below their surface

## limb darkening
The opposite effect to **limb brightening**, and more common since most stars, including the Sun, cool towards the outside without having layers of hot material on top of cooler ones

## limb profile
Detailed outline of a spectral line, used for determining the abundances of particular elements in stars

## liquid mirror
Telescope mirror which might be created by spinning a pool of mercury (the metal) to produce an optical surface capable of forming an image. The notion is over a century old and has the attraction that the ideal shape for a telescope mirror, a paraboloid, is assumed automatically by a spinning liquid surface. Using modern methods – including smooth electric motors to guarantee a good image – it might be possible to build cheap liquid mirrors much larger than practicable solid ones. Problems would include the toxicity of mercury. A 2.7m test mirror at the University of British Columbia in Canada has shown that the principle works and can provide a cheap mirror capable of producing good images. But it only does so while the telescope points at the zenith: tilt it and the parabola is distorted by gravitation

## LMC
The Lesser Magellanic Cloud
*See* MAGELLANIC CLOUDS

## LMO
*See* LOW MASS OBJECT

## LMT
*See* LARGE MILLIMETRE TELESCOPE

## lobe
Area of radio emission observed far to one side of the optically visible part of some galaxies

## Local Group
Assembly of over 30 dozen galaxies including our own and forming a

discrete group in space. Its three biggest members are our own galaxy, M33 and M31, the Andromeda nebula. Smaller members include the Greater and Lesser Magellanic Clouds. Spiral, elliptical and irregular galaxies are all to be found within the local group, of which new members are still being found. Members range in distance up to five million light years from our galaxy

## Lockyer, Norman (1836-1920)
British astrophysicist and pioneer of solar spectroscopy. He discovered helium in the Sun and founded the scientific weekly **Nature**

## Loki
Most powerful of the volcanoes of **Io**. It is more powerful than all the Earth's volcanoes combined. Other Io volcanoes have been named Pele and Prometheus

## Long Duration Exposure Facility (LDEF)
10-tonne spacecraft placed in orbit in 1984 to test long-term effects of exposure to space. Its exposure was even more long-term than anticipated because of the 1986 space shuttle Challenger disaster, which postponed its recovery until 1990. It provided data on the concentration of dust in interplanetary space

## longitude
Position of an object on a sphere east or west of some arbitrary meridian line – in the case of Earth, one running through Greenwich in London, England. On the celestial sphere longitude is called Right Ascension. Other objects in the solar system have also had longitude systems defined in recent years – Mercury's answer to Greenwich is a crater called Hun Kal, and for Venus a point called Alpha Regio

## long period comet
Comet with an orbital period of over 200 years. About 500 long period comets have been observed, but these are only a fraction of the huge number presumed to exist in the **Oort Cloud**

## Lorentz Transformations
Equations derived from special relativity which describe ways of relating measurements made by observers in motion relative to each other. The transformations contain the mathematics describing, for example, the change in the apparent size of physical objects, and the change in the apparent rate at which clocks run, near to the velocity of light

## Low Mass Objects
Possible objects – also called Brown Dwarfs – several times the size of Jupiter which might be one of the forms of dark matter in galaxies. LMOs in our galaxy might be detected by observing their gravitational lensing of light from more distant stars

## Lowell, Percival (1855-1916)

US astronomer best-known for championing the idea that Mars had artificial canals and therefore life. His books **'Mars as an Abode of Life'** and **'Mars and its Canals'** were his main works defending this idea, which led Lowell (a man of great private wealth) to set up a special observatory at Flagstaff, Arizona. He had outstandingly clear eyesight, and his long linear features on Mars were plausible enough to survive on maps for many decades after his death. They are now regarded as optical illusions and Mars maps produced from space probe photographs show little resemblance to Lowell's Mars drawings. Some of his other work, including his Saturn observations, have stood the test of time better and the Lowell Observatory is a highly-rated centre for solar system science

## luminosity

Light output of a celestial object corrected to allow for its distance from Earth, and measured by means of **absolute magnitude**

## Luna

Latin for the Moon, and the name of a Soviet programme of lunar exploration with unmanned space probes from 1959 to 1976, including three (Luna 16, 20 and 24) which returned moonrock to the Earth

## Lunar Orbiter

Series of five US spacecraft which between 1966 and 1968 revolutionised lunar science by returning detailed photography of the about 80% of the Moon's surface. They provided detailed information used in choosing landing sites for the **Apollo missions**

## Lunik

Soviet spacecraft series which opened up the far side of the Moon to human knowledge when Lunik III returned the first images of it in 1959

## Lunokhod

Lunar roving vehicles used on some of the **Luna** missions of the 1970s

## Lupus

Constellation of the southern hemisphere, crossed by the Milky Way. *(Genitive is **Lupi;** means the 'wolf')*

## luxon

Fundamental particle travelling at the speed of light – and therefore possessing no mass – such as the photon or the neutrino

## Lyman

Proposed NASA/ESA space telescope to operate in the far ultraviolet, planned for service in the 1990s. It would allow observations to be made in the promising 900-1200 Angstrom region of the spectrum and elsewhere in ultraviolet frequencies. It is named after Theodore Lyman, discoverer of the **Lyman lines**

### Lyman Alpha Light
Ultraviolet light observed from stars and attributable to energy emitted
by the electron of a hydrogen atom falling from the first excited level to
ground state or absorbed when it travels in the opposite direction

### Lyman Forest
Area of the spectrum in visible light where a dense mass of spectral
lines – fancifully compared to trees in a forest – are seen in the spectra
of distant galaxies. The lines are **Lyman Lines** displaced into the
visible spectrum by the redshifting of light from the galaxies caused by
their recession due to the expansion of the universe

### Lyman Lines
Series of **hydrogen transition** lines in the spectrum of hydrogen
observed in the ultraviolet, most notably the Lyman Alpha line
hydrogen transitions

# Mm

## M
Prefix for object designations in the **Messier Catalogue**

## M (Star type)
M type stars are the coolest of all, with surface temperatures of less than 3500°. Such stars are cool enough to allow some molecules – rather than just isolated atoms – to exist in their outer layers. M stars tend to be orange in colour and Betelgeuse in Orion is the classic member of the class

## M1
The Crab Nebula in Taurus

## MACHO
Massive Compact Halo Object. One proposed form which **dark matter** in galaxies could adopt, MACHOs would be planet-sized objects in deep space. They could be observed by the gravitational lensing effect they might have on light from distant stars

## Magellan[1]
US Radar mapping mission which provided detailed mapping of the entire surface of Venus with a resolution of about 120m. Magellan was launched in 1989 and arrived at Venus in August 1990. A stripped-down version of a bigger planned mission, the Venus Orbiting Imaging Radar (VOIR), Magellan ceased operating in October 1994. Towards the end of its life, after the end of the radar imaging programme, Magellan was placed into a low orbit and used to provide detailed data on Venus' gravitational field by observations of its orbital movement

## Magellan[2]
Pair of 6.5m telescopes run by the US Carnegie Institution at Las Campanas in Chile

## Magellanic Clouds
The Greater and Lesser Magellanic Clouds are the nearest members of the **Local Group** of galaxies to our own, and are seen in the southern constellations of Dorado and Mensa and Tucana respectively. The gravitation of the Magellanic clouds is thought to distort the geometry of our own galaxy. Both galaxies were found in the 1980s to be vigorous seats of star formation, according to observations by the **IRAS** satellite which revealed the presence of dust, heated in some areas by radiation from young, very hot stars. In 1987 a supernova visible to the

naked eye was observed in the Lesser Magellanic Cloud

## magnetic fields
Magnetic fields are caused by motion of some kind involving charged or magnetic material, and arise in the universe on every scale from the atomic to the galactic. The Earth's magnetic field results from the convection of the Earth's core, which contains large amounts of iron. On a larger scale, whole galaxies are thought to have magnetic fields on the evidence of systematic alignment of interstellar particles, like so many compass needles under the influence of a weak magnet. This magnetism probably arises from the interaction of charged particles in electric fields. In the solar system, the Earth has much the most powerful magnetic field of the terrestrial planets, although Mercury also has a magnetic field and there is a weak spiral magnetic field throughout the solar system spreading outwards from the Sun itself. At the Earth's orbit the solar magnetic field is thousands of times weaker than the Earth's. Magnetic fields cause splitting of spectral lines and other spectral effects, allowing them to be detected and measured in many stars. They are especially strong in some types including the **T Tauri** stars

## magnetic mirror
Curved electromagnetic field capable of trapping charged particles. The Earth's **Van Allen** belts are an example. Magnetic mirrors have been proposed as containers for the charged material within possible fusion reactors for power generation on Earth

## magnetic monopole
Particle bearing a single magnetic pole rather than the paired north and south poles of a normal magnet

## magnetism
Permanent magnets attract and repel because of the unbalanced electron spin in the atoms of some elements, notably iron. The movement of charged particles, normally electrons, in electric fields produces the same effect. Magnetism is the study of these effects and how they are produced

## magnetograph
Device for measuring magnetic fields. A network of magnetographs has been installed all over the Earth for decades, yielding huge amounts of data, and versions of these instruments have been sent into orbit and to other planets since the 1960s

## magnetometer
*See* MAGNETOGRAPH

## magnetopause
Limit of the Earth's magnetic field in the direction of the Sun, where it interacts with the **Solar Wind**. The magnetopause is not a thin line but a

layer of variable thickness. Its distance from the Earth varies with the amount of activity on the surface of the Sun, coming closer when the Sun's output of charged particles increases

## magnetosheath

Three-dimensional volume around the Earth, stretching over 1000 Earth radii out into the Solar System, where particles in the Solar Wind stream around the Earth's **magnetosphere**. A similar structure of magnetopause and magnetosheath has been found around other planets, especially Jupiter, which have significant magnetic fields

## magnetosphere

The area of magnetic influence of the Earth in space. The Earth's magnetosphere is a volume stretching a short and variable distance towards the Sun, meeting its magnetic influence at the magnetopause, but running out deep into the solar system behind the Earth within the **magnetosheath**. The Earth is not completely isolated from the Sun's magnetism by its own magnetic field. Instead, charged particles penetrate it in significant numbers, supplying the **Van Allen** belts with material and causing effects like the **Aurora**. The term is also applied by analogy to the space around other planets with significant magnetic fields

## magnetotail

The part of the magnetosphere pointing away from the Sun, which because of the 'shadow' effect of the Earth and its magnetic field is far more voluminous than the part facing the Sun

## magnification

The increase in the size of an image provided by a telescope (or microscope). Magnification is measured in linear rather than area terms, so that a planet viewed under a magnification of 200 will seem 200 times larger than with the naked eye (to which it would in fact appear as a point source of light) and would have 40,000 times the apparent area – 200x200. Some small telescopes and binoculars are specified in terms of magnification and lens size, so that 10x50 binoculars have a magnification of 10 and objective lenses 50mm across

## magnitude

Measure of the brightness of any object in the sky, according to a geometrical scale set up by **Hipparchos** in about 120BC and refined in the 19th century after the development of photometry. The basis of the magnitude system is a 100-fold difference in brightness between objects separated by five magnitudes. This means that each magnitude is equivalent to a change of just over 2.5-fold in the amount of light received by an observer. The numbers get smaller as the objects get brighter. The original basis was that the brightest star in the night sky would be set at zero magnitude, although in fact Sirius, the brightest star in the sky, has a magnitude of -1.4 and there are two other negative-magnitude stars, Canopus and Arcturus. The Sun has a magnitude of -26.8 and the full Moon -12.6. There are about 2000 stars of naked-eye magnitude, generally set at 6.5, although at many dark sites, fainter stars can be observed. The largest telescopes now in use will reach objects below the 25th magnitude and the **Hubble Space Telescope** can stretch this to about the 31st magnitude. The magnitude system is a means of assessing the full influx of light from a celestial object. For extended objects, like comets or the Moon, or moving or continuous ones, like meteors, the total amount of light must be added up as if from a single point source. The magnitude system was devised to allow stars to be compared as seen from the surface of the Earth. Since the distances to celestial objects began to be known – mostly during this century – these **apparent magnitudes** have been supplemented by **absolute magnitudes**, the magnitude an object would have at a standard distance of 10 parsecs

### main sequence
The band across the centre of the **Hertzsprung-Russell Diagram**, which contains most of the stars in the sky. Main sequence stars include all stars except giants, white dwarfs and some unusual types This provides insights into the relationship between star types and allows their distances to be determined, because the relationship between brightness and spectral type is well-known for stars on the main sequence

### major axis
The longest diameter of an ellipse, such as a planetary orbit

### Maksutov
Type of **Cassegrain** telescope which uses lenses as well as mirrors to produce small telescopes of long focal length

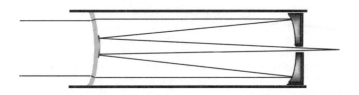

*Maksutov telescope*

### mantle
Layer of the Earth between the core, the innermost part, and the crust, the part stretching to the surface. The mantle of the Earth begins a few tens of kilometres below sea level, varying between oceanic and

continental areas, and its convection is responsible for the drifting of the continents

## Mare

Dark, low lying, lava-filled, circular plain on the surface of the Moon: plural maria. The maria are filled with basalt and are generally thought to be the result of collisions with large asteroid-sized objects early in the history of the solar system. Mare means Sea, after an earlier theory of their nature. The maria appear, on the evidence of the numbers of craters counted on their surfaces, to have ages of about four billion years, making them a few hundred million years younger than the more heavily cratered lunar **highlands**

## Mariner

Series of ten US spacecraft launched for planetary exploration between 1962 and 1973. Mariners 1, 3 and 8 were failures. Of the others, 2, 5, and 10 were sent to Venus and 4, 6, 7 and 9 to Mars, and Mariner 10 also visited Mercury

## Mars[1]

The fourth planet of the Solar System, orbiting the Sun at an average distance of 228 million km in an orbit taking 687 days. Mars is accompanied by two small satellites, Phobos and Diemos. It rotates on its axis in about half an hour longer than the Earth, and has white polar caps reminiscent of the Earth's. But Mars is unlike the Earth in several key ways. It is far colder, with about 15° the warmest summer surface temperature at the equator. It also has far less atmosphere, with a surface pressure of 0.7 per cent that of the Earth, and its atmosphere consists mostly of carbon dioxide, with only small amounts of oxygen, nitrogen, water vapour, argon and other constituents. It is possible that the martian atmosphere has been steadily declining in pressure, with carbon dioxide and water being removed from it without the recycling machinery available on the Earth to place it back in the atmosphere later. They would then be trapped within the planet as ices, and their removal would cool the planet as their greenhouse effect was diminished. The martian atmosphere is dense enough, however, to sustain large dust storms which periodically make the surface all but invisible from space. The planet itself seems to be geologically inactive but the surface exhibits large extinct volcanoes and erosional features showing that there has been liquid water on Mars massively beyond the amounts of water now visible there. The surface of Mars exhibits two main types of terrain. The northern hemisphere is dominated by cratered plain' below the average martian 'sea level', while the southern has more craters, is older, and stands 1-3km above the general level of the Martian surface. Mars has about 10 per cent the mass of the Earth, making it about twice the size of Mercury but distinctly smaller than Venus or the Earth, and has an equatorial radius of 3398km, half that of the Earth. Its average density is 3.94 gm/cc, compared to 5.52 for the

Earth. Over the years, much effort has been expended on searching for life on Mars. In 1996 it was claimed that traces in a **Mars Meteorite** indicate the possible presence of life on Mars – but in the form of microscopic animals only. In 2000 it was claimed that some erosion features on the Martian surface imply the presence of liquid water in recent times.

## Mars[2]
Series of Soviet spacecraft sent to one of the planets of the solar system between 1962 and 1973

## Mars Climate Orbiter
NASA Mars mission lost on arrival at Mars in 1999

## Mars Global Surveyor
NASA Mars mission which arrived in Mars orbit in 1997 and allowed the surface of Mars to be mapped in unprecedented detail as well as analysing its surface composition, mapping its magnetic field and producing a detailed altimetric map of its surface elevation, using a laser instrument called MOLA, the Mars Orbiting Laser Altimeter

## Mars Meteorites
Like the Moon, Mars has gravity low enough for major meteorite impacts on its surface to blast material into space, some of which later appears as meteorites on the Earth. Such meteorites, classed as the SNC group (**shergottites, nakhalites** and **chassignites**) have been used to provide evidence about the composition on Mars and the presence of water at its surface

## Mars Observer
US mission to Mars which arrived there in August 1993 and promptly ceased transmitting due to an irreparable fault

## Mars Pathfinder
NASA mission to Mars which landed in 1997 and placed a roving remote-control vehicle, Sojourner, on the Martian surface.

## Mars Polar Lander
NASA Mars mission lost on arrival at Mars in 1999

## Marsquake
Martian answer to an Earthquake. Seismometers carried by US landers on Mars show that Mars has very little seismic activity compared to the Earth

## Martian
referring to Mars

## Mascons
Mass concentrations detected below the surface of the Moon by their effect on the orbits of the Lunar Orbiter spacecraft. A dozen Mascons have been found underlying the nearside maria, and they seem to

indicate a high density for maria basalt. They provide data about the physical state of the Moon's interior – if the interior were molten they would sink instead of being at the surface. Anomalous regions of high gravity have also been detected by Mars orbiters

## maser

Microwave Amplification by Stimulated Emission of Radiation – the microwave version of a laser. Celestial masers of great power are observed by radio astronomers and are the result of microwaves being trapped and amplified in gas clouds

## 2MASS

The Two-Micron All-Sky Survey, an infrared sky survey carried out during the 1990s with ground-based telescopes.

## mass driver

Device using electromagnetic fields to propel mass to high speeds. Mass drivers have been built on a small scale and fairly detailed engineering proposals have been drawn up for mass drivers which could shift lunar material to space colony sites by means of magnetic levitation. A mass driver would consist essentially of electric coils through which a phased current would pass, accelerating material in metal buckets

## mass loss

Removal of material from stars, especially from heavy stars which can shrink from 50 to 3 solar masses during supernova explosions, with a dramatic effect on their later evolution. The mass loss leaves them below the mass required to collapse into a black hole. On a less dramatic scale, mass is lost to stars when companions nearby suck it away, especially in contact binary stars where the stars are close together

## Mass-Luminosity Relationship

The almost straight-line link between the mass and **absolute magnitude** of **main sequence stars**

## Master

Proposd ESA mission designed to be launched between 2005 and 2009 to fly past the planet Mars and visit asteroids in the main asteroid belt between Mars and Jupiter.

## Maunder Minimum

Period of the late 17th century when very few sunspots seem to have been visible. Western and oriental evidence for the Maunder Minimum seems to confirm independently that it was a real event, not just the result of astronomers failing to observe the Sun rigorously

## Maxwell Gap

Gap in the C ring of Saturn 87,500 km from the centre of the planet

## James Clerk Maxwell Telescope

UK/Netherlands telescope for **submillimetre wavelength** observations, opened in 1987 and sited on Hawaii. It is named after the founder of the science of electromagnetism and the discoverer of the laws of energy distribution in gasses. James Clerk Maxwell (1831-1879) also provided the first mathematical demonstration that the rings of Saturn must consist of a large number of small particles rather than being solid sheets like a gramophone disc, as had been thought

## Medieval Minor Minimum

Period of low sunspot activity which lasted from AD1280 to 1350

## Mensa

Constellation of the southern hemisphere which contains part of the Greater Magellanic Cloud
*(Genitive is **Mensae;** means the 'table')*

## Mercurian
*referring to*  MERCURY

## Mercury[1]

The innermost planet of the solar system, orbiting the Sun in 88 days at an average distance of 58 million km. Mercury has a radius of 2439 km, making it intermediate in size between the Moon and Mars, although its mean density of 5.42 gm/cc is nearer to those of Venus and the Earth. Mercury has the least circular orbit of the major planets, with an eccentricity of 0.2. Almost all our knowledge of Mercury was gained by three flybys carried out by Mariner 10 in 1974 and 1975, in an exquisite piece of celestial snooker. Mariner showed Mercury as a cratered planet like the Moon without the maria, although there is one major basin structure aptly called the Caloris (hot) Basin. There are also the inter-crater plains where there are few large craters, perhaps indicating a more recent surface. Mercury has a magnetic field about 1% as strong as the Earth's, indicating a possible metal core, although this seems not to be hot enough to be liquid. Mercury also rotates very slowly, in a special version of captured rotation. Its day of 57 Earth days means that it makes three turns on its axis for every two orbits of the Sun. (Telescopic maps of Mercury were drawn until the 1960s on the basis of true captured rotation, assuming an 88-day spin, and so were wildly inaccurate.) Mercury has an exceptionally thin atmosphere, about a thousand trillionth as dense as the Earth's, dominated by hydrogen and helium, possibly captured from the solar wind, as well as sodium and other components. Its eccentric orbit and spin provide hot and cold poles. At the cold poles the Sun is at its highest when Mercury is farthest from the Sun, and at the warm poles when it is nearest Surface temperatures on Mercury can go to over 400° and fall to perhaps -200° during the mercurian night, since Mercury has too little atmosphere to moderate either the huge influx of solar energy or the cold of deep space by moving heat to the parts of the planet where no solar energy is arriving. It is even possible that ice is present in the coldest zones. Mercury has no satellites

## Mercury[2]
First US manned spaceflight campaign, involving four manned orbital flights, and one carrying a monkey, along with suborbital and test flights, between 1959 and 1963

## meridian
Line of longitude running from pole to pole, on the Earth, another solid body or the celestial sphere

## meridian telescope
Telescope set up to observe only on a north-south axis, to allow the times when objects cross the meridian, and their elevation above the horizon, to be measured precisely, giving their exact position in the sky

## Merlin
Array of seven radio telescopes in Britain used for interferometry

## mesopause
Thin layer of cold air separating the mesosphere from the ionosphere in the Earth's upper atmosphere

## mesosphere
Part of the Earth's upper atmosphere stretching from the top of the **stratosphere** at about 50km above sea level to the base of the **ionosphere** at about 90km

## Messier Catalogue
List of 109 objects in the sky, from M1, the Crab Nebula, to M109, a galaxy in Ursa Major, drawn up by Charles Messier. The list's prominent members also include M31, the Andromeda Nebula, M42, the great nebula in Orion, M45, the Pleiades, and M44, Praesepe. The passage of time means that there is now some controversy over the exact identity of some of his 109 objects

## Messier, Charles (1730-1817)
French astronomer who in the 1770s compiled the first systematic list of nebulae and other extended objects in the sky. His main interest was not in nebulae but in comets, of which he discovered 13. His aim in drawing up the catalogue was to avoid confusion when comet hunting, not provide a list of objects for nebula and galaxy fanciers

## META
MEGA-CHANNEL EXTRATERRESTRIAL ASSAY
A project current at the time of writing with a 26m radio telescope to scan eight million radio channels at a time for evidence of transmissions by extraterrestrial civilisations. Run by Harvard University, the project has been privately funded for lack of government money. It began in 1985 and has been supplemented by a southern-hemisphere counterpart

based in Argentina.
*See* SETI, META

### meteor

The visible flash of light produced by a meteoroid entering the Earth's upper atmosphere. The term is also applied to the streak of electrons produced by the same effect, which can be observed because it reflects radar signals. Meteors can be sporadic – not associated with a known shower – or can travel in packs with the same orbits, in which case they are named after the constellation in which the shower's **radiant** appears. The radiant effect is a practical demonstration of perspective. The meteoroids are travelling on parallel courses so that they appear to come from the same spot, like railway tracks appearing to converge towards the horizon

### meteor crater

Any crater formed on the Earth's surface by meteorite impact – especially **Arizona Meteor Crater**, the first to be recognised. The two main types are impact craters, formed when the meteorite simply digs a hole in the Earth's crust, of which the Arizona crater is an example, and larger types called explosion craters, rarely accompanied by meteorite fragments since they are formed by the impact of large meteorites which are totally vaporized in the process of forming the crater. Several large craters on the Canadian shield, like Lake Manicougan, are examples

### meteorite

Rock deposited on the Earth from space. Meteorites can be divided into rocky and stony types, but most are chondrites, a class of rocky meteorites of granular structure, which may be samples of material almost unchanged from the origin of the solar system. Other types of meteorites seem to have undergone some form of geological processing. Meteorite orbits seem to resemble those of asteroids, as do their physical properties, which is further evidence that meteorites are messengers bearing powerful evidence of the early days of the solar system before the formation of the planets

### meteoroid

Piece of material in interplanetary space but too small to be viewed as an asteroid – from dust grain size up to several hundred tonnes

### meteor shower

Increased level of meteor activity caused by the Earth's crossing a meteoroid stream, typically associated with the orbit of a comet. Many sporadic meteors, those not associated with known showers, may be members of unknown or decayed faint showers

### methane

Gas of formula $CH_4$, emitted from volcanoes on the Earth and common in the atmospheres of the giant planets

## Metis

Satellite of Jupiter discovered in 1979 from images returned by
**Voyager 1**

## Metonic Cycle

19 year cycle with which sequences of solar eclipses repeat. Meton of
Athens found in 430BC that 235 lunar orbits take almost exactly 12
lunar years of 12 new moons and seven of 13 new moons take almost
exactly 19 years, allowing lunar and solar calendars, which otherwise
diverge heavily, to coincide after 19 years

## Michelson Interferometer

Device used in 1880 to show that the Earth does not move through an
ether filling the universe. The Michelson-Morley Experiment which
proved the absence of the ether shows that beams of light act in the
same fashion even if they shine in different directions, so that the
ether's structure is not apparent and there is no medium present for light
to travel through as there is, for example, to carry waves through the
ocean. This putative ether is not related to the organic chemical of the
same name

## microgravity

Low level gravitation obtaining in Earth orbit, which offers potential for
novel types of research and manufacturing in space

## micrometeorite

Tiny meteorite, capable of filtering through the Earth's atmosphere to
the surface of the Earth. On planets like the Moon without a dense
atmosphere, micrometeorites can carry out considerable feats of erosion
over long periods of time

## micrometeoroid

Virtually synonym of micrometeorite

## Microscopium

Constellation of the southern hemisphere. Dog Latin for the
microscope.
*(Genitive is **Microscopii**)*

## Milankovitch Cycle

Variation in time of the amount of solar radiation arriving at the Earth
and its distribution through the year, caused by the precession of the
equinoxes, the varying eccentricity of the Earth's orbit, and the
changing angle of the Earth's equator to the ecliptic. Milutin
Milankovitch (1879-1958) published his work in 1930 and he and his
followers have tried to explain Ice Ages in terms of the Milankovitvch
Cycles, including most prominently cycles of 21,000 and 40,000 years
associated respectively with the precession of the equinoxes and the
inclination of the Earth's axis

## Milky Way
Band of light stretching across the sky and caused by the high concentration of stars in the plane of our galaxy. The Milky Way can be resolved into its constituent stars and other objects by telescope. The name is also applied to the Galaxy itself – the only visible galaxy not present in even the most reliable catalogues of nebulae. The Milky Way Galaxy seems to be about 20,000 parsecs across, making it a large but not giant galaxy, of about 100 billion stars. The solar system is about 8,500 parsecs from its centre. The centre of the galaxy, in the constellation **Scorpius** is obscured from view by dust and gas but is now able to be observed in infrared light by spacecraft such as the **Infrared Space Observatory** which has observed hundreds of thousands of stars at the galactic centre

## Miller-Urey Experiment
Demonstration that electric discharges simulating lightning can cause common chemicals to form life-like materials or materials needed for life to commence, especially amino acids. An encouragement (although of unknowable significance) to **exobiologists**

## Millimetre Wavelength Astronomy
Branch of radio astronomy of especial value for viewing interstellar gas clouds and the molecules they contain. Millimetre wavelength signals do not pass freely through the atmosphere so that millimetre wave telescopes, which can operate via interferometry or as single dishes, have to be sited on high mountains like optical telescopes, and may ultimately go into space

## Mimas
400km diameter satellite of Saturn discovered by **William Herschel** in 1789. Mimas has a 186,000km orbit taking 0.9 days to travel, not far beyond the rings of Saturn. Mimas is revealed by **Voyager** photography as having an immense 100km crater a quarter of the diameter of Mimas itself. Its surface is densely cratered and presumably old. Its low density of about 1.2 gm/cc indicates an interior dominated by ice rather than by rock

## mini black hole
Possible black hole of asteroid-like mass – millions of tonnes – and pinhead size

## minor axis
Smallest diameter of an ellipse, such as a planetary orbit

## minor planet
Archaic synonym for asteroid

## minute of arc
*See* ANGULAR MEASURE

## Mir

Soviet space station launched in 1986. Mir (Peace) is capable of supporting up to 10 people in space and has a mass of about 20 tonnes

## Mira

Variable star in Cetus, remarked upon since ancient times. Mira has a period of about a year and can be seen with the naked eye at about the third magnitude when at its brightest. Mira-type stars have been observed pulsating into elliptical rather than circular shapes

## Miranda

Satellite of Uranus discovered by **Kuiper** in 1948. The innermost of the five major satellites, Miranda is about 160km across and orbits 130,000km from Uranus in a circular 1.4 day orbit. Its surface is scarred by heavy faulting which has so far not been explained. It has even been suggested that Miranda may have been smashed into pieces by an asteroid impact and later reassembled by gravitation

## mirror

Device for reflecting light or other radiation. Curved mirrors can be made to form images, a principle exploited by **Newton** to create the first reflecting telescope and which is now applied in the construction of all large telescopes. Since his time, the ability to grind large mirrors accurately to within a small fraction of the wavelength of light has increased, and with it the ability to make large mirrors of use in astronomy. There is controversy over whether to make larger single mirrors for major telescopes or to concentrate on multiple-mirror types where the light from a number of smaller mirrors is added together

## missing mass

Proposed large amount of matter present in galaxies but not visible. It has been proposed that 90-98% of the mass of many galaxies may be 'missing,' especially on the basis of studies of the orbits of stars around galactic centres. But other lines of investigation, including hunts for the **gravitational lensing** effects which such mass ought to produce, imply that reports of its existence may have been greatly exaggerated. It has been variously proposed that the missing mass may exist in the **haloes** above and below the galaxies' planes of rotation and that it may be present in the form of exotic atomic particles, or exist as **MACHOs**, planet-sized objects in deep space. The presence of this material, if it exists, has immense cosmological importance, especially for the expansion and possible future contraction of the universe

## mission specialist

Individual carried into space (especially via the space shuttle) as an expert for a particular experiment rather than as a professional astronaut. Medicine, science and espionage are their preferred skills

## Mixmaster Universe

Theoretical model of the universe just after the big bang, with violent gyrations in all directions to smooth out the cosmic background radiation left over from the big bang. This model has the merit that it accounts for the highly isotropic (uniform) appearance of the background radiation in all observable directions

### Mizar
Star in Ursa Major (next to the end among the visible stars of the Plough, away from the Pointers), which has a visible companion, Alcor, and is itself a telescopic double star

### MMT
*See* MULTIPLE-MIRROR TELESCOPE

### mock sun
Spot of light sometimes seen to the left or right of the true Sun and at the same height above the horizon, caused by the reflection of sunlight by ice crystals high in the atmosphere

### moldavite
Type of tektite found in Slovakia

### molecule
Assembly of atoms in a stable form. Atoms cannot form molecules under the extreme conditions found in hot stars, but they are found in cooler stars, and elsewhere throughout the universe **(interstellar molecules)**. Molecules are hard to identify by means of the same spectroscopic techniques used to uncover atoms in stars, and infrared astronomy comes into its own for molecular studies because of the way in which many of the atom to atom bonds which characterise molecules can be examined in the infrared

### momentum
Energy which a body possesses due to its motion. The principle of the Conservation of Momentum states that momentum cannot be created or destroyed – if one body loses momentum, another must have gained it

### Monoceros
The constellation of the Unicorn, spread across the celestial equator and adjacent to Orion. Crossed by the Milky Way.
*(Genitive is **Monocerotis**)*

### month
The time taken for the Moon to orbit the Earth. Several types of month are defined for different purposes, including the draconitic month, the time the Moon takes to reappear at the same node of its orbit on the celestial equator, which is the most realistic measure and totals 27.21 days, and the sidereal month of 27.32 days, the time the Moon takes to reappear at the same point in the sky relative to the fixed stars. This differs from the draconitic month because of the motion of the Earth and Moon around the Sun. The Anomalistic month of 27.55 days is the total time needed for the Moon's cycle of slowing and speeding up in its

orbit as it is carried nearer and farther from the Earth

## Moon

The Earth's natural satellite, orbiting the Earth, and rotating on its axis, once per lunar month of 27.3 days. The Moon has a diameter of 3,500km and a surface area about equal to that of Africa. Six US space missions have taken a total of 12 people to the Moon, and three unmanned Soviet missions have returned moonrock to the Earth. The Moon has little if any magnetic field and a limited amount of seismic activity, and is geologically quiet compared to the Earth. Its surface consists of two main types of terrain, the Maria, smooth, dark plains of up to 4 billion years of age, and the Highlands, which are older and more heavily cratered. Apart from meteorites, highland rocks are the most available souvenirs we have of the earliest days of the solar system. They are not much younger than the Moon itself, which seems to have formed some 4.54 billion years ago. Most of the Moon's craters were formed by meteorite impact, but there is ample evidence that the Moon has also had internal forces shaping its own surface, with volcanic craters and other volcanic structures visible in the Highlands and elsewhere. The side of the Moon away from the Earth has fewer large Maria structures and is a few kilometres higher than the near side, so that the Moon is shaped like an egg, pointing away from us. At the time of writing the great era of lunar exploration, the late 1960s and early 1970s, is over and manned lunar studies have gone quiet – so much so that no rocket system capable of launching people to the Moon is now in existence. But the subject has been revived by the **Clementine** space probe, which supplied huge amounts of data about the Moon's surface very cheaply. In addition, the European and US space agencies are collaborating on studies of a return to the Moon, starting with robotic probes and working up to permanent habitation. A range of scientific problems, like the possible existence of a molten lunar core and the existence of water at the Moon's surface, remain to be solved. However, there may be ice near the lunar surface, especially in shaded craters near the poles.

### Moon-orbiting observatory (MORO)

ESA plan for an observatory which might be placed in Moon orbit early in the 21st century for photographic, radar and spectroscopic measurements of the Moon, as part of ESA's long-term planning for a permanent manned presence on the Moon

### Moonquake

Seismic event on the Moon. Seismic detectors left on the Moon by Apollo astronauts show that there are few Moonquakes – a few thousand per year compared to up to ten times as many for the Earth. They tend to occur deep down, up to 800km below the lunar surface, and cluster in a monthly cycle, suggesting a link to frictional and tidal forces set up by the Moon's orbital motion around the Earth

### MORO
*See* MOON-ORBITING OBSERVATORY

### Mossbauer Effect
Atomic vibration used to construct very precise atomic clocks, which in turn can be used in astronomy and in experiments (such as tests for general relativity) where very precise timing is indispensable

### Multiple-Mirror Telescope (MMT)
Telescope on Mount Hopkins in Arizona which used six 183cm mirrors to imitate a single 6m mirror. The development of the MMT led to multiple mirrors becoming an accepted part of telescope technology, although the MMT mirrors themselves were later replaced by a single 6.5m mirror.

### multiple star
Any star system with more than one star, from binaries on up

### Musca
Small constellation of the southern hemisphere.
*(Genitive is **Muscae**; means the 'fly')*

### Mysterium Lines
Lines found in radio spectra which were at first baffling, and which turned out to be due to maser action on hydroxyl groups in interstellar space

# Nn

### N (galaxy type)
Unusual type of galaxy with extremely bright core, related to **Seyfert** galaxies and **quasars**

### nadir
The point on the Earth or the celestial sphere directly below the observer's feet and 180° above the zenith

### naked singularity
A singularity resembling a black hole but not surrounded by an event horizon concealing it from view. It has been proposed that singularities cannot be exposed to the rest of the universe with no outer horizon, in which case a naked singularity would in practice never occur

### nakhalite
One of the three types of meteorite found on the Earth which are thought to have originated on the surface of Mars *(see* **SNC***)*. The first to be identified fell at Nakhla in Egypt in 1911 in a shower of meteorites, one of which is reported to have killed a dog upon impact

### names
Naming systems in astronomy have come under pressure in recent decades because of the huge amount of detailed knowledge of the solar system produced by space probes. In theory, the objects of the solar system with a visible solid surface, like asteroids, satellites and the inner planets, could require millions of names for their hills, mountain ranges, craters, valleys and other features. The problem began in the 17th century with the Moon, where most features are named after scientists of the past. The space age has brought similar problems including Venus (whose surface is 'visible' in radar wavelengths), where features have been named mainly after prominent real and fictional women, Mercury, where artists and authors figure, Mars, where scientists and place names dominate, and the satellites of the outer solar system, where mythological characters associated with the satellite names are preferred. The process is in the hands of a committee of the **International Astronomical Union**. *Sky and Telescope magazine* (May 1995) has an exhaustive description of the state of play

### nanometre
One billionth of a metre: the usual measure of light wavelengths

### NASA
*See* NATIONAL AERONAUTICS AND SPACE ADMINISTRATION

## NASDA
*See* NATIONAL SPACE DEVELOPMENT AGENCY

## National Aeronautics and Space Administration (NASA)
US government agency which carries out aviation and space research projects. Among these have been Apollo, the space shuttle, many successful planetary missions, satellite observatories and the development of communications and remote sensing satellites

## National New Technology Telescope (NNTT)
Proposed US optical telescope for the 1990s, which would use four 7.5m mirrors to mimic the optical effect of a single 15m mirror or a 25m interferometer

## National Oceanic and Atmospheric Administration (NOAA)
US government agency responsible for weather satellites and other forms of remote sensing

## National Optical Astronomy Observatories
Arm of the US National Science Foundation responsible for running the **Kitt Peak** observatory

## National Radio Astronomy Observatory (NRAO)
US radio astronomy institution which runs the **Very Large Array,** the world's largest integrated set of radio telescope dishes

## National Space Development Agency (NASDA)
Japanese space agency responsible for launchers and for scientific and commercial satellites. It has a launch centre at Tanegashima in southern Japan

## neap tide
Tide at the Moon's first or third quarter, when the lunar and solar tides do not add up, and so is lower than spring tides

## NEAR
NEAR-EARTH ASTEROID RENDEZVOUS
NASA mission to visit asteroid 253 Mathilde in 1997 and spent a year from February 14 2000 orbiting asteroid 433 **Eros** in an orbit 35Km above its surface, one of the Apollo-Amor asteroids which can approach the Earth closely. Its images revealed craters, boulders and other small-scale features of the surface of Eros. Near 2 was being planned in 2000 at the time of writing.

## nebula
Latin for Cloud, plural **nebulae**. The term was originally applied to any non-point source of light from outside the solar system, but is now no longer used to describe galaxies. A wide range of types of nebulae are recognised, including dark and bright types, some dominated by gas and others in which dust is a major component. Dark nebulae are seen as dark outlines against bright objects – the Coalsack being a prime example. Among bright nebulae are reflection nebulae which shine by

light reflected from other objects, emission nebulae which glow, usually from emissions from hot, young stars, and planetary nebulae, which are expanding gas bubbles resulting from nova explosions. The solar nebula is the term for the mass from which the Sun and the rest of the solar system have condensed. The types of nebula merge into each other and a given nebula can have parts which absorb radiation, and others which reflect or retransmit it

## nebular hypothesis

Theory that the Solar System condensed from the Solar Nebula. This theory is now generally accepted, which is why objects like comets and meteorites are regarded as primitive material from the early days of the solar system and therefore of great significance to solar system studies. The nebular hypothesis is undergoing constant mathematical refinement to improve our knowledge of the processes which made the solar system adopt its present distribution of matter and energy

## negative space

Region of space with unusual physical laws which might theoretically be encountered after an (equally theoretical) journey through some kinds of black hole

## NGC

*See* NEW GENERAL CATALOGUE

## Neptune

The eighth planet of the Solar System and the last of significant size, being the outermost of the **gas giants**. Neptune was discovered by Johann Galle and Louis d'Arrest in Berlin in 1846, on the basis of calculations by **Leverrier**. Numerous cases have since come to light of earlier unrecognised observations of Neptune, including two by **Galileo**, who in 1612 noted the 'star's' motion but failed to realise that he was looking at a new planet. Neptune has a diameter of 48,600km and a mean distance from the Sun of 3OAU, and takes 165 years to make one orbit of the Sun. Neptune weighs 17 times as much as the Earth. Neptune seems to have an atmosphere dominated by hydrogen, helium and methane, but probably has a core of heavier materials, perhaps including iron and silicates, to account for its density of 1.66 gm/cc. This core may be surrounded by a mantle with water ice and other frozen materials including methane and ammonia. Neptune's upper atmosphere rotates in a period of some 17 hours. Observations of an occultation of a faint star by Neptune in 1984 led to the discovery of a thin ring some 20km wide about 76,000km from the planet's centre. Neptune was the last planet apart from Pluto to be visited by a space probe, **Voyager 2** in August 1989. It found since new satellites including Proteus, the second largest after Triton and larger than Nereid, the satellites discovered telescopically from Earth. The green-blue clouds of Neptune when observed by Voyager – or Hubble – are seen to be accompanied by high, bright clouds and to be darkened by spots, one named the Great Dark Spot by analogy with Jupiter's Great Red Spot

## Nereid

Satellite of Neptune discovered by Gerald Kuiper in 1949. Under 500km in diameter, it has a 5.6 million km, 359 day orbit of high eccentricity and inclination, which takes it within 1.4 million km of Neptune at its closest and over 9.7 million km away at its most distant

### neutrino

Massless, uncharged nuclear particle whose main property is spin. Neutrinos are given off in immense numbers in nuclear reactions – a flood of uncounted billions of them pours off the Sun, for example – and they have immense importance in astrophysical and cosmological calculations. Because they are massless (or according to some cosmological theories possess a very tiny mass), they interact hardly at all with matter, and neutrinos generated in the Sun's core pass out of the Sun with almost no probability of being affected by the rest of its matter. This means that solar neutrinos are the most direct form of information we can receive about the very centre of the Sun. The problem is that anything which will not interact with matter is hard to detect. Neutrino telescopes are the answer. They bear no resemblance to any other type of telescope. Instead they usually consist of a large cavern, perhaps a disused mine working, filled with a material like cleaning fluid. On the very rare occasions when a neutrino interacts with a chlorine atom in the fluid, the atom is transformed into an atom of argon which is then detectable. Assigning a very small mass to the neutrino is one possible solution to the missing mass problem

### neutron

Neutral nuclear particle of essentially the same mass as the proton, and together with protons accounting for most of the mass of atomic nuclei

### neutron star

Object produced by the death of a star weighing 1.4-2.3 solar masses. As soon as there is too little radiation emerging from stars of this mass to prevent their collapse, they shrink until the pressure between neutrons in the star's atomic nuclei will not allow them to become any smaller. Neutron stars are still able to emit energy, as observations of pulsars confirm

## New General Catalogue (NGC)

Widely-used catalogue of nebulae and galaxies published in 1888, and much more comprehensive than Messier's. The NGC is an updated version of the General Catalogue begun by **William Herschel** and finished by his son **John Herschel**, and produced in its final form by **Dreyer**. The NGC includes about 2500 objects to Messier's 109 and includes information about the southern hemisphere sky, based mainly on work by John Herschel in South Africa

## Newton, Isaac (1642-1727)

English scientist and philosopher. Newton's influence on astronomy cannot be overstated. It ranged from the highly practical invention of the reflecting telescope to the theoretical insight of the universal theory of gravitation. The Newtonian reflector design is still in common use, mainly for small to medium-sized telescopes. It involves a primary mirror sending light back up the telescope tube to a flat secondary, which sends the light to an eyepiece at the side of the tube. Newton also carried out experiments with prisms which demonstrated the nature of light and colour by showing that white light consists of light of the colours of the rainbow, and that heat is a form of light of a wavelength close to that of red light. This was the start of the discovery of the electromagnetic spectrum. Newton was the discoverer of the laws of motion which control all physical objects. The first of these states that objects continue in rest or uniform motion unless some outside force affects them. The second states that a force produces an acceleration in a body in proportion to its size. The third states that all action produces equal but opposite reaction – the basis for all rocketry, since it is the reaction to the gases emerging from a rocket which drives it in the opposite direction. Newton discovered the law of gravitation – that all objects attract each other with a force proportional to the product of their masses and inversely proportional to the square of the distance between them He proved that this result was consistent with **Kepler's** laws. Newton was one of a group of influential English scientists which also included **Halley**, but his interests ran far beyond what we would view as 'science,' into biblical chronology and into being Master of the Mint. The Newton is also the standard unit of force in the Système International of measurement. The Isaac Newton telescope, first sited in Sussex, England, and relocated in 1984 to Palma in the Canaries, Spain, is the largest optical telescope produced in the UK, with a 2.5m main mirror, and is used mainly by British and Dutch astronomers

## Next Generation Space Telescope (NGST)

Planned replacement for **Hubble** which is scheduled for launch in about 2008.

## NGST

*See* NEXT GENERATION SPACE TELESCOPE

## NNTT

*See* NATIONAL NEW TECHNOLOGY TELESCOPE

## NOAA

*See* NATIONAL OCEANIC AND ATMOSPHERIC ADMINISTRATION

## noble gases

*See* RARE GASES

### noctilucent cloud

Cloud seen shining at night, just after dusk or before dawn, high in the Earth's atmosphere, especially from high latitudes. The name means 'night-shining.' Noctilucent clouds have little in common with normal clouds. They consist of ice crystals some 80km above sea level. They commonly have a blue colour and are interesting as clues to the nature of the upper atmosphere and because they probably form by a complex process whereby ice accumulates about nuclei of meteoritic dust

### non-baryonic matter

Proposed form of matter consisting of atoms whose components are not the protons, neutrons and electrons found in the material familiar on Earth. Non-baryonic material has been proposed as a candidate for **dark matter**. Prime suspects are **neutrinos**, which may prove to have a small but significant mass, contrary to the long-held view that they are massless

### non-thermal radiation

Radiation such as **synchrotron radiation** which is not related to the temperature of the body emitting it and so cannot be used as a guide to the temperature of its source

### NORAD

The North American Aerospace Defence Command, a part of the US military whose duties include the maintenance of a large optical and radar system designed to keep track of the thousands of objects in orbit around the Earth

### Norma

Constellation of the southern hemisphere.
*(Genitive is **Normae;** means the 'levelling square', as used by builders and others)*

### Northern Lights

*Synonym for* AURORA BOREALIS

### Nortvedt effect

Test of **general Relativity** whereby the mass of a body as determined from its gravitation should equal that from its inertia. Laser ranging, which yields precise data about the Moon's distance from the Earth, seems to confirm general relativity via the Nortvedt effect, at the expense of the rival **Brans-Dicke** theory

### nova

Star which exhibits a sudden rapid increase of brightness, short of the massive brightening associated with a supernova. The Latin word nova (meaning 'new') implies a new star, but in fact novae are old stars prone to sudden brightening, not new-born ones. Most novae are thought to be double stars in which material is transferred from one star to another, probably from a main sequence star to a white dwarf. Most novae are seen to erupt only once, and in these cases, thermonuclear burning, set off when a critical mass of material accumulates in a gas layer around the white dwarf, is probably responsible. These stars may become novae at long intervals. Dwarf novae brighten at intervals from days to years, with greater brightening after longer intervals, and the brightening is probably due to energy being released periodically as it builds up in a gas disk around the white dwarf. There are also recurrent novae, which seem to involve red giants as the companion to the dwarf, and which may erupt via complex processes involving magnetic fields building material up in energetic columns above the surface of the white dwarf, from which it is released in occasional enormous bursts. A nova can become 5-15 or even more magnitudes brighter during an eruption *(plural is **novae**)*

## Nozomi
Japanese spacecraft launched to Mars in 1998 and due to arrive after a troublesome journey in 2003. First Japanese interplanetary mission.

## NRAO
*See* NATIONAL RADIO ASTRONOMY OBSERVATORY

## nuclear bulge
The sphere of stars and other material at the heart of our galaxy. The bulge has never been observed, but seems to be about 4000 parsecs across, about a fifth of the total spread of the spiral arms of the galaxy

## nuclear burning
Inaccurate but commonly used synonym for nuclear fusion in stars

## nuclear reactions
Reactions which lead to new species of atomic nuclei being formed in stars or elsewhere

## nucleogenesis
*See* NUCLEOSYNTHESIS

## nucleosynthesis
The process of creation of nuclei in stars. Nucleogenesis is a less common synonym. The biggest single act of nucleosynthesis occurred in the first minute of the universe's history, when helium (which makes up 23 per cent of the universe) and lithium were formed from hydrogen. Now nucleosynthesis occurs only within stars: the main categories are the hydrogen to helium reaction which drives most stars, the formation of heavier elements up to and including iron which occurs in older stars, and the formation of elements beyond iron, which occurs during supernova explosions

## nucleus [1]
The central, positively-charged, part of an atom, containing almost all of its mass. The nucleus's positive charge arises because it consists of positive-charged protons and neutral neutrons, and is balanced by the

negative charge of orbiting electrons

## nucleus [2]

The small solid body at the centre of the head of a comet. Comet nuclei in the inner solar system are hidden from view by glowing gas and dust. The first detailed view of one was obtained by sending the **Giotto** spacecraft into **Halley's Comet** on March 13, 1986

## nutation

Tiny, gyroscope-like motion of the Earth's polar axis, which occurs on a 19-year cycle and is caused by variations in the solar and lunar gravitational forces acting on the Earth.

# Oo

## O (Star Type)
The hottest type of star, with surface temperatures of 30,000 to over 60,000, so that almost all atoms at the surface are more or less heavily ionised. O type stars are rare because they have short lifetimes by comparison with the cooler members of the other spectral classes

## OAO
*See* ORBITING ASTRONOMICAL OBSERVATORIES

## Oberon
Outermost satellite of Uranus, in a retrograde, 13-day orbit 583 000km in radius and precisely in Uranus's equatorial plane. Discovered by **William Herschel** in 1787, Oberon was first viewed clearly by **Voyager 2** in 1986 and turns out to be a cratered world some 1500km across, marked by crater rays like those seen emanating from some lunar craters. Oberon, unlike the inner satellites of Uranus, shows little sign of internal geological activity

## objective
The light-gathering lens of a refracting telescope

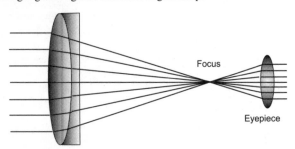

Focus

Eyepiece

Object glass

## Occam's Razor
The principle, set out in the Middle Ages by William of Ockham (a village in Surrey, England) that explanations should not be more complex than necessary. William of Ockham lived approximately 1285-1349 and was a student of motion and mechanics

## occultation
The cutting off of an astronomical body from an observer by some other

body. The most usual is an occultation of a star by the Moon.
Occultations are a fruitful source of astronomical data, yielding precise
positions (for example of the Moon in its orbit) and other information.
Occultations of stars by asteroids allow asteroid sizes to be determined,
and the ring systems and atmospheres of the outer planets can be
investigated by observing the dimming of starlight as the planet passes
in front of a star

## Octans
Constellation of the southern hemisphere which contains the southern
celestial pole.
*(Genitive is **Octantis;** means the 'Octant')*

## Olbers' Paradox
Paradox attributed to Wilhelm Olbers (1758-1840) who posed it in 1823
– but apparently also considered by **Halley** and perhaps earlier
astronomers. Why is it dark at night? Or, more formally, why if the
universe is infinite does the light from distant stars not add up to make
the whole sky infinitely bright? The answer is in the size and age of the
universe. There has not been enough time for light to get here from
regions beyond the finite observable universe, and if it did it would be
redshifted into invisibility by the expansion of the universe

## Olympus Mons
Volcano on the surface of Mars, apparently active within the last few
hundred million years and therefore evidence of comparatively recent
martian vulcanism. At about twice the size of the Hawaiian volcanic
system, Olympus Mons may be the solar system's biggest volcano

## Oort Cloud
Flock of many millions of comets presumed to exist far beyond the
planets and marking the outermost reaches of the solar system. Jan Oort
(1900-1992) estimated in 1950 that the cloud must contain about 100
billion comets, of which a few a year are diverted by the gravitation of
stars near the Sun into the inner solar system. The cloud probably lies
some 40,000AU from the Sun

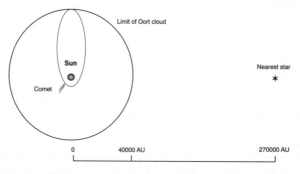

### open cluster
*Synonym for* GALACTIC CLUSTER

### open universe
Possible condition of the universe in which it is of low enough density for the mutual gravitation of the different components not to overcome the momentum established in the big bang. An open universe therefore goes on expanding indefinitely

### Ophiuchus
Large constellation which straddles the celestial equator and contains a stretch of the ecliptic (although it is not one of the recognised signs of the Zodiac) and an expanse of the Milky Way. Opiuchus was a serpent-bearer in ancient legend
*(Genitive is **Ophiuchi**)*

### 70 Ophiuchi
Double star some 17 light years from the Earth which may be accompanied by a large planet

### opinaut
Putative traveller through a black hole, who would risk dismemberment by almost infinitely large forces, followed by the opportunity of emerging into new and bizarre universes

### opposition
Position of a planet opposite the Sun in the sky as seen from Earth. A planet at opposition is at its closest approach to the Earth and is visible all night, making opposition the ideal time for observation of the superior planets

### optical astronomy
Astronomy making use of observations of visible light

### optical axis
The centre line of a telescope or other optical instrument, joining the main mirror or lens to its focal point

### optical flashes
Flashes of light seen by astronauts, caused by cosmic rays releasing **Cerenkov** radiation in their eyeballs

### Optical SETI (OSETI)
The Search for Extraterrestrial Intelligence (see **SETI**) using optical frequencies rather than radio, which is chosen for most SETI experiments. Some scientists have suggested that interstellar messages in laser light might be widespread, and detectable using sensors on existing ground-based telescopes, but none of the limited experiments tried so far have yielded positive results.

### optics
Science and technology of light, and the colloquial term for equipment

used to collect and handle light

## orbit

Path of one celestial body around another or of a pair of bodies
mutually about each other. Bodies are bound in orbit by gravitation and
when one body has a negligible part of the mass of the other, the orbit it
adopts is subject to **Kepler's Laws**. Within the solar system, orbits
range from the highly eccentric paths of comets to the compass-perfect
orbits of the satellites of Uranus. In some circumstances, energy rather
than mass can take up an orbit, as when light is captured by the
gravitation of a black hole. Technologists are adept at putting artificial
satellites of the Earth into precisely tailored orbits designed to match the
Earth's rotation or allow them to observe particular parts of the Earth's
surface at close quarters. The two orbits which most affect the Earth are
the Moon's around the Earth and the Earth's around the Sun, although it
is possible to speculate on the possible effects on the Earth of the Sun's
240 million year orbit around the centre of the galaxy

## orbital velocity

The velocity of a body at a particular point in its orbit. The Earth moves
about the Sun at an average 30km per second, while the Moon moves at
only about 1km per second around the Earth

## Orbiter

The reusable aircraft-type part of the **Space Shuttle**, used to house the
crew and payload and containing the main engines

## Orbiting Astronomical Observatories (OAO)

Series of four US astronomy satellites launched between 1966 and
1972. OAO1 lasted only three days in orbit. OAO2 was a two-tonne
satellite which made observations for just over four years from 1968 to
1973, with an array of seven ultraviolet and four optical telescopes.
OAO-B, the third of the series, never reached orbit. The fourth of the
series, OAO3, also called Copernicus, carried a large ultraviolet
telescope, an X-ray telescope and optical telescopes

## Orbiting Solar Observatories (OSO)

Series of nine US orbiting observatories mainly meant for solar
observation, launched between 1962 and 1975. OSO1 and OSO2
observed mainly solar flares. Confusingly, there were two satellites
called OSO3. The first failed to reach orbit but the second was
highly successful at observing the Sun in X-ray, ultraviolet, gamma
ray and other wavelengths. OSO4 to 8 had similar equipment,
although OSO8 made X-ray observations of Milky Way sources as
well as of the Sun

## organic matter

Organic matter – complex molecules including carbon – is so-called
because it is the stuff of life on Earth, but in space it appears to be
present in a vast variety. Observations in the infrared, where the

vibration patterns of organic molecules can be seen, have shown that
organic molecules up to the complexity of amino acids, which have at
least ten atoms, exist in space, a finding confirmed by their being found
in meteorites. Over 100 **interstellar molecules** have been observed in
space and their presence in comets and asteroids means that they must
have been present on the early Earth when life was beginning here,
although they seem not to have been involved directly in the
development of terrestrial life forms

### Orion
One of the most spectacular constellations in the sky, Orion includes the
bright stars Betelgeuse and Rigel, the Orion Nebula M42, a bright gas
nebula where stars are now forming, and Orion's Belt, three bright stars
straddling the celestial equator. Orion is the hunter of Greek legend
*(Genitive is **Orionis**)*

### Orionids
Meteor shower with radiant in Orion, observed in October

### orrery
Mechanical model of the solar system, often driven by clockwork. At
their peak of popularity in the 18th and 19th century, the first was built
for the 4th Earl of Orrery (Ireland), Charles Boyle, by George Graham
in the early 18th century

### oscillating universe
Possible condition of the universe in which a cycle of big bang,
expansion, contraction and renewed expansion is repeated many times

### osculation
Literally 'kissing,' but used in astronomy to denote the path, touching
the actual one taken by a comet or other body in the solar system, which
it would adopt if every body in the universe except itself and the Sun
were removed. This allows the perturbation due to the planets'
gravitation to be discounted. In studies of the outer solar system it is
sometimes necessary to use osculating elements of the orbits of the
giant planets and Pluto to correct for their gravitational influence on
each other

### OSETI
*See* OPTICAL SETI

### OSO
*See* ORBITING SOLAR OBSERVATORIES

### outer planets
The planets of the solar system beyond Mars – the gas giants plus Pluto

### OWL
THE OVERWHELMINGLY LARGE TELESCOPE
*See* EUROPEAN SOUTHERN OBSERVATORY

### Ozma
US project to search the sky in radio frequencies for transmissions produced by intelligent life Starting in 1960, two phases of Ozma searching with radio telescopes yielded no sign of extraterrestrial intelligence

### ozone
Oxygen organised in molecules of three oxygen atoms rather than the usual two

### ozone layer
Layer of the Earth's upper atmosphere which shields the Earth's surface from ultraviolet radiation. The ozone layer is thicker and closer to sea level at low latitudes and thinner and higher nearer the Poles. Its depletion by human-made chemicals is currently being fought because of the effects of ultraviolet radiation on life, especially increased skin cancers

# Pp

### P
P Signifies a **periodic comet**, like Comet P/Encke (Encke's Comet) or P/Halley (Halley's Comet)

### P-P
*See* PROTON-PROTON CHAIN

### Pallas
Asteroid number 2, second in size only to Ceres – and perhaps Vesta – and some 500-600km in diameter. Pallas is comparatively spherical in shape, in contrast to the more irregular small asteroids, and rotates every 7.9 hours

### parabola
One of the **conic sections**. Parabolic sections have the property of being able to bring light to a focus at a single point, so that telescope makers aspire to create parabolic optical surfaces

### parallax
The change in apparent position of an object caused by movement on the part of the observer. Parallax errors in reading a gauge are those caused by looking at it at an angle rather than from the front. The parallax of a star is the alteration in its position caused by the Earth's annual movement in its orbit. Parallaxes were the first means of determining stellar distances, although the method only works for nearby stars

### parking orbit
Orbit in which planetary probes are placed before being boosted away from the Earth

### parsec
Distance at which a star would have a parallax of one second, and equal to 3.26 light years, 31 trillion kilometres or 206,000AU. Parsecs are the standard measure of distances in the universe beyond the solar system, although parallax is rarely used as a means of establishing stellar distance

### Parsons, Williams (1800-1867: the third Earl of Rosse)
Irish astronomer whose six-foot telescope at Birr Castle, County Offaly, Ireland, was used for the first observations of the spiral structure of the galaxies

### partial eclipse
Eclipse of the Sun in which the Moon does not totally cover the Sun's disc – so that the Sun's atmosphere remains invisible – or of the Moon in which the Earth's shadow covers only part of the visible surface of the Moon

### particle
Any constituent part of an atom, such as the proton, neutron and electron, or of a possible atom, like the positron, as well as muons, mesons and other components of atomic nuclei. These are sometimes called elementary particles although some appear more fundamental than others. Photons are the elementary particles of electromagnetic radiation

### Pasiphae
Small satellite of Jupiter discovered in 1908, and orbiting Jupiter every 735 days in a highly inclined and eccentric orbit an average of 23.3 million km from the planet. Very little is known about Pasiphae apart from the elements of its orbit. It seems to be under 40km across

### patterned ground
Type of terrain on the surface of the Earth and of Mars. Patterned ground is characterised by polygonal shapes on a large scale, caused by the freezing and thawing of surface parts of permafrosted areas of terrain

### Pauli Exclusion Principle
*See* EXCLUSION PRINCIPLE

### Pavo
Constellation of the southern hemisphere.
*Genetive is **Pavonis**; means the 'peacock')*

### peculiar galaxies
Galaxies which do not belong in any of the normal categories, spiral, barred spiral, elliptical or irregular. Some peculiar galaxies defy simple explanation, while others appear to be members of the usual galaxy types distorted by explosions and collisions. Those related to galaxy types in the **Hubble classification** are given the addendum (pec) to the Hubble type they most resemble

### Pegasus
Large constellation of the northern hemisphere named after the winged horse of legend.
*(Genetive is **Pegasi**)*

### penumbra
Derived from the Latin from 'almost a shadow,' the term is used in two ways in astronomy. The first applies to eclipses and refers to the area which is partially rather than wholly in shadow. During an eclipse of the Sun there is a narrow area of totality in which the completely eclipsed

sun is seen. Surrounding this is a much larger area where the Sun is only partly shadowed, where the penumbra reaches the Earth's surface. In an eclipse of the Moon, two types of darkening of the lunar surface are seen. The central darkest area is in the umbra and the area of lesser darkening around it in the penumbra. The second usage relates to sunspots, where the paler area surrounding the darker centre of the spot is the penumbra

## Penzias, Arno (born 1933)
German-born US physicist and co-discoverer with Robert Woodrow Wilson of the cosmic background radiation. Now a senior executive of Lucent, the US telecommunications group

## Perfect Cosmological Principle
The rule that apart from local irregularities, the universe is homogeneous in form over both space and time. This rule is hard to test because it applies only on the largest scale, where clusters of galaxies are mere local disruptions, but has been questioned on the basis of plots of the distribution of all known galaxies. In these, elements of structure like bubble walls can be seen, although their significance is not agreed upon

## perigee
Point in a satellite's orbit where it is closest to the Earth

## perihelion
Point in the orbit of a planet, or other body orbiting the Sun, where it is closest to the Sun

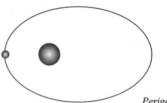

*Perigee*

## period
The time taken for a single cycle of some regular event, such as a complete sequence of the light curve of a variable star, a single journey of an object around its orbit, or between two pulses from a pulsar

## Period-Luminosity Relation
Link between the **absolute magnitude** of a **Cepheid variable** and the period of its light curve, discovered by **Henrietta Leavitt**. She found that brighter Cepheids have longer periods, in a mathematically precise fashion, so that as soon as a Cepheid's period and apparent magnitude are known, its distance can be worked out simply. This is the key to the determination of all stellar distances beyond the small range of parallax measurements

## periodic comet
Comet in an orbit which brings it into the inner solar system at regular

intervals. There are short and long period comets, short in this context being defined as under 200 years

## permafrost
Permanent freezing of ground on Earth, found in the Arctic and Antarctic regions, sometimes to depths of many hundreds of metres. Permafrost has also been postulated as the cause of the **patterned ground** seen on the surface of Mars

## Perseids
Meteor shower seen in August, with radiant in Perseus

## Perseus
Large constellation of the northern hemisphere, named after the mythical character, containing the famous variable star **Algol**, and crossed by the Milky Way.
*(Genitive is **Persei**)*

## Phaethon
Asteroid 3200, thought from its orbit to be the probable remainder of the comet which was the source of the Geminid meteors

## phase
State of illumination of the Moon or another celestial object as seen from Earth. Phases can be expressed as new, full, half, etc or in percentage terms – a full Moon is 100% illuminated

## phase angle
The angle between the Sun, another body and the Earth. The larger the phase angle the more of the surface of the body is illuminated from the point of view of an earthly observer

## Phobos[1]
Larger of the satellites of Mars, discovered by **Hall** in 1877 and having an ellipsoidal shape of some 20km average size. Phobos is an average 9380km from Mars, taking about eight hours per orbit, and has been revealed by space probes as a lumpy, cratered body. Its spectrum resembles those of some asteroids, suggesting that it may be a captured asteroid, like Mars's smaller satellite Deimos

## Phobos[2]
Pair of unmanned space missions sent to Mars by the former Soviet Union. Phobos 1 was an almost complete failure, shutting down, perhaps because of a faulty command from Earth, as soon as it reached Mars in 1988, while Phobos 2 lasted 57 days in 1989 and provided infrared, gamma ray and magnetic data as well as photographs of Mars and its namesake satellite

## Phoebe
Outermost satellite of Saturn, discovered by Pickering in 1898 in an orbit taking 550 days to travel, an average of 12.9 million km from the planet. Phoebe is in a steeply inclined orbit to the general plane of

Saturn's rings, its rotation, and its other satellites, and seems to be some 150km across. Phoebe is dark, unlike the ice worlds of the inner Saturnian system, and may be a captured object from the outer solar system. Dark material blasted by impact from the surface of Phoebe has been cited as a possible cause of the dark area on the surface of Iapetus, the next satellite towards Saturn after Phoebe

### Phoenix[1]
Constellation of the southern hemisphere.
*(Genitive is **Phoenicis**)*

### Phoenix[2]
**SETI** programme run at the **Arecibo** telescope in Puerto Rico

### photocell
Device for sensing light by detecting an electric current released when it strikes a suitable surface. Widely used in astronomical equipment

### photochemistry
The study of chemical reactions occurring under the influence of incident light. Examples of astronomical interest include the Earth's upper atmosphere, where sunlight catalyses the production of ozone from conventional oxygen molecules, and that of Titan, where molecules including ethylene, acetylene, hydrogen cyanide and others are produced by photochemical reactions involving the nitrogen and methane which make up most of Titan's atmosphere

### photometry
Measurement of the intensity of incoming light, using a photometer. Photometric methods are indispensable for magnitude determinations and other observations which provide numerical underpinning for astronomical theory

### photomultiplier
Device which uses electronics to increase the intensity of incoming light. Photomultipliers use materials which emit electrons when light falls on them (the photoelectric effect) and an electronic 'cascade' to increase the number of electrons before they are counted by a sensor

### photon
Fundamental particle of electromagnetic radiation. Different problems require radiation to be thought of as a particle or as a wave, and the shorter the wavelength of the radiation the more energetic the equivalent photon

### photon sphere
The sphere of light and other radiation orbiting a **Schwarzschild** black hole. The light in the photon sphere (or photon circle) comes not from the black hole itself but from other stars and celestial objects whose light is intercepted at the correct angle by the hole's gravitation

## photosphere
The visible surface of the Sun, which has a temperature of some 6000K.
The photosphere marks a comparatively sharp boundary between the
solid body of the Sun and the solar atmosphere. Observations of the
photosphere tell us only about the top few hundred kilometres of the
Sun's body. The term is also used for the visible surface of other stars

## Piazzi, Guiseppe (1746-1826)
Italian monk, professor of mathematics and astronomer who on January
1, 1801 discovered Ceres, the first asteroid to be found, while observing
from Palermo, Sicily

## Pictor
Southern hemisphere constellation, meaning the painter.
*(Genitive is **Pictoris**)*

## piggyback launch
Use of a single launcher to place more than one satellite in orbit

## Pioneer
Series of US spacecraft. The Pioneers launched between 1958 and 1969
were mainly designed for experiments in Earth orbit, to do with the
Earth's particles and fields, and for solar observations, apart from some
Pioneers intended, without much success, for lunar orbit. In 1973
Pioneer 10 was the first spacecraft to visit Jupiter, and has since become
the first spacecraft to leave the solar system. Pioneer 11 passed near
Jupiter and Saturn. Later members of the series are Pioneer Venus 1 and
2, large probes sent to Venus to make observations from above the
atmosphere of Venus and to send probes to the planet's surface. Pioneer
Venus 1, the orbiter, arrived at Venus in 1978 and Pioneer Venus 2, the
landers, in 1979. The orbiter made radar maps of the Venusian surface
and observed its cloud cover while the five landers from the sent
short-lived probes to investigate the planet's atmosphere and surface

## Pisces
Constellation of the Fishes, on the ecliptic in the northern hemisphere
(apart from a small area in the southern).
*(Genitive is **Piscium**)*

## Piscis Austrinis
Constellation of the southern hemisphere containing the bright double
star Fomalhaut
*(Genitive is **piscis austrini**; means the 'southern fish')*

## plage
Bright, high energy region of the solar chromosphere, associated with
activity in the Sun's magnetic field

## Planck, Max (1858-1947)
German physicist who set out quantum theory – the science of energy in
discrete quanta rather than continuous radiation – in work first

published in 1900. Planck's Constant (usually represented by the symbol h) gives the relationship between the frequency of a particular photon and its energy. Planck also set out the formula for the energy distribution in the spectrum of a black body

## planet

Astronomical body larger than an asteroid but too small to support fusion reactions and so qualify as a star. We have direct knowledge of only the nine planets of the solar system. Of these one, Pluto, is so small that it is sometimes viewed as a large asteroid. But several of the major planetary satellites, especially Titan, are so large that they would be viewed as planets if they were in their own orbits around the Sun. Callisto and Titan, the largest satellites of Jupiter and Saturn respectively, are almost as massive as Mercury, and more massive than Pluto. The solid solar system planets all seem to have their own internal processes which are more important than meteorite impact in forming their surfaces, and are massive enough to take up near-spherical shapes. Planets are aggregations of material formed in the early days of the solar system, while the comets, meteorites and asteroids are fundamental pieces of the early solar system never gathered into planets. It seems from close observation of their proper motions that other nearby stars may have large planets much bigger than Jupiter, the largest planet in the solar system, although this method does not allow smaller planets to be detected. But nobody knows how often planets might form near other stars and whether multiple star systems, which are very common, could form planets as the Sun, a lone star, did some 4.5 billion years ago. Detecting stars around other planets relies on hunting for small **Doppler effects** in their **spectra.** A planet orbiting a star displaces it away from and towards the Earth during its orbit. This movement can be detected by **blue** or **red shifts** in starlight received at the Earth. But the effect is very small and means detecting movement of under 100m/s which has only become possible in recent years. A listing in July 2000 showed 53 **main-sequence** stars with planets or **brown dwarfs** in orbit around them, plus two **pulsars** with planets orbiting them, plus 14 doubtful objects and, for comparison, 21 stars which had been examined in detail without stars being discovered. Three stars were positively identified as having dust discs indicative of planet formation, the best-known being Beta Pictoris. The technique of observing planets indirectly by their gravitational effects on stars means that very large planets are most likely to be detected and some have apparent masses of over 50 times that of Jupiter, the biggest planet in the **solar system**. These must be very different world from the familiar planets of the solar system. Other methods now being tried, such as hunting planets by spotting them transiting in front of the stars they orbit, might yield data on smaller objects.

## planetary nebula
Nebula formed by a **red giant** star emitting its outer layers into space after they start burning helium. The observable planetary nebulae are a few tens of thousands of years old at most, since once the gas which forms the nebula expands too far it ceases to be visible. Early observers of these nebulae thought that their round form made them look like planets, to which they are unrelated. They are often thought to be simple spheres of gas which look ring-like because we observe them through the thickest part of the gas bubble, but detailed observation shows that they have complex structures.

## planetesimal
Small dust and gas body, abundant in the early solar system, from which the terrestrial, and possibly gas giant, planets seem to have formed

## Planet X
Name used for the undiscovered planet of the solar system in the early decades of the 20th century, the search for which led to the discovery of Pluto. In recent decades the term has been applied to other putative planets of the outer solar system which might be needed to explain anomalous drifts in the movement of Uranus, although it seems that the explanation may instead lie in the use of imprecise figures for the masses of the planets. A wealth of interesting solar system bodies remains to be discovered but none is likely to be of significant mass

## Plaskett's Star
Large binary star in Monoceros in which two stars totalling nearly 100 solar masses orbit each other. It was discovered by John S Plaskett (1865-1941), a Canadian astronomer and head of the Dominion Astrophysical Observatory, in 1922

## plasma
Ionised atomic material, common in astronomical contexts where large amounts of energy are available – stars and their atmospheres, the Earth's outer atmosphere, the tails of comets when in the inner solar system, the magnetosphere of Jupiter, and others

## plate tectonics
The mechanism that drives continental drift on the Earth, whereby large 'plates' of the Earth's crust move relative to each other. Signs of plate tectonic action have also been sought on Mars and Venus, without success

## Plato (427BC-347BC)
Greek philosopher who lived in Athens and is best remembered in astronomy for pursuing the idea that celestial bodies and their motion are not subject to the imperfections of Earthly objects

## Platonic bodies
The five geometrical shapes which can either contain a sphere perfectly or be perfectly surrounded by one. They are the tetrahedron, the cube, the octahedron, the dodecahedron and the isocahedron. The Platonic bodies were a feature of various now discarded western cosmologies

## Pleiades
Conspicuous open star cluster in Taurus, M45, containing some 350 stars and large amounts of gas. At least six Pleiades are visible to the naked eye – the exact number you can see is a good test of eyesight

## plume
Spiky plasma column seen near the Sun's pole at periods of high solar activity, also known as polar plumes. The plumes' shape is probably controlled by the Sun's magnetic field

## Pluto
The smallest and most distant planet of the solar system, discovered by **Tombaugh** in 1930. Pluto's exact mass is a matter of debate, although it seems to be about 0.25percent that of the Earth. Pluto is the only planet of the solar system not visited by space probes and is not scheduled to be, so that our knowledge of it is limited. Pluto's satellite **Charon** was discovered in 1978 and orbits 19,000km from Pluto. It is the largest satellite in the solar system relative to the planet it orbits, being about 1,300km across to Pluto's 2,300km. Observations of the interaction between Pluto and Charon have allowed our information on the planet to be enhanced. It has a density of about 2 gm/cc, which is consistent with a mix of rock and ice. Solid nitrogen appears to dominate its solid surface. Pluto also has the oddest orbit of any planet in the solar system, with an eccentricity of 0.25, so that it spends part of its time nearer to the Sun than Neptune, including the period from 1979 to 1999. Pluto's mean distance from the Sun is 39AU, and it takes 248 years to orbit the Sun. Pluto's minute size and its strange orbit have encouraged the idea that it is an escaped satellite of Neptune. Some satellites, including Neptune's satellite Triton, are bigger than Pluto. With the discovery of other large objects in the outer solar system, such as **Chiron** and the other **Centaurs**, Pluto and Charon look increasingly like members of a new group of remote members of the solar system, not a planet and satellite as they have traditionally been understood. A **Hubble Space Telescope** view in 1996 finally revealed that Pluto, which rotates on its axis in 6.4 days, has a surface with dark and bright spots and linear markings, whose nature is at present unknown. A 'Pluto Express' plan, for a mission which could visit Pluto after a 10-12 year spaceflight, has been drawn up by US and Russian scientists.

## Pointers
The pair of stars in the **Plough** which point somewhat imperfectly – but well enough to be useful if you are lost in the northern hemisphere –

towards **Polaris**

## polar axis
Axis of rotation of an **equatorially-mounted** telescope, parallel to the Earth's own **axis of rotation**

## polar caps
Regions of frozen matter in the polar regions of planets. The Earth's polar caps are made of snow and ice. The only others known are on Mars, and are composed of a mix of water ice (mainly) and solid carbon dioxide

## polarimetry
The study of polarised light, which yields a wealth of information about the physical condition of objects which have transmitted or reflected it. Light which is reflected or scattered generally becomes polarised, like sunlight scattered in the Earth's atmosphere. Cutting out this light is the principle of Polaroid sunglasses. The **polarisation** of light has been used to yield information about planetary surfaces which have reflected it or about interstellar dust which has scattered it

## Polaris
The bright star Alpha Ursae Minoris, so-called because it is situated near the north celestial pole. Polaris is a **Cepheid** variable star which is notable for the rapid decline in its variability, which has a period of about four days. It varies now only by a visually imperceptible 0.01 magnitudes

## polarisation
Preferential distribution of the waves in electromagnetic radiation so that the waves are parallel to each other rather than randomly distributed around the line of travel of the wave. Radiation can start out polarised, like **synchrotron** radiation, or have polarisation thrust upon it, by reflection or scattering

## polar plume
*See* PLUME

## pole
Fixed point on a rotating body where its axis of rotation intersects with its surface. Poles inherently come in pairs, 90° away from the equator of the body. The **celestial poles** are the stationary points about which the **celestial sphere** appears to rotate, and are the points at which the Earth's axis extended into space cuts the celestial sphere. The **poles** of the **ecliptic** are the points on the celestial sphere where a line drawn vertically to the ecliptic rather than to the Earth's equator cuts the celestial sphere – the northern is in Draco and the southern in Mensa. The **galactic poles**, on the same principle, are the points where the axis of rotation of the galaxy meets the celestial sphere. The northern is in Coma Berenices and the southern in Sculptor

**Pole Star**
*Synonym for* POLARIS

**Pollux**
The 17th brightest star in the sky and the brighter of the twins Castor and Pollux. Pollux (Beta Gemini) has an apparent magnitude of 1.16, absolute magnitude 1.0, is 35 light years from Earth and is of spectral type K0

**populations**
Distinct categories of stars found in our own and other galaxies. Population I stars are the younger, being found in spiral arms of galaxies, and are comparatively rich in heavy elements formed in **supernova** explosions. Population II stars are older and occur preferentially in galactic haloes rather than in spiral arms. They have far lower abundances of heavy elements, by at least tenfold, since the universe contained far fewer such atoms when they formed. There is also a postulated Population III, a hypothetical group of stars in the early universe which would have produced some of the heavy elements we see today

**pore**
Dark area of the Sun's surface which can be the precursor of a sunspot

**positional astronomy**
The study of the location of objects on the **celestial sphere** and the way in which they change over time

**positron**
Particle identical to an **electron** but bearing a positive rather than negative electric charge

**Potassium-Argon (K-Ar) Dating**
Method of finding the ages of rocks by determining their abundances of potassium 40 and argon, working on the principle that potassium 40 (an isotope of potassium) decays to argon 40 over a known **half life** of 1.26 billion years

**potential energy**
Energy which an object possesses by virtue of its position in a gravitational or electromagnetic field, like a boulder ready to topple from a cliff or an electron about to plummet through an electric field

**Poynting-Robertson Effect**
Relativistic effect whereby solar radiation causes dust particles in the inner solar system to spiral very gradually into the Sun. This vacuum cleaner effect is counteracted by comets constantly bringing new material into the inner solar system

**Praesepe**
The open cluster M44 in Cancer

**Prairie Network**
System of cameras in the US Midwest designed to give detailed information about the orbits and magnitudes of incoming **fireballs**

**precession**
Drift of the celestial coordinate systems across the celestial sphere over a 26,000-year cycle. Precession is the visible manifestation of a top-like movement of the Earth's axis in space

**prefixes**
Units used in astronomy and in science generally are often modified with prefixes, usually running in three powers of ten. The most important are kilo, mega, giga and tera for a factor of a thousand, a million, a billion and a trillion (a trillion is a thousand billion) and milli, micro, nano and pico for a factor of a thousandth, a millionth, a billionth and a trillionth

**primary**
The main light-collecting mirror of a reflecting telescope; or the principal star of a multiple star system

**primary cosmic ray**
**Cosmic ray** arriving in the Earth's atmosphere from space, as opposed to the secondary rays produced by the interaction of primaries with the Earth's atmosphere

**prime focus**
The point at which light is brought to a focus by the main mirror or lens of a telescope

**prime meridian**
The line of 0° longitude on the surface of a planet. In the case of the Earth, a line running through Greenwich in London is accepted as the prime meridian, and in recent decades the equivalent points have also been nominated on Mercury, Mars and Venus **(longitude)** and on many solar system satellites. The equator and poles of a rotating body are decided by nature, but the prime meridian has to be decided arbitrarily

**primeval nebula**
*Synonym for the* SOLAR NEBULA
**Primitive solar nebula** is another little-used alternative

**'Principia Mathematica'**
**Isaac Newton's magnum opus,** in which he set out his work on motion, gravitation, and the mathematical methods needed to describe them. Published in 1687, the book's full title was 'Philosophiae Naturalis Principia Mathematica'

**prism**
Triangular-sectioned glass cylinder which can be used to split light into its spectral components or to recombine it once divided, because of the differential rate at which glass refracts light of different wavelengths.

**Diffraction gratings** have largely replaced them in astronomical equipment

## Procyon
The bright star Alpha Canis Minoris, and the eighth brightest star in the sky. Procyon is 11.3 light years from the Earth and of spectral type F5. It has an apparent magnitude of 0.37 and an absolute magnitude of 2.7

## prominence
Glowing mass of gas seen in the Sun's corona at eclipses and with coronagraphs. Prominences can be active or passive, and are bright only by comparison with the darkness of deep space. Photographed against the Sun's disc they appear dark. Prominences are huge structures, sometimes much larger than the Earth, and some last for many weeks. Their shape is influenced by solar magnetic fields

## proper motion
Motion of a star or some other celestial object caused by its own movement rather than that of the Earth. Stars with large proper motions in the sky are certain to be comparatively close to the Earth. **Barnard's Star** has the fastest proper motion of any star in the sky, but even this is only 10 arc seconds per year, so that it would take 180 years to travel the diameter of the full Moon in the sky

## protogalaxy
Galaxy in the process of formation by gravitational contraction

## proton
Positively-charged particle with mass almost identical to that of the neutron, and found with neutrons in the nuclei of atoms

## Proton
Russian (and former Soviet) rocket launcher used extensively in manned and unmanned spaceflight The name was also used in the 1960s for a series of Soviet satellites used to investigate cosmic rays

## proton-proton chain
Process whereby protons are assembled into helium nuclei, the normal energy production process for stars like the Sun. The **carbon cycle** dominates in larger, hotter stars. The proton-proton cycle also produces neutrinos, and photons of energy

## protoplanet
Planet in the process of accreting from **planetesimals** or by **gravitational contraction**

## protostar
Star in the process of formation by **gravitational contraction.** Protostars become stars once fusion commences. Protostars have been observed in several sites of star formation in our own galaxy and in the **Greater Magellanic Cloud**

### Proxima Centauri
The nearest star to the solar system, at a distance of some 4.3 light years. Proxima Centauri is a member of the triple star system which we see as Alpha Centauri

### Psyche
Probably the sixth largest asteroid, some 300km across and of comparatively high albedo

### Ptolemy, Claudius (120-170)
Egyptian astronomer who developed the theory of **deferents** and **epicycles** to explain the apparent movements of the Moon and planets in an Earth-centred universe. His main work on astronomy is now known by its Arabic title of the **Almagest**, and was the definitive work on western astronomy until the time of **Copernicus**. Ptolemy also worked on optics and astrology, and has been accused on faking observations on a virtually industrial scale

### pulsar
Star emitting radio, optical or other radiation in regular pulses, usually many per second. Pulsars (the best-known of which is the one hidden in the **Crab Nebula)** are rapidly rotating **neutron stars** formed in **supernova** explosions, and produce energy in pulses because energy is emitted from them in a tight beam, often compared to the beam from a lighthouse, along the axis of rotation of the neutron star left over from the explosion. A pulse is observed each time the beam sweeps over the Earth. The supernova remnants seem in some cases to be slowing in their rotation, so that the extraordinarily unvarying interval between pulses becomes slightly longer over a period of years

### Puppis
Constellation of the southern hemisphere. One of the constellations formed by the breakup of the huge constellation of Argo Navis, the ship Argo, it is still large, and crossed by the Milky Way
*(Genitive is also **Puppis**; means the 'ship's stern')*

### Pyrex
Type of glass favoured for telescope mirrors because of its low expansion with increased temperature

### Pythagoras (6thC.BC)
Greek philosopher remembered mainly for his famous theorem about the properties of right-angled triangles. He was an adherent of the idea that the Earth is round. His religious and mathematical school produced ideas about the relative distance of objects from the Earth, based on their relative velocities across the sky

### Pyxis
Constellation of the ship's compass in the southern hemisphere, one of

the constellations formed by breaking up the massive constellation
Argo Navis.
*(Genitive is **Pyxidis**)*

# Qq

## QSO
*See* QUASAR

## Quadrantids
Often-impressive meteor shower observed in the first few days of
January. Their radiant is in Draco but they are named after the now
defunct constellation Quadrans. The Quadrantids are distinguished by
being the 'sharpest' major meteor shower, with very high hourly rates
for a period of just a few hours on January 3, implying a very narrow
stream of meteoroids

## quantum theory
Theory developed by Danish physicist Neils Bohr (1885-1962) which
states that at the smallest scale, energy exists in discontinuous 'lumps'
or quanta rather than being infinitely divisible. Thus lines in the spectra
of stars mark the quantum of energy separating two different energy
levels of a particular electron in an atom, the energy of the transition
being given by h, **Planck's** constant, multiplied by the frequency of the
spectral line

## quark
Type of subatomic particle (several different quarks are known) which
form the 'building blocks' of protons, neutrons and other nuclear
particles

## quasar (QSO or Quasi-Stellar Object)
Quasars are apparently starlike objects characterised by enormous
redshifts. They have been among the most discussed objects in
astronomy and cosmology since their high redshifts were identified in
1963. Several thousand are now known. Quasars are so distant that they
must be the nearest objects we can see to the origin of the universe,
because of the time taken for light they have emitted to reach the Earth.
They are now generally thought to have been extreme examples of
active galactic nuclei, the energetic centres of unusual galaxies like
**Seyfert** and **N galaxies**. They are observable in optical and radio
wavelengths and the alteration of their light on its journey to us is a
powerful probe of intergalactic space. Despite their name, quasars (the
term is derived from 'quasi-stellar radio source') also exhibit structure,
including jets of matter to one side of the starlike source. There is a
school of thought that insists that some quasars are far nearer to us than
their redshifts might imply, in other words that the redshifts are not
'cosmological,' caused by the general expansion of the universe. This

theory relies on the fact that more quasars than might be expected are seen near other comparatively nearby galaxies with which they appear to interact. Quasars are employed as a probe of the deep (and therefore early) universe: light from them reveals spectral lines characteristic of gas clouds and galaxies between them and the Earth. If the theory that they are distant objects from the early universe is correct, quasars were characteristic of the early universe and none are now shining

## Quasi-Stellar Object
*See* QUASAR

## quiet sun
The Sun as observed between **solar maxima**, with few sunspots, and a low level of magnetic and radio effects on the Earth

# Rr

## R Process
Nucleosynthesis process whereby heavy elements, beyond iron in nuclear size, are formed in **supernovae**

## R Coronae Borealis
Giant variable star with a carbon-rich atmosphere

## RA
*See* RIGHT ASCENSION

## radar astronomy
Radar is the use of radio waves reflected from distant objects to yield information about them. For astronomers, it has the disadvantage that radar methods can only be used on objects near enough for a usable return to be recorded. In the days before space probes were available, radar was useful as a means of discovering details of the surface topography of the Moon and the terrestrial planets. Radar signals are also reflected by meteors in the upper atmosphere, since the flash of light seen by optical astronomers is accompanied by a streak of ionised air which returns radar waves. The use of this method allowed daylight meteor showers invisible to optical astronomy to be discovered, revealing **meteoroids** coming towards the Earth from the direction of the Sun, in contrast to the nighttime showers whose members approach us moving towards the Sun. The **Magellan** spacecraft, used to map Venus in radar wavelengths, was spectacularly successful. Radars are also used on earth-orbiting satellites to observe the surface of the Earth, since they can 'see' at night and through cloud

## radial velocity
The velocity of an object towards or away from the observer, along a straight line connecting the object and the observer. Radial velocities can be measured by means of the **Doppler effect**

## radian
*See* ANGULAR MEASURE

## radiant
The point in the sky from which **meteors** of a particular shower appear to come. The **meteoroids** which produce the meteors in the upper atmosphere are in the same orbit around the Sun, and enter the Earth's atmosphere parallel to each other, so that they appear to come from a single radiant by the perspective effect. The constellation in which the radiant is found gives its name to the shower, unless there is room for

ambiguity in which case some more specific name (like the April and June Lyrids) is adopted

## radiation

The transmission of energy by electromagnetic means rather than by mechanical ones including conduction or convection. Electromagnetic Radiation is the more commonly-used term. In addition, emissions from radioactive decay are usually described as radiation even when they are generally viewed as particles (like alpha or beta particles) rather than waves

## radiation belts

Layers of ionised material captured from the solar wind and trapped by the magnetic fields of planets. The Earth's **Van Allen Belts** are the best-known example, but they pale by comparison with that of Jupiter, whose magnetic field is far more powerful. Planets with little magnetism, like Mars, are unable to hold a significant radiation belt

## radiation pressure

The pressure pushing outwards from the centre of a star because of the energy generated at the star's core which is transmitted out of the star and into space. Radiation pressure counterbalances the gravitational forces due to the star's mass which tend to make it contract. When the star's energy production ceases and the radiation pressure is removed, the star will start to collapse

## radioactivity

Particles and radiation emitted by the fission of unstable atomic nuclei

## radio astronomy

Powerful branch of astronomy, now over 60 years old, in which astronomers use radio waves to examine the same objects as optical astronomers, and new ones which are visible only or mainly at radio frequencies. Radio astronomy feeds from (and contributes to) the rapid technical change in telecommunications and information technology. **Interferometric** methods allow radio telescopes of immense size to be simulated, and moving radio telescopes into space allows radio emissions to be detected outside the frequencies which can penetrate the Earth's atmosphere. Radio astronomy has already increased our knowledge of the universe in fundamental ways, ranging from the discovery of **pulsars** and the **cosmic background radiation** to the observation of lightning in the atmosphere of Jupiter. Radio waves can penetrate interstellar gas clouds which are opaque to light, allowing us to observe the centre of the galaxy directly, and permit the universe to be viewed at different temperatures and energies from those seen with optical telescopes. The birth of radio astronomy, whose founder was **Jansky**, was the start of the process of recent decades by which astronomy has expanded to observe the universe across virtually the whole of the electromagnetic spectrum

## radio galaxies
Galaxies observed entirely or mainly in radio frequencies. Galaxies like our own emit little radio energy by comparison with their optical emissions, but some peculiar galaxies emit large amounts of radio energy. They tend to emit radio waves from lobes to either side of the main optical galaxy, although there are also cases where radio signals come from jets where strong **synchrotron** processes are at work

## radioisotope
Isotope of an element which is unstable and prone to radioactive decay. Because the decay occurs at a known rate **(half-life)**, some radioisotopes can be used for dating rocks and meteorites

## radio telescope
Telescope used to observe the radio sky. Radio telescopes look profoundly different from optical ones. Most resemble radar or satellite communications dishes instead, although older-fashioned types use extensive wire antennae. The dish types work by scooping up incoming radiation from the sky and bringing it to a focus where it can be recorded. The signals received can be amplified many billions of times, or added to those received from other radio telescopes for **interferometry**. Because of the rise of interferometry as a technique, few new radio telescopes are being built in the form of single large dishes, and instead arrays (such as the **Very Large Array** in the US) are the pattern. But single receivers are still being built for use in unusual frequencies, like the **James Clerk Maxwell Telescope** on Hawaii, designed for use in **submillimetre wavelength** astronomy

## radius of curvature
The radius of the sphere of which a lens or mirror surface forms a part

## radius vector
The line joining a planet or satellite to the star or planet which it orbits

## raisin cake model
Model of the expansion of the universe based on the analogy of a raisin cake being cooked. As the cake is cooked, it expands by rising and the raisins are pushed farther apart. Provided the cake is of generous proportions, the expansion looks similar no matter which raisin the observer sits on, just as the expansion of the universe looks the same from every galaxy

## Randomicity Principle
Notion that a **singularity** producing emissions of matter and energy does so entirely at random, rather than obeying a predictable set of rules about the balance between the two. **Hawking** first outlined the Randomicity Principle, which arises because at a singularity the familiar laws of physics, including the partition laws about the distribution of matter and energy, lose their usual meaning, along with **spacetime** itself

## Ranger

Series of nine US satellites designed to return close-up photography of the Moon. Rangers 7, 8 and 9 were the only successful members of the series, arriving at the Moon in 1964 and 1965

## rapid bursters

X-ray sources whose output of radiation increases and decreases very rapidly over a wide range, sometimes many times per day. Also known as X-ray bursters, rapid bursters are thought to give out X-ray bursts when a **neutron** star sweeps up a critical mass of material from a companion star. This mass collapses at once onto the star's surface and releases its energy in a single X-ray burst. Bursters have also been detected in other frequencies than X-rays

## rare gases

The gases Helium, Neon, Argon, Krypton, Xenon and Radon, sometimes called the noble gases because they do not normally take part in chemical reactions

## ray

Line of pale dust thrown up by meteorite impact, observed on the surface of the Moon and Mercury, leading back to the crater whose creation produced the ray. Ray craters are thought to be the youngest on the Moon, some as recent as a few hundred million years

## Rayleigh Criterion

Formula for the resolving power of telescopes, stating that two point sources cannot be resolved if they are closer together than 1.22X/D, where X is the wavelength of light and D the lens or mirror size

## Rayleigh Scattering

The effect whereby light of different colours is scattered differentially in gas or by suspended particles. The Earth's sky is blue because the Rayleigh scattering affects blue light most. In the thin Martian atmosphere, the sky is red, because the slight blue colour due to light scattered by the air is far less powerful than the red colour due to scattering by dust particles suspended in the atmosphere

## recombination

Assembly of neutral atoms from ions and electrons as old stars swell and cool

## recurrent nova
*See* NOVA

## red giant

Type of star which has left the main sequence, ceased burning hydrogen at its core, and swollen to many millions of kilometres in diameter. Red giants produce energy from burning helium in their cores and hydrogen in their outer layers. Stars enter the red giant phase when they exhaust the supplies of hydrogen in their cores. At this point in their history, the star changes fundamentally, as the core shrinks and heats up, allowing helium fusion to start there, and allowing the area around the core to become hot enough for hydrogen burning. At the same time, the amount of heat being produced increases so much that the star swells massively, its surface cools and it turns red, because it emits less heat per unit of its surface area than before

## redshift
Movement of the spectral lines of an astronomical object towards the red, caused by the object moving away from the Earth. Redshifts are observed on all scales from galactic redshifts caused by the expansion of the universe to others produced by the rotation of planets on their axes

## red spot
*See* GREAT RED SPOT

## red supergiant
**Red giant** of many solar masses, and subject to even more massive expansion that normal red giants. Such stars can swell to the size of the Earth's orbit around the Sun or even larger. Betelgeuse in Orion is the best-known example. Red supergiants are so large that their average densities are very low, but they are among the brightest stars known

## reflector
Telescope which uses a mirror, rather than a lens, as the prime optical component to collect light. There are a variety of reflector configurations, including **Newtonian, Cassegrain** and others, which account for most of the world's large telescopes. Reflectors have ousted refractors partly because it is cheaper to make a mirror of the desired accuracy – there is only one surface to get right – and partly because telescope engineering is rendered far simpler by having a main optical surface which can be supported from behind and which is sited at the bottom rather than the sky end of the telescope

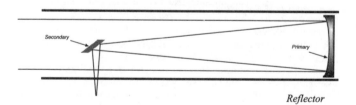

*Reflector*

## refractor
Telescope with a lens rather than a mirror as the main light-collecting component. Refractors have been surpassed by reflectors among the biggest telescopes but are sometimes used for work in areas like

astrometry where immense light-gathering capacity is not critical. A good refractor's main lens is a compound of several lenses designed to preserve natural colour faithfully **(achromatic)**, and in which each piece of glass must be optically flawless. This accounts for the high cost of good telescope lenses and the fact that no refractor larger than 1m has ever been built

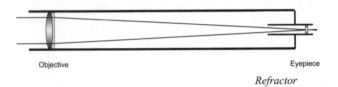

Objective                                      Eyepiece

*Refractor*

### refractory elements
Elements of high melting and boiling points, such as most metals. They tend to concentrate in the inner planets while their opposites, the volatiles, are found preferentially at a tactful distance from the Sun, in the outer solar system, especially in the gas giant planets and in comets

### regolith
The fine-grained 'soil' of the lunar surface, formed by the gradual action of meteorite impact and solar radiation on moonrock

### Regulus
Alpha Leonis, the brightest star in Leo and the 20th brightest star in the sky, sited virtually on the ecliptic. Apparent magnitude 1.36, absolute magnitude -0.7, type B7, distance from Earth 84 light years

### relativity
A pair of theories about the nature of gravitation and of motion, respectively called General and Special Relativity, and developed mainly by **Einstein**. The **General Theory** was confirmed by astronomical observations of the effect of the mass of the Sun on passing starlight, while the **Special Theory** remains controversial, although evidence for some of its predictions, like the increase in mass of particles approaching the velocity of light, has been obtained in particle accelerators. The effect of relativity on astronomy cannot be underestimated. It starts by showing how stars shine and continues with the whole field of relativistic astrophysics, the content of which covers **black holes**, the **big bang**, and almost all other major issues surrounding the origin, large-scale structure and evolution of the universe. **Gravity Probe B**, also called the Relativity Mission, is a NASA space probe due to be launched in 1999 which is designed to test the general theory of relativity by looking for the twisting of spacetime caused by the mass of the Earth

### relay telescope
Telescope using a spherical primary mirror, secondary mirror and lenses, sometimes built by amateur telescope makers

### remote sensing
The use of satellites (and aircraft) to obtain information about the Earth's surface, waters and atmosphere

### resolution
The minimum separation between two objects capable of being distinguished by a particular telescope. Angular resolution is a synonym. For a particular instrument, the theoretical resolution is given by the **Rayleigh Criterion**, which telescope makers can approach but not beat

### resonance
Time coincidence of astronomical importance, for example between the orbital periods of satellites or between rotational periods are entrenched by the repeated periodic action of gravitation. Resonances abound in the solar system. The most obvious is the way in which the Moon revolves on its axis in exactly the same time period as it takes to orbit the Earth, so that we only see one face of the Moon from the Earth. Other resonances are now being discovered throughout the solar system including the many responsible for the **Kirkwood Gaps**, and the ratio of three to two between the orbital periods of Pluto and Neptune

### rest wavelength
The observed wavelength of a spectral line when there is no relative motion between the observer and the source of the radiation containing the line. **Redshifts** and **blueshifts** caused by the Doppler effect are measured with reference to the rest wavelength

### Reticulum
Small constellation of the southern hemisphere.
*(Genitive is **Reticuli;** means the 'net')*

### retrograde motion
Movement in the solar system contrary to the direction of the Earth's rotation. Retrograde motion is rare in the solar system and examples are regarded as needing explanation. Venus turns on its axis in a retrograde direction, and some comets and some of the satellites of the outer solar system have retrograde orbits

### reversing layer
Lower part of the Sun's **chromosphere**, where the dark absorption lines seen in the Sun's spectrum are formed

### Rhea
Satellite of Saturn discovered by **Cassini** in 1672. Rhea has a circular, 4.5 day orbit almost exactly in the plane of Saturn's equator and 527,000km in radius. Rhea is a bright, icy world with impact craters

dominating its surface, and is some 1500km across with a density of only about 1.3, implying that it consists mainly of ice mixed with a little rock

## Rheticus, Georg Joachim (1514-1576)
Austrian astronomer now remembered mainly as a supporter and biographer of Copernicus

### rich field telescope
Telescope of short focal length, designed not to resolve very close objects or see very faint ones but to allow a good view of comparatively large areas of sky. Used especially by comet and nova hunters and observers of telescopic meteors

### Rigel
The bright star Beta Orionis, the second brightest star in Orion and the seventh brightest in the sky. Rigel is a variable star with an average apparent magnitude of 0.14 and an average absolute magnitude of -7.1. It is 900 light years from Earth and is of type B8, one of the brightest types of star known

### right ascension (RA)
The equivalent of **longitude** on the **celestial sphere**, usually measured in hours, minutes and seconds across the sky to match the rotation of the Earth, from the point in Pisces where the ecliptic crosses the celestial equator

### Rigil Kentaurus
Alpha Centauri, the fourth brightest star in the sky and the brightest in Centaurus. With an apparent magnitude of 0.01 and an absolute magnitude of 4.39, Rigil Kentaurus belongs to spectral type G2 and is 4.3 light years from Earth, making it the nearest star to the Sun apart from **Proxima Centauri**, another member of the same star system

### rille
Narrow valley on the lunar surface, of variable length up to tens of kilometres long. Many are thought to be former tunnels in lava flows, whose roofs have collapsed as the lava cooled. Similar structures are observed in volcanic areas of the Earth

### rings
Bands of dust and rock orbiting planets. Saturn's is the most spectacular in the solar system, but others are known to orbit Jupiter, Uranus and Neptune. Ring systems are found within the **Roche limits** of large planets and have a number of characteristics in common. One is that they are paper-thin by comparison with their diameter: another is that the rings are always divided by gaps containing little or no material, swept clear by **resonances** with satellite orbits. There are also wave systems in rings caused by gravitational forces concentrating material at particular points along them. Spoke-like structures in the rings of Saturn

appear to be due to electromagnetic forces

### ring basins
Large impact basins on the surface of the Moon and Mercury, examples
being the Mare Orientale and the Mare Caloris respectively

### ring nebula
The planetary nebula M57 in Lyra

### Ritchey-Chretien Telescope
Type of **Cassegrain** telescope with a specially wide field of view, used
mainly for stellar photography

### Roche Limit
The zone near to a star, planet or other body within which its gravitation
is too powerful for solid bodies to exist. Its size is given by Roche's
Law

### Roche Lobe
Figure-of-eight shape showing the zones of gravitational influence of
the individual members of a binary star system. Roche Lobe diagrams
help solve problems like deciding when material ejected from one star
will fall into the other

### rocket
Device which moves by means of the force generated under **Newton's
Third Law of Motion**, which states that actions – pushing material out
of the rear of a rocket – generate equal and opposite reactions – the
rocket moves forward. Rockets normally travel by burning fuel to
produce hot gases, which are ejected from the rocket engine, but there
are also types which eject cool gas or even streams of electrons

### ROSAT
Joint German/UK/US satellite launched in 1990 and used to produce a
map of the sky at wavelengths in **X-rays** and the extreme **ultraviolet**
especially in the 5-10 Ångstrom range. Called the Roentgen Satellite in
honour of Wilhelm Roentgen, discoverer of X-rays. It has identified
tens of thousands of new X-ray sources and helped elucidate processes
including the latter stages of solar evolution such as supernova
explosions and the formation of **starburst galaxies**

### Rosetta
**ESA** mission planned for the year 2003 and designed to land on and
sample the nucleus of a comet. Original plans to return cometary
material to the Earth have been abandoned to save money. The lander
will probably be called Champollion and the comet to be visited is
Comet Wirtanen in 2013

### Rosse, Earl of
*See* PARSONS

## RR Lyrae

Variable star which has given its name to a group of similar stars, also known as cluster variables because they are often found in **galactic clusters**. They all have an **absolute magnitude** of about 0.5 at the peak of their light curve, which means that as soon as one is observed and its apparent magnitude is found, its distance can be found by simple arithmetic. All RR Lyrae stars have periods of variation of under a day

## RR Lyrae Gap

Gap in the **Hertzsprung Russell diagram** for **globular clusters**, at about zero magnitude for stars of about type F. There are no stars except RR Lyrae variables in this area of the H-R diagram for such a cluster

## Rudolphine Tables

Tables of planetary positions compiled by **Kepler**, mainly from observations by **Brahe**, and used by astronomers for about a century after their publication. Funded by (and named after) Emperor Rudolph II, they were finally published in 1627 after interruptions due to wars and many other difficulties. They also included a comprehensive table of the positions of the fixed stars

# Ss

### S Process
**Nucleosynthesis process** by which heavy elements are produced in Red Giant stars

### Sagan-Ward Cyclical Climate Theory
Theory that Mars may sometimes be far less hostile to life than at present. The theory – a kind of Martian version of **Milankovitch cycles** – depends upon the irregularity of the Martian orbit, which can sometimes allow the temperature at the poles of Mars to be higher than now, releasing water locked up there. The terraced appearance of the Martian north polar cap, redolent of repeated freezing and thawing, is indirect evidence for this theory, as is the presence of large water-cut features on the surface of Mars. But the Sagan-Ward theory may not be enough to account for these features, since there now seems to be very little water available in the Martian polar caps even were they to melt

### Sagitta
Small constellation of the northern hemisphere, crossed by the Milky Way
*(Genitive is **Sagittae;** means the 'arrow')*

### Sagittarius
Zodiac constellation of the Archer, at the southernmost point of the ecliptic, in the southern hemisphere.
*(Genitive is **Sagittarii**)*

### Sakigake
The first Japanese spacecraft to leave Earth orbit for interplanetary space, in 1985. Sakigake was equipped to observe the solar wind and to make a flyby of Comet Honda-Mrkos-Pajdusakova in early 1996

### SALT
*See*  SOUTH AFRICAN LARGE TELESCOPE

### Salyut
Series of Soviet manned space stations, culminating in Salyut 7, launched in 1982. Salyut 7 was a 35m long structure when rockets were docked to it, with a mass of 47 tonnes

### Sampex
The Solar, Anomalous and Magnetospheric Particle Explorer, launched by NASA in 1992. It was used to explore phenomena such as the **South Atlantic Anomaly** and particles from cosmic rays and solar flares

### Sandage, Alan (born 1926)
US astronomer best-known as the discoverer of **quasars** in 1960

### SAO
*See* STAR CLASSIFICATION

### Saros
The period of just over 18 years in which the movements of the Sun and Moon in the sky coincide. The Saros has been known since antiquity and is of value because it allows eclipses to be predicted

### SAS
*See* SMALL ASTRONOMICAL SATELLITE

### satellite
Any natural or artificial body in orbit around another, usually a planet. The terms 'Earth satellite' and 'artificial Earth satellite,' used early in the space age to describe artificial satellites of the Earth, are now archaic

### saturation[1]
State of old planetary surfaces in which so many impact craters are present that they cover the surface completely. The crater count on a saturated surface would not be increased by more impacts. The Highlands of the Moon are saturated, as is most of the surface area of Mercury, but the younger surfaces of the lunar maria and the mercurian inter-crater plains are not

### saturation[2]
State of a camera film which has been so overexposed that more exposure would yield no more image

### saturation[3]
Measure of the amount of colour in light from a particular source. White light has zero saturation, because it includes the full range of frequencies of visible light, while light from a single spectral line, of effectively a single wavelength, is 100% saturated. The term is applied analogously to radiation of other wavelengths

### Saturn
The sixth planet of the solar system and its largest apart from Jupiter. Saturn has an equatorial diameter of 120,000km, but its polar diameter is 10 per cent less, giving it much the greatest polar flattening of any planet of the solar system. Saturn is also the least dense of the planets, at about 0.7gm/cc. Saturn is accompanied by its famous ring system and by a large family of satellites, and is 95 times as massive as the Earth. Its globe has a system of cloud belts and zones like those of Jupiter but on a smaller scale and displaying more gradual change. Saturn rotates on its axis in 10 hours and has a 29-year orbit at an average of 1427 million km from the Sun. Most of our knowledge of Saturn and its satellites comes from brief visits by the US Pioneer 11 and Voyager 2

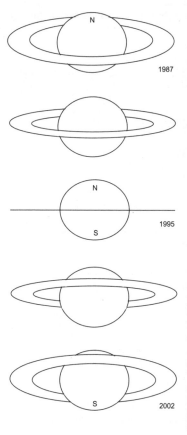

spacecraft. At its immense distance from the Sun, the 'surface' temperature at the cloud tops is only about 95K, but the observed cloud zone takes up less than 1% of the planet's radius. Beneath the clouds is thought to lie a deep layer of gas, mainly hydrogen and helium, which lower still turns into solid metallic hydrogen. At the planet's very heart there is likely to be a core of rocky and/or icy material. Both this and the metallic hydrogen layer are likely to be much smaller than their equivalents within Jupiter, since Saturn has less mass and hence less of the internal pressure needed to form these zones. Its lower overall density also limits their possible sizes. The outer cloud layers of Saturn contain methane and ammonia as well as hydrogen and helium. Saturn has nine major satellites: **Mimas, Enceladus, Tethys, Dione, Rhea, Titan** (itself bigger than Mercury), **Hyperion, Iapetus** and **Phoebe** and a large number of smaller satellites, some of which dictate the gaps in Saturn's ring system. First identified correctly by **Huygens,** smaller versions of the ring system have since been found at other gas giant planets, but none are as large or as spectacular as Saturn's. The rings of Saturn may have formed by the breakup of a large asteroid-like object within the last few million years

### scale factor
Factor used by cosmologists to represent the change of large distances with time: symbol R

### scarp
Step in the topography of a surface. Examples abound on the solid

surfaces of the solar system, including some on the surface of Mercury which appear to be fossil traces of the planet's original cooling from the molten state

## scattering

Diversion of light by matter. such as the effect of the Earth's upper atmosphere on incoming sunlight – which causes the sky to look blue – or the scattering of starlight in dust or gas nebulae. Sunlight is scattered very effectively by electrons in the solar atmosphere, and pictures taken on the surface of Mars show that the Martian atmosphere, which contains large amounts of dust, tends to scatter light in such as a way as to make red rather than blue skies

## Schiaparelli, Giovanni (1835-1910)

Italian astronomer who discovered the link between comets and meteor showers. He is best-known for his observations of Mars, in describing which he used the term 'canali' for markings he thought might be channels of some sort. These were taken up as 'canals' in the English-speaking world, although he had not intended to imply artificiality. This gave rise to scientific and fictional speculation **(Lowell)** about life of Mars

## Schmidt Camera

Photography-only telescope used mainly for wide-angle sky surveys. Schmidt cameras use a thin non-spherical lens, the correcting plate, at the skyward end of the telescope to capture light from a wide sky area faithfully. The principal technical problem with Schmidt optics is the correcting plate, which is designed to match the optical properties of the telescope mirror and which is complex to grind exactly. Schmidt telescopes are also long for their light-gathering power because the lens needs to be at the **centre of curvature** of the mirror, while most large refractors are only half this length, as the focal length of a mirror is only half of its radius of curvature

## Schmidt-Cassegrain

Type of **Cassegrain** telescope which uses a Schmidt-type correcting plate

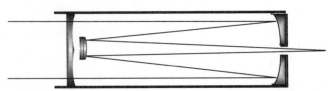

*Schmidt-Cassegrain Telescope*

### Schwarzschild Black Hole

Black hole with mass but no rotation or electric charge. This makes the Schwarzschild black hole the simplest type to analyse mathematically. A Schwarzschild black hole formed from a star of four solar masses would have an **event horizon** some 20km in diameter and a **photon sphere** surrounding it of about 25km diameter

### Schwarzschild Radius

The radius of a Schwarzschild black hole to the event horizon. The **singularity** forms when a sufficient mass of material has collapsed within the event horizon and is trapped there by its gravitation

### Schwarzschild Solution

Solution to the **General Relativity** formulae describing a Schwarzschild black hole

### Schwassmann-Waschmann, Comet

Notable **periodic** comet 1925 II, orbiting the Sun in an almost circular orbit just beyond Jupiter, in contrast to the highly eccentric orbits of most comets, and prone to sudden increases in brightness

### scintillation

Technical term for 'twinkling,' the fluctuations in brightness of stars caused by atmospheric instability. Radio scintillation is a similar effect seen in radio astronomy, but is caused by fluctuations in the solar wind rather than in the Earth's atmosphere

### Scorpius

Constellation on the ecliptic in the southern hemisphere, including the bright star Antares, and the best-known X-ray source in the sky, **Sco X-1**. *(genitive is **Scorpii**; means the 'scorpion')*

### Sco X-1

Conspicuous X-ray source, the first ever detected, and found in the sky near the centre of the galaxy. Sco X-1's radiation does not have the regularity of highly predictable **pulsars**. Instead it may be releasing X-rays at random as it sweeps up comparatively dense interstellar material from the area at the heart of the galaxy

### Sculptor

Constellation of the southern hemisphere in which lies the southern galactic pole. *(Genitive is **Sculptoris**)*

### Scutum

Small constellation of the southern hemisphere, crossed by the Milky Way and the site of a nova in 1970. *(Genitive is **Scuti**; means the 'shield')*

### Sea

Archaic term sometimes used for the lunar Maria **(Mare)**, which are in fact extremely dry plains of lava

## seasons

Periods of annual variations in the Earth's weather caused by the geometry of the Earth's orbit, which leads to varying amounts of sunlight falling on different parts of the Earth's surface. The same term is applied by analogy to Mars and other planets

## secondary cosmic rays

Rays produced by the impact of **primary cosmic rays** on the Earth's atmosphere. Secondary cosmic rays are not really cosmic in origin at all

## secondary crater

Crater produced by the impact of debris which thrown up from the formation of a primary crater produced by meteorite impact

## secondary mirror

Mirror used to handle light within a telescope, rather than to collect it in the first instance from outside, the task of a **primary mirror** or system of mirrors

## second af arc

*See* ANGULAR MEASURE

## sector

In **Kepler's Laws**, which govern the orbits of planets, a sector is the area swept out by the **radius vector** of a planet – the line joining it to the Sun – in a given period of time. It does not change in size since the planet moves faster the nearer it comes to the Sun, so that the effect of the eccentricity of the planet's orbit is self-cancelling

## secular

Changing steadily with time, as opposed to cyclical change which repeats over some cycle

## seeing

One of the favourite conversational topics among observational astronomers, seeing is the state of stillness or turbulence of the atmosphere. Good seeing – a very low level of turbulence – is one of the characteristics most sought after when telescope sites are being considered, since poor seeing increases the apparent size of images produced by a telescope, lowering its resolving power and in effect giving it the performance of a poorer instrument. Mountain sites for major observatories are selected only after exhaustive tests of their seeing quality

## Semimajor Axis

Distance from the centre of an **ellipse**, such as an orbit, to its most distant point

## Semiminor Axis

Distance from the centre of an **ellipse** to the nearest point on its circumference

## Serendip

**SETI** experiment in which radio astronomy data gathered at the **Arecibo** telescope and the 64m Parkes telescope in Australia (Southern Serendip) is searched for artificial signals.

## Serpens

Constellation of the Serpent, mainly in the northern hemisphere and also called Serpens Caput, the Serpent's Head.
*(Genitive is **Serpentis**)*

## SETI

Search for Extra-Terrestrial Intelligence, the activity of looking for celestial signals of artificial origin, usually in radio wavelengths, and for other signs of intelligent life beyond the Earth. About 50 such searches had been carried out at the time of writing, with no success. SETI experiments active at the present time include **BETA, META, Phoenix** and **Serendip**. Most concentrate on the region of the radio spectrum around 1-10 gigahertz, where signals can travel well both in space and in the Earth's atmosphere and where numerous key spectral lines, such as the 21cm hydrogen line, are to be found which might (the theory goes) suggest themselves to other species as markers near which transmissions might be sent. The US Congress has traditionally targeted SETI experiments for high-profile budget cuts, leaving it to be resurrected by private donors and scientific societies. Although most SETI experiments depend upon searches for radio signals, **optical SETI** is growing in acceptance.

## Sextans

Constellation straddling the celestial equator and meaning the Sextant.
*(Genitive is **Sextantis**)*

## Seyfert Galaxy

Type of galaxy with bright cores and known to emit X-rays. Seyferts are disrupted spiral galaxies and are related to **quasars** and **BL Lacertae** objects, although their activity is on a less massive scale. They were discovered by Carl Seyfert in 1943. It seems that many large spiral galaxies may have a Seyfert stage, and that our own galaxy may once have been a Seyfert. The Seyfert process may be related to material being sucked into black holes at the hearts of galaxies, and our galaxy appears to contain a massive black hole at its centre

## shadow bands

Dark bands seen travelling across the Earth's surface during total eclipses of the Sun, following the eclipse track, and caused by the heating and cooling of the Earth's atmosphere as the sun's heat is cut off and restored

## Shapley, Harlow (1885-1972)

US astronomer who used Cepheids to determine the size of the galaxy

## Shaula

The bright star Lambda Scorpii, the 23rd brightest star in the sky, with an apparent magnitude of 1.6 and an absolute magnitude of -3.3, both averages since Shaula is a variable star. Type B1, 310 light years from Earth

## shear wave

Type of wave encountered in earthquakes (and seismic events in other celestial bodies) which are useful in determining interior structures of planets because they are not able to travel through any liquid core which the body may have. Shear waves are propagated by a movement of the particles in which they are travelling at right angles to the direction of propagation, which is only possible in a rigid material

## shell burning

Burning of hydrogen outside the cores of old stars. Shell burning starts when stars have consumed the hydrogen in their cores and begin to contract. At this stage the gravitational energy released in contraction allows hydrogen burning to begin outside the core. Then the energy released by shell burning and gravitational collapse causes the star's outer layers to swell up, producing a **red giant** or **red supergiant** star

## shergottite

One of the types of meteorite of Martian origin found on the Earth
*See* SNC

## shock metamorphism

Alteration of rocks by severe shocks, especially meteorite impact. Several minerals are known to be characteristic of severe shock processes and are regarded as indicators of meteorite impact, including forms of quartz known as Coesite and Stishovite

## shock wave

Wave found in solid and fluid materials and consisting of successive compressions and rarefactions of material along the line of travel of the wave. Shock waves are produced by explosions and other causes. In astronomy they are important because in stellar gas and dust clouds they can prompt star formation by triggering the gravitational collapse of material into a protostar. Mass concentrations in stellar dust and gas clouds are often observed in patterns indicative of the effects of shock waves. They are also thought to be important in the processes occurring in **nova** and **supernova** explosions and in galaxies which are the seat of unusual energetic events

## Shoemaker Levy 9

One of many comets discovered by David Levy and Carolyn Shoemaker in Arizona, USA, this one found short-lived fame in July 1994 during its impact with the planet Jupiter, of which the effects on Jupiter's cloud system were widely observed from the Earth. The comet had already been broken up by Jupiter's gravitation and many scars on the Jovian cloud system were observed as its pieces hit the planet

### Shooting Star
Synonym for **meteor**: shunned by the cognoscenti

### short-period comet
Comet which orbits the Sun in under 200 years, the most famous example being **Halley's Comet**, with a 76-year orbit. Of the approximately 600 comets known, some 100 are short-period

### SI
*See* SYSTÈME INTERNATIONAL

### sidereal
Relating to the stars. As well as being used in a general fashion, the term is applied to definitions of the day, month or year measured in terms of the stars. Thus a Sidereal Day is the period needed for the stars to return to the same position in the sky as they were the day before, about 23 hours 56 minutes. The Sidereal Month (27.32 days) is the time taken for the Moon to reappear at the same point relative to the stars, and the Sidereal Year is the time taken for the Sun to reach the same point in the sky relative to the stars, 365.26 days

### sidereal time
The time in the Sidereal Day for a particular point on the Earth's surface. The Sidereal Time equals the **Right Ascension**, measured in hours, minutes and seconds, of the **Meridian** at a particular time and place

### siderite
Little-used term for iron meteorite

### Simplicity Principle
Less attractive name for **Occam's Razor** – the idea that theories should not be more complex than is essential to explain the observations which prompt them

### simultaneity
The condition of two events occurring at the same time. One of the key findings of **relativity** is that all simultaneity is in reality only apparent – a second observer would not see the same events as occurring at the same time as the first one did, or at the same time as each other

### singularity
Point where the curvature of spacetime is infinite. Singularities are aptly named – they are the most 'singular' and bizarre objects in astronomy, since all the normal rules of physics cease to have effect there. A singularity must lie at the heart of a **black hole**, surrounded by an **event horizon** and **photon sphere** preventing its being observed from the outside universe. At the singularity, matter entering the black hole has no hope of being sustained by its physical strength, even including the forces which hold atoms themselves together. Instead, all material

sucked into the hole, including the original matter making up the star which collapsed to make the black hole, is crushed into an infinitely tiny 'pinhead' at infinitely high pressure

## Sinope

Small satellite of Jupiter discovered in 1914 by Nicholson and thought to be less than 20km in diameter. Sinope orbits Jupiter in a highly inclined and eccentric orbit an average of 24 million km from the planet, making it the outermost of Jupiter's satellites and encouraging the assumption that it is a captured asteroid. It takes 758 days for a complete orbit of Jupiter

## Sirius

Alpha Canis Majoris, the brightest star in the night sky. Sirius has an apparent magnitude of -1.47 and an absolute magnitude of 1.45, and is 8.7 light years from Earth. The main star is of type A1, and is accompanied by a much smaller **White Dwarf** companion, Sirius B. There have been reports of other possible members of the Sirius system. Sirius is much the brightest star in Canis Major and is found by extending the line of the stars of **Orion's Belt** south-westwards. Sirius is white and there have been numerous debates about whether its colour has changed in the last 2,000 years, since descriptions of its colour from antiquity, especially by **Ptolemy**, seem to refer to it as red. Translation difficulties and misunderstood astrological usages appear to be the explanation, not changes in the star itself

## SIRTF

*See* SPACE INFRARED TELESCOPE FACILITY

## Skylab

US science laboratory placed in space in 1973 and used for many astronomical observations, especially of the Sun, in a wide variety of wavelengths. Skylab broke up on reentering the atmosphere in 1979. The basic design of Skylab was based on the fourth stage of a Saturn rocket, which yielded a structure about the size of a small house, making it significantly larger than the early Soviet space stations

## slit

Narrow, long gap through which light enters a **spectrometer**

## Small Astronomy Satellites (SAS)

Series of three astronomy satellites of both scientific and political interest. Also called Explorer 42, SAS-A was launched by Italy from a platform off the Kenyan coast in 1970 and named Uhuru, the Swahili for freedom. SAS-B and C (Explorers 48 and 53) complete the series. Uhuru was the first satellite to construct a systematic survey of the X-ray sky and its results will be of use to astronomers for many years. SAS-B in 1972 carried much the most sensitive gamma-ray telescope ever placed into orbit, and operated until 1980. SAS-C again looked mainly at X-ray sources. All of these satellites weighed under 200kg each and only one was over a metre in any dimension, and they produced results out of all proportion to their cost

## SMM
*See* SOLAR MAXIMUM MISSION

## Smooth Plains
Areas of the surface of the Moon and Mercury which are almost free of craters and which are thought to be of volcanic origin. The term was first used in the context of Mercury, but similar areas of the Moon show clearer indications of volcanic action

## SNC
The Shergottite, Nakhalite and Chassignite meteorites, which have come to the Earth from Mars. The shergottites are thought to have suffered most alteration during the impact process which led to their ejection into space. They have been used to provide information on the geological history of Mars and on its atmosphere and water resources. They seem to be igneous rocks 200 million to 1.3 billion years old, and the isotope composition of nitrogen bubbles in them seems to resemble that in the atmosphere of Mars

## snowball model
Model of a comet as a murky snowball of ice and dust, emitting tails and other features only upon making a close approach to the Sun. This model was largely confirmed by the 1986 space probes to **Halley's Comet**

## SOFIA
STRATOSPHERIC OBSERVATORY FOR INFRARED ASTRONOMY
a US-German aircraft-based observatory with a 2.7m telescope, due to enter service in 2002

## SOHO
*See* SOLAR AND HELIOSPHERIC OBSERVATORY

## solar activity
Phrase applied to everything other than the normal emission of radiation by the Sun, especially the appearance of **sunspots** and disturbances of the Sun's magnetism. This activity is associated with **flares** and increased emissions of energetic particles from the Sun, and has direct effects upon the Earth, especially upon radio reception and the appearance of the **aurora**

## solar array
Assembly of silicon cells used on satellites to convert sunlight into electric power. Solar arrays have grown during the space age into structures capable of producing many kilowatts of power from areas of many tens of square metres of material. In the future, space stations will demand even more electricity, and larger arrays will be used along with

new technology, including a change to new materials like gallium arsenide instead of silicon, and the use of focussing mirrors to concentrate more light on a given area of material

## solar atmosphere

The part of the Sun above the visible **photosphere**, merging eventually into the **solar wind**. The solar atmosphere contains only a negligible fraction of the Sun's mass and consists mainly of the **chromosphere**, the part of the atmosphere seen at solar eclipses and visible in between by users of special telescopes designed to cut out the Sun's disc from view. The solar atmosphere is in constant motion, most notably a five-minute oscillation of its outer layers caused by **pressure waves** of energy resonating in the gas of the atmosphere. The outer part of the Sun's atmosphere, the very low-density **Corona**, has a temperature of up to about 2 million K, far higher than the surface temperature of even the hottest star. Much effort has been put into determining the composition of the Sun's atmosphere from the strength of the **spectral lines** within it. This work has shown that within limits, it has the same composition as the most primitive classes of meteorite, which seem to be remnants of the solar nebula from which the solar system formed

## solar constant

The rate at which solar energy arrives at the Earth, equal to about 13.5 Watts per square metre in space just above the Earth's atmosphere. The solar constant is not constant, and in recent years there have been many attempts to discover whether its day-to-day and year-to-year variations are accompanied by long-term variations which could have important effects on the evolution of life on Earth, modern-day climate change and the incidence of ice ages

## solar cycle

The 22-year period over which the pattern of sunspots on the Sun's surface repeats itself. The solar cycle was long thought to last 11 years, but analysis of sunspot records shows that the 11-year peaks seem to come in pairs, so that a 22-year cycle is now often thought of as being more correct. Many attempts have been made to find possible longer cycles of several 22-year periods. There have also been lengthy periods in the 300-year-plus history of solar observation when few if any sunspots have been visible

## solar day

The day measured in terms of the time taken for the Sun to return to the same point in the sky, and equal to about 24 hours 4 minutes

## solar flare

Bright flash of **plasma** in the Sun's atmosphere, capable of affecting radio traffic on Earth when particles of the plasma arrive at the Earth. Flares are most common at peak periods for sunspot activity, and are accompanied by ultraviolet and X-ray emissions as well as bright

flashes of light. Flares seem to operate by a mechanism in which energy
is stored by the Sun's magnetic field and then released in a single
sudden burst

## solar eclipse
*See* ECLIPSE

## Solar and Heliospheric Observatory (SOHO)
**ESA** space mission to examine the Sun's oscillations and luminosity,
the solar wind, and the outer layers of the Sun. SOHO was launched in
1995, carrying 12 instruments, and sited at the first **Lagrangian** point
of the Earth/Moon system, from which the Sun is always visible. The
SOHO satellite is intended to work closely with ESA's **cluster** satellites
launched in 2000 for examining the Earth's geomagnetic field. Its main
objectives were to examine the solar interior, the Sun's atmosphere and
the **solar wind.** It obtained information about the solar interior by
measuring the oscillations of the Sun's **photosphere,** its visible surface,
caused by sound waves in the Sun's interior. It has provided a
revolutionary increase in our knowledge of solar activity and its images
have led to over 100 comet discoveries

## Solar Maximum Mission (SMM)
US satellite launched in 1980 for X-ray, gamma ray, ultraviolet and
other studies of the Sun at a time of peak solar activity. SMM worked
well for 10 months and then broke down, and was repaired in orbit by
two astronauts from the space shuttle Challenger in 1984. This repair
worked well and the SMM was later used for more solar observations
and for viewing **Halley's Comet** and other objects

## solar nebula
The cloud of dust and gas from which the solar system is believed to
have condensed, mainly by gravitational attraction. Studies of the origin
of the solar system and the evolution of the solar nebula suggest that the
solar system did not simply condense from a homogeneous cloud.
Instead, there seem to have been areas of varying composition to
account for detailed differences between the atomic composition of the
Sun, the Earth, the other planets, meteorites and other solar system
objects

## Solar Orbiter
Proposed ESA mission to take a spacecraft within about 30 million km
of the Sun, allowing to observe the Sun's surface and the solar wind
with unprecedented closeness.

## solar oscillations
Slight 'shivering' of the body of the Sun, with a period of 52 minutes,
plus various harmonics of this and longer period oscillations, and
discovered in the search for slight variations in the Sun's shape

## solar parallax

Average angular radius of the Earth as seen from the Sun, about 9 seconds of arc. This is equal to the difference in the position of the Sun in the sky as seen from opposite sides of the Earth

## solar sailing

Possible technique for travelling through the solar system, or beyond, propelled not by rockets but by the **solar wind** and solar radiation caught in a sail many kilometres across. A favourite of science fiction writers, solar sailing has also received detailed attention from spacecraft engineers

## solar system

Collective term for the Sun and all the objects under its gravitational influence. The last few decades have increased our knowledge of the solar system massively, because of the availability of spacecraft to visit planets and other solar system objects. Since the 1960s, our knowledge of the solar system's planets and satellites, and its asteroids and comets, and of the Sun itself, has increased many millions of times. We also know that the idea of the solar system as a star, nine planets, and some other miscellaneous objects, is mistaken. Pluto, the ninth planet, is seen to be little more than a hefty asteroid: while the relationship between the many categories of object in the solar system is becoming steadily clearer. It is now thought that the smaller solar system objects – asteroids, comets and meteoroids – are closely related and are the solar system's most primitive objects, while the planets and the larger satellites have condensed from material of roughly the same composition as these primordial objects. The formation of planets and large satellites seems to have been a complex process, ranging from the formation of Jupiter – essentially a small-scale act of star formation – down to the glueing together of a small number of planetesimals to form the larger asteroids. As solar system specialist Carl Sagan has said, our era has had the great good fortune to be the one in which the objects of the solar system have been transformed from points of light in the sky to familiar worlds whose nature and origin are well understood

## solar-terrestrial physics

Study of the interaction between the Earth and the Sun, with particular emphasis on the effect on the Earth of charged particles and energy from the Sun and of the interactions of solar and terrestrial magnetism. The **ionosphere** – the zone of charged particles around the Earth – is sustained by solar activity and is of particular importance in solar-terrestrial relations. The whole field of solar-terrestrial physics is being altered by space missions like **SOHO** and **Cluster**, designed to amplify greatly our knowledge of the processes by which the Sun influences the Earth

**solar time**
Time measured through an average 24-hour day, corrected to allow for the eccentricity of the Earth's orbit and other factors which affect the length of actual days of the year

**solar wind**
The stream of particles being driven constantly off the surface of the Sun and into interplanetary space. The Earth is protected from the solar wind by its own atmosphere and its magnetic field. In the outer reaches of the solar system the solar wind becomes indistinguishable from the rest of the **interstellar medium**. The existence of the solar wind was first surmised from observations of the gyrations of comet tails. The material of the solar wind is moving at several hundred km per second, and consists largely of **protons** and **electrons** plus a few per cent of **alpha particles**. The blizzard of **neutrinos** constantly flowing from the Sun is not usually regarded as part of the solar wind

**solar year**
The year measured in terms of the time it takes the Sun to return to a fixed point in the sky, the **Vernal Equinox**, and at 364.24 days, slightly shorter than the **Sidereal Year**. Also called the Tropical Year

**solid rocket booster**
Solid fuel rocket used in pairs to provide part of the power for **Space Shuttle** launches. The boosters are jettisoned and parachuted into the sea for reuse, improving the economics of the Shuttle. The boosters were redesigned after being blamed for the 1986 Challenger shuttle disaster, which was caused by their leaking burning material which destroyed the rest of the Shuttle

**solstice**
Times of the year when the Sun is at its southernmost and northernmost points on the ecliptic, called respectively – with no deference to southern hemisphere residents – the summer and winter solstice. They fall on about June 21 and December 22 respectively

**sounding rocket**
Rocket launched into the Earth's upper atmosphere, but not into space, to allow measurements or observations, or to create periods of microgravity for materials experiments

**South African Large Telescope**
9.1m telescope under construction in Sutherland, South Africa, and due to enter service in 2003

**Southern Atlantic Anomaly**
Region above South America and the South Atlantic where the Earth's magnetic field traps charged particles in large numbers at a height of several hundred kilometres, and where the charged particles can interfere with the electronic systems of satellites

## Southern Lights
*Synonym for the* AURORA AUSTRALIS

## Soyuz
Lengthy series of Soviet and now Russian manned spaceflights which started in 1967

## Spacehab
Cylindrical module designed to be fitted in the Space Shuttle payload bay to increase the Shuttle's ability to carry people into space

### Space Infrared Telescope Facility (SIRTF)
Space Infrared Telescope Facility US space telescope with an 85cm telescope, planned for launch in 2001 to examine infrared-emitting objects in the 3-180 micron wavelength range

## Spacelab
**ESA** laboratory carried into orbit by the **Space Shuttle.** Spacelab can be configured for experiments in biology, medicine, remote sensing, astronomy, materials science and other subjects

## Space Law
The growing mass of legal knowledge and precedent on law in outer space, including the ownership of celestial bodies, rights to privileged space sites like geostationary orbital slots and mineral rights in space

### spacelike path
Path on a **spacetime** diagram in which so much space is covered in so short a time that the velocity of light would be exceeded. Although diagrams of such journeys can be drawn on spacetime diagrams with equipment no more complex than a pencil, actual objects are forbidden from reaching or exceeding the velocity of light, so that such journeys cannot be accomplished

### space manufacturing
The processing in space of material, derived from the Earth or procured in space, for use in space or on Earth. Although space methods have immense potential in theory, there are severe economic barriers to the profitable bulk manufacture of goods in space

### space platform
Crewed orbiting structure for applications such as telecommunications, remote sensing and science. The first space platforms may start to appear in the 1990s. In practice there is no clear dividing line between them and space stations, but space platforms, being smaller, would be better for applications requiring low gravitation and an undisturbed environment

## Space Shuttle
Reusable space launcher developed in the US by **NASA** and first used in 1981. The Shuttle was meant to lead to low launch costs by providing a launcher whose component parts were all reusable apart from the

large external tank. In fact costs spiralled, damaging the economic case, and seven people were killed when the Challenger Shuttle was destroyed on launch in 1986. Shuttle flights resumed but the disaster caused the US to recreate its ability to carry out unmanned launches with expendable rockets. Now only missions needing human supervision, or too large for other launchers, make use of the Shuttle

## Space Telescope
*See* HUBBLE SPACE TELESCOPE

## Spacetime
*See* SPECIAL THEORY OF RELATIVITY

## spaghettification
The lengthways stretching of objects as they approach a black hole, which would extend any possible material so much that it was utterly ripped apart before it was able to enter the hole

## Special Theory of Relativity
One of the two theories of relativity theories proposed by **Einstein**, the other being the **General Theory**. Special Relativity is of lesser scope than General, and is less controversial because it has proved more amenable to experimental proof. It concentrates upon the theory of motion, and especially upon the effects caused by the velocity of light acting as an absolute speed limit on every kind of motion. Its predictions include the **Lorentz** transformations of time and distance with increasing velocity, which have been verified experimentally **(Fitzgerald Contraction)** . They lead to the idea of a single entity, spacetime, in which measurements can be made on a consistent basis despite the problems posed for normal measurement systems by relative motion at velocities which are a significant fraction of the velocity of light

## speckle interferometry
Process for determining the surface features of stars, which would normally be unresolvable by standard telescopic methods. Instead of lengthy photographic exposures, where details of a star's surface are blurred by atmospheric turbulence, many very short exposures of bright stars are taken and combined by computer. This can produce images detailed enough to show features and to allow star diameters to be measured

## spectral lines
Dark or bright lines seen in the spectra of astronomical objects. The lines – emission lines if bright and absorption lines if dark – are observed at frequencies which represent the difference in energy levels between possible electron configurations of different atoms. It follows that the lines can be used to determine the presence or absence of different elements, and by observing their thickness the abundance of different elements can be determined. In addition, the velocity with

which the emitting body is approaching or receding from the Earth can be found by measuring **Doppler** effects on the wavelengths of spectral lines. Spectral lines were first observed in optical astronomy but are now observed across almost the whole **electromagnetic spectrum** and are the very core of the methodology of modern astronomy and astrophysics

### spectral type
*See* STAR TYPES

### spectrobolometer
Device for measuring the energy distribution across a **spectrum**. This device is applied mainly to the solar spectrum and those of nearby objects like the Moon, since distant stars provide too little energy at the Earth to give spectrobolometric readings

### spectrograph
Device for producing a permanent record of a **spectrum**. Modern examples consist generally of a **diffraction grating** fed by a telescope and in turn feeding a camera or some other recording device

### spectroheliogram
Recording of the Sun's spectrum, produced by means of a spectroheliograph, a spectrum machine adapted for solar use

### spectrometer
Instrument for measuring (and sometimes recording) a spectrum

### spectrometry
Measurement and analysis of spectra for the determination of composition, motion etc of astronomical objects

### spectroscope
Any device used for obtaining spectra

### spectroscopic binary
Double star whose components cannot be told apart visually or photographically. Instead, its spectrum reveals the presence of more than one star via the **Doppler effect** caused by the orbital motion of one or both of the stars in the pair. There are also spectroscopic multiple stars with more than two members

### spectroscopic parallax
Means of finding the distance to a star by spectroscopic methods. It relies upon finding the distance of one member of a star type by normal parallax measurement, after which other members' distances can be determined by comparing their apparent magnitude with that of the first star. The relation between spectroscopic parallax and the normal or trigonometric **parallax** is loose

### spectroscopy
The use of **spectra** to yield data about celestial objects. Almost the

same thing as spectrometry except that spectrometry is more quantitative

### spectrum

The distribution of energy from a body in terms of its frequency, in any part of the electromagnetic spectrum or the whole of it. Spectra in visible light were the first to be observed and are the most informative for most kinds of celestial objects. Spectra of astronomical objects are interpreted in the light of measurements made in Earthly laboratories. Their role in astronomy and astrophysics is fundamental because the spectrum of an object provides most of the information obtainable on most astronomical objects, with rare exceptions like the few stars with substantial **proper motions**. Normally, almost everything we can find out about the composition, distance, velocity and other characteristics of a celestial body is derived in some way from its spectrum.
*plural is* SPECTRA

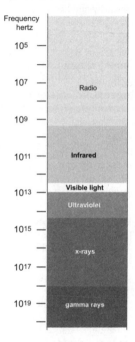

### speculum

Latin for mirror. Speculum metal was the raw material of astronomical telescope mirrors from the time of Newton until the 19th century, and was an alloy of copper, tin and other materials according to various formulae

### speed enhancement

Process of making a camera film faster – more sensitive – by special methods like baking it, treating it with novel chemicals or altering the method by which it is processed

### spherical aberration

Distortion caused by the use of spherically-shaped surfaces in mirrors or lenses in optical equipment. Spherical shapes do not bring light to a precise focus, and it is necessary to use a more complex **paraboloidal** shape to produce precise images

### spherical astronomy

The study of the distribution of celestial objects on the celestial sphere

## spherules
Glassy beads found in moonrock and produced by melting caused by meteorite impact

## Spica
The bright star Alpha Virginis, the 14th brightest in the sky. A variable star of type B1, with average apparent and absolute magnitudes of 0.91 and -3.3 respectively, Spica is 220 light years from Earth

## Spicules
Bright features seen at the Sun's limb. Found in the low **Chromosphere**, they mark the edges of **supergranules** in the Sun's upper layers

## spider
Device for holding a secondary mirror in place in a reflecting telescope, so called for its shape which involves several arms with a round body at the centre

## spin-flip
Change in the orbital direction of the electron of a hydrogen atom, from moving in the same direction as the nucleus itself spins to its opposite. The slight difference in energy between these two states gives rise to the 21cm radio emissions characteristic of hydrogen and central to radio astronomy

## spin-orbit coupling
**Resonance** effect by which bodies can match their spin periods to the orbital periods of other astronomical bodies. The most conspicuous example – visible even to the naked eye observer – is that of the Moon, which turns on its axis once per monthly orbit so the same face, that of the Man in the Moon, is always visible. Spin-orbit coupling arises from gravitation acting over long periods on small asymmetries like the non-spherical shape of the Moon. Some cases are more complex, such as the rotation of Mercury (three spins on its axis per two orbits of the Sun). Another remarkable case from the inner solar system is Venus's day, which is equal in length to two thirds of an Earth year, so that the same face of Venus is pointed towards the Earth at each of its **conjunctions.** Similar couplings are observed in many cases in the outer solar system, a notable example being the orbital period of Charon, which matches the length of the day on Pluto. So Charon seems to hover above the same spot on Pluto's surface, making it the solar system's first geostationary satellite

## spiral galaxy
The most common type of galaxy in the **Hubble classification**, with spiral arms emerging from a central core. In recent years much work has been carried out on the formation of the spiral structure, which seems to be due to pressure waves moving around the galaxy. Our own galaxy, of about 100 billion stars, is a comparatively large member of

the class. Spiral Nebula is an obsolete synonym

## sporadic
Meteor not associated with a meteor shower. Many sporadics are
thought to be members of showers which have decayed away, but others
may be genuinely unassociated with meteoroid streams or may be
members of weak, unidentified showers

## Sporer Minimum
*See* LATE MEDIEVAL MINIMUM

## spring tide
Tide experienced when the gravitation of the Sun and Moon are added
together, giving the largest possible tidal effect

## Sputnik
Soviet unmanned space programme which began the space age with the
launch of Sputnik 1 on October 4, 1957, and ran until Sputnik 10 in
1961. It weighed five tonnes to Sputnik 1's 84kg

## sputtering
Erosion of surfaces exposed to space by cosmic rays and the solar wind,
e.g. at the surface of the Moon and Mercury and on meteorites

## SS
*See* STAR CLASSIFICATION

## SS 433
Star in the SS Catalogue **(Star Classification)** which emits two
powerful beams of radiation into space and which seems to be a rare or
unique source of X-ray, radio and optical emissions. SS 433, a 14th
magnitude star in Aquila, appears to consist of a star of about three solar
masses orbited by a smaller star, less massive than the Sun, surrounded
by a disc of material which it is drawing from the larger star. Material
falling from the disc onto the star forms jets which emit X-rays and
other radiation

## Standard Time
Uniform time observed within a given time zone on the Earth's surface

## star
Celestial body whose temperature and density is high enough to allow
energy to be generated by **nuclear fusion**. A massive range of star types
have been catalogued and described, ranging in size from less than 0.1
solar masses to about 100. Most stars follow a simple, almost
straight-line, relationship linking their mass to their light output or
luminosity, the **Hertzsprung-Russell diagram**. Stars are the basic
study of most astronomers and astrophysicists, who in recent years have
addressed issues including star formation, the later lives of stars after
the major process of energy production – the production of helium by
fusing hydrogen – has ceased, and the dynamics of interacting multiple
stars, especially those involving a collapsed star and a normal one

## starburst galaxy

Type of galaxy which exhibits bright emissions in infrared and other wavelengths, possibly caused by major episodes of stellar formation. The nearly simultaneous formation of millions of stars may be prompted by pressure waves caused by severe disturbances to the galaxy, perhaps a collision with another galaxy. Very large examples have been dubbed Super Starburst Galaxies and seem to involve quantities of energy comparable to those needed to produce a complete galaxy of stars. The galaxy M82 in Ursa Major is a noted example

## star classification

Numerous overlapping systems are used to identify the stars in the sky. The oldest is simply to give conspicuous stars a name. Most proper names for stars are old, in many cases handed to us via Arab countries in the Middle Ages, and such names are replete with history and meaning. The first systematic approach to the names of stars was pioneered by **Bayer** in the 17th century. He gave the stars designations consisting of a letter of the Greek alphabet – usually starting with Alpha for the brightest – and the genitive of the name of its constellation. So Alpa Canis Minoris is the brightest star in Canis Minor. (This is why the genitives of constellation names are given in this dictionary under the entry for each constellation.) This system works well for the brightest stars but collapses completely for the large number of stars which became apparent once telescopes entered use. In this century the Henry Draper (HD) catalogue and its extension (HDE) have described by position over 250,000 stars with their spectral type and magnitude. There are also catalogues of variable stars, which begin obscurely at R for each constellation and run to Z, then starting with SS to SZ, TS to ZZ etc, then starting again with AA to AZ, BA to BZ etc. When this runs out – at the 334th variable per constellation – the followers are simply called V335 etc, which might have been a better idea to start with. There are also special catalogues like SS (of strong spectral line stars, called for the authors' initials), of nebulae (**Messier** and the **New General Catalogue**), of radio objects (3C for the third Cambridge catalogue), X-ray sources (numbered by constellation eg Sco X-1 for the first source found in Scorpius), a variety of modern catalogues which list objects simply by position, and a number of catalogues of particular classes of object drawn up by astronomers and often called after their surnames

## star cluster

Any grouping of stars which runs beyond a multiple star. The main types are **globular** and **open** (or galactic)

## Stardust

US space mission designed to return interstellar and cometary material to Earth after an encounter with Comet Wild 2 in 2004

## starspots

The equivalent of **sunspots** on stars other than the Sun. Spots are suspected of existing on variable stars whose brightness dips as they turn comparatively spotted faces towards Earth. By analogy with the Sun, where sunspots are associated with strong magnetism, starspots would indicate strong magnetic fields for the stars in question. Starspots covering a quarter of the surface of **Proxima Centauri** have been detected by the Hubble Space Telescope, accounting for a 41-day variability in its output

## star trails

Circular paths of the stars around the celestial poles, due to the Earth's rotation. One of the easiest targets for astronomical photography

## star types

Stars are classified according to spectral types in order of their surface temperature. From hottest to coolest the types are O, B, A, F, G, K and M. Within each type are subtypes 0 (hottest) to 9 (coolest), so that B9 is slightly hotter than A0. Most stars occupy positions on the main sequence of the **Hertzsprung-Russell diagram**, where the relation between star type and magnitude and mass is simple, but there are also groups like the **giants, supergiants** and **white dwarfs** which do not obey this relationship

## Steady State Theory

Theory of the universe whereby material appears continuously. Under Steady State Theory the expansion of the universe would not alter its appearance significantly, since new material would appear as the old receded. The discovery of the cosmic background radiation, apparently the remains of the big bang, destroyed the Steady State Theory

## Stefan-Boltzmann Law

Rule connecting the peak frequency of radiation from a black body source with the fourth power of its temperature. The Stefan-Boltzmann Constant links the two and has a value of $5.69 \times 10^8$ Watts per square metre per Kelvin$^{-4}$

## stellar evolution

The processes of birth, change, and death of stars. The term is applied to the changes through the lifetime of a single star, making it quite different from the use of the term in biology, where it is applied to change occurring across generations. The evolution of a star is described by a track showing its temperature and luminosity, which vary over time as the star forms, when its temperature increases rapidly, occupies a position on the main sequence, and leaves it after normal **hydrogen** burning ceases. The time taken for this process depends on the star's mass, from billions of years for the Sun down to a few tens of millions for the most massive stars

### stellar parallax
The **parallax** of a particular star as seen from the Earth

### stellar wind
Flux of material from stars into interstellar space, analogous to the **solar wind** from the Sun

### Stephan's Quintet
Group of five galaxies which are regarded as anomalous because they seem to be associated, except that one has a far larger redshift than the other four

### steradian
Unit of solid angular area, for example on the **celestial sphere**, consisting of a square one radian **(angular measure) on a side**

### STORMS
Proposed ESA mission designed to use three spacecraft to examine the "ring current" of electrons, which orbits the Earth at several Earth radii above the equator and is a hazard to spacecraft. The satellites would be placed up to 50,000km above the Earth.

### Stratoscope
US experimental programme of the 1960s and 1970s in which large telescopes were carried to the upper atmosphere by balloon

### stratosphere
The part of the atmosphere bounded by the tropopause below and the stratopause above, about 12-50km above the Earth's surface. Although the gases of the stratosphere are very thin, they can be warm – sometimes over 30° – because of the presence of stratospheric ozone, which captures the energy of the Sun's ultraviolet light

### strewn field
Area of the Earth's surface where a large number of meteorites, from a single meteorite fall, are found

### Strong Force
*See* FORCES

### Struve, Friedrich Georg Wilhelm (1793-1864)
Prussian astronomer who founded the Pulkova observatory in Russia and did original observational work on double stars, spherical astronomy and other subjects. He also founded a considerable astronomical dynasty including his son Otto, also director of Pulkova

### Subaru Telescope
Japanese national telescope on Mauna Kea, Hawaii, with 8.2m main mirror. Named after the Japanese for the **Pleiades**.

### subgiant
Star type intermediate between the **main sequence** and the **red giants**

### submillimetre wave astronomy
Branch of astronomy which uses radiation in the 0.3-1mm wavelength band, to which the Earth's atmosphere is transparent, between radio and infrared radiation. The interstellar medium and its molecular components are a particular target of this school of astronomy

### Submillimetre Wave Astronomy Satellite (SWAS)
NASA satellite for submillimetre wave astronomy planned for launch in the mid-1990s

### Sudbury Structure
Geological structure in Canada, best-known as a source of nickel ore and thought to have been formed by meteorite impact

### Suisei
The Japanese word for comet, and the name of the Japanese spacecraft sent on a mission near Halley's Comet in 1986

### Summer Triangle
The three stars **Vega, Deneb** and **Altair**, so-called because they are a conspicuous feature of the summer sky in the northern hemisphere

### Sun
The star which dominates the solar system and contains most of its matter. The Sun is by far the most familiar star to astronomers, and is known to be a fairly ordinary G2 star **(star classification)** with a surface temperature of some 6000K. It is about 329,000 times as massive as the Earth and is notable among other stars for being solitary rather than part of a multiple system. During this century, the energy source which powers the Sun has been identified as nuclear fusion, ending millennia of speculation, and models of the Sun's formation have been produced as part of wider studies of the origin of the solar system. The Sun is known to be a variable star with regular cycles of sunspot activity over 22 years, although its the total variation in energy output is far less than that of other variables observed by astronomers. This variation is closely linked to the Sun's intense magnetism, which is also intimately involved in the other surface and atmosphere effects studied by the many astronomers who study the Sun. In the last few decades, their work has been expanded by the use of telescopes to observe the Sun in a wide variety of wavelengths. The Sun was one of the first objects observed by radio astronomy and has since been viewed with telescopes operating across almost the whole of the electromagnetic spectrum, as well as more arcane instruments like **neutrino telescopes**. As well as being fascinating in its own right – and as the energy source for life on Earth – the Sun fascinates astronomers because it is close and well-known enough to provide the baseline to which observations and theories of other stars are referred

### Sun Dog
Bright spot sometimes seen in the sky and caused by sunlight reflected

from ice crystals high in the atmosphere

### Sungrazers

Class of comets which approach very close to the Sun. Many collide with it and cease to exist The commonest Sungrazer class is the **Kreutz group**, whose retrograde orbits take them very close to the Sun. Our knowledge of Sungrazers has been vastly expanded by US Air Force satellites used to view the Sun, which also spot Sungrazers

### sunspot

Dark patch seen on the surface of the Sun. Sunspots look dark only because they have a temperature about 2000° lower than the 6000°C of the Sun's surface. They can be larger than the Earth, and have been known since ancient times because they can become large enough to be seen with the naked eye. (Do not try it, or you risk damaging your sight.) Sunspots are now known to be associated with solar magnetism, whose lines of force give them their shape, and with more general disturbances of the Sun's atmosphere and surface. They are thought to appear as a result of the Sun's magnetic field interacting with the rotating gases of the Sun's body, and models have been produced on this basis which also encompass the 22-year cycle of sunspot activity and the way in which sunspot activity starts at the Sun's polar regions and spreads from there towards the solar equator (*see* **Butterfly Diagram**), Reversals and weakenings of the Earth's magnetism are familiar to geophysicists: it is possible that the historical periods of low sunspot activity are a sign that the Sun's magnetism also varies in some way

### sunspot cycle

The **solar cycle**, the 22-year period over which sunspot activity varies

### sun-tan age

Age of a meteorite, Moonrock, etc., determined from the density of cosmic ray tracks near its surface. This indicates not the age of the rock since its formation but the length of time for which it has been exposed to space

### supercluster

A cluster of clusters of galaxies. Superclusters are the largest objects so far described apart from the universe itself. An example is a supercluster centred on the Virgo cluster of galaxies, which is of special interest because our own galaxy, and the other members of its **local group**, are members of this supercluster. Superclusters typically have a sheet or filament shape when mapped in three dimensions

### supergiant

Type of very large red giant star at the top right-hand corner of the **Hertzsprung-Russell diagram**. Betelgeuse in Orion is the most conspicuous example. Supergiants (also red supergiants) are among the brightest of stars, with **absolute magnitudes** many times greater than those of **main sequence** stars like the Sun

### supergranulation
Large-scale polygonal structure of the Sun's surface, with units tens of thousands of kilometres across. This structure is related to the convection patterns associated with the flow of heat from the Sun's interior into space

### superior conjunction
Condition for Mercury or Venus in which it is precisely on the opposite side of the Sun from the Earth. At superior conjunction the planet's illuminated face is fully presented to the Earth, but the planet is then at its smallest and hardest to observe, since it is at its farthest distance from the Earth and close to the Sun in the sky

### superior planets
The planets of the solar system farther from the Sun than the Earth. Now an obsolescent usage

### supermassive black hole
Black hole weighing millions or billions of solar masses. Emissions from active galaxies, apparently caused by radiation from matter in rapid orbits around massive objects in galactic nuclei, appear to confirm their existence although they cannot be observed directly

### supermassive star
Possible star hundreds or thousands of times as massive as the Sun. At the time of writing various possible supermassive stars had been identified, but later discounted as being close clusters of normal stars, so that the existence of supermassives was still not established

### supernova
The catastrophic and explosive disruption of a heavy star late in its evolution. Some supernovae are bright enough to outshine the galaxy in which they erupt. Supernovae are now known to be major sources of material erupted into interstellar space. They are the origin of all the universe's heavy elements – those beyond iron in atomic weight – as well as producing intense cosmic rays and severe shock waves. They can only arise from stars of more than some 9 solar masses, and result from shock waves sent out as the core of such a star collapses. There is also a second category of supernova explosion, less well known than this classic type, apparently affecting smaller stars with white dwarf companions. A galaxy as large as ours has a supernova every few decades, although it may be impossible to observe if it is hidden by the centre of the galaxy

### supernova remnant
The remains left over by a supernova explosion. These burnt-out stars sound dull but are in fact among the most exciting objects in the sky. A supernova sheds huge amounts of its mass in the course of exploding,

leaving behind a core which collapses to a **neutron** star, which may can be visible as a **pulsar**, if it is of less than about three solar masses. Beyond that the core is subject to complete gravitational collapse and becomes a **black hole**. The best-known such remnant is the **Crab** nebula in Taurus, the remains of a supernova observed in 1054AD

### superradiant scattering
Effect which amplifies light passing near a **black hole**. It could in principle produce strange physical effects like the explosion of a black hole into which large amounts of energy are drawn

### Superstring Theory
A development of the **General Theory of Relativity**, superstring theory arises from relativistic theories of matter and postulates the existence of superstrings – multi-dimensional defects in spacetime, left over from the early universe. Their effects might in theory be observed by looking for manifestations like **gravitational waves**, or perturbations of the very steady signals from **pulsars**

### Surveyor
Series of five successful and two unsuccessful US spacecraft sent to carry out soft landings on the Moon between 1966 and 1968

### SWAS
*See* SUBMILLIMETRE WAVE ASTRONOMY SATELLITE

### Swift
NASA spacecraft for detecting gamma-ray **bursters**, under development at the time of writing and due for launch in 2003

### Swift-Tuttle, Comet
The large comet 1862 III, the source of the Perseid meteors, rediscovered by the Japanese amateur astronomer Tsuhuhiko Kiuchi in 1992

### synchronous
Adjective meaning in time: thus a geosynchronous orbit for a satellite matches the Earth's rotation, keeping the satellite stationary in the sky from the point of view of an observer on the Earth, while a Sun-synchronous one matches the Sun's apparent route through the sky to allow a satellite to observe the Earth consistent illumination

### synchrotron radiation
Radiation emitted by charged particles travelling at speeds near that of light through magnetic fields, and observable in both optical and radio astronomy. Electrons travelling at near-light speeds in strong magnetic fields are the usual source of synchrotron radiation in astronomy

### synodic period
A period of time measured with respect to the Earth. Thus a synodic month is the period of 29.53 days in which the Moon makes a complete orbit of the Earth from New Moon to New Moon as seen by an observer

on the Earth, allowing for the Earth's rotation around the Sun. A planet's synodic period is the time it takes to return to the same position - such as **opposition** or **conjunction** - with respect to the Earth, allowing for the orbital movement of each around the Sun

## Système International

The system of units in general use among scientists, using as its basic units the metre (length), second (time), kilogramme (mass), plus other basic units like the Candela (for illumination), and derived units such as the Newton for force. The basic units are those not defined in terms of the others, while the derived units are defined from the basic ones. Thus a Newton is the force which accelerates a mass of one kilogram by one metre per second per second

## syzygy

An alignment of three celestial bodies. Examples include eclipses, which are syzygies of the Earth, Moon and Sun, or a planetary opposition or conjunction, when the Earth, the Sun and a planet are aligned

# Tt

### T Tauri Stars

Category of erratic **variable** stars which have yet to reach the main sequence of the **Hertzsprung-Russell diagram**. T Tauri itself is at the centre of a **Herbig-Haro Object**, which confirms its youth and the fact that Herbig-Haro Objects are associated with star formation. The variability of these stars is probably linked to changes which occur before the star can become a stable, **main-sequence** star, and involves massive emissions of glowing gas into space. It is possible that most or all main sequence stars have passed through a T Tauri stage. This possibility has been taken up in studies of the origin of the solar system, where the Sun's T Tauri stage has been implicated in the distribution of **angular momentum** in the solar system

### tachyon

Putative particle travelling at a velocity greater than that of light. Tachyons are unknown to science and if discovered would involve odd logical consequences – like events happening before their causes – as well as a fundamental revision of relativistic physics

### tail

Dusty or gassy material trailed from a comet in the inner solar system under the influence of solar radiation. A comet tail is only slightly denser than deep space itself, and shines by reflection of sunlight from dusty material and by the fluorescence of gas molecules. The dusty and gassy types of tail often separate out as forces of differing strength and type act on them

### Tarantula Nebula

Nebula notable because it apparently houses one of the most massive stars known, possibly weighing up to 200 solar masses

### tardyon

Particle moving at less than the velocity of light. This category includes all known particles except for those such as photons and neutrinos which travel at the velocity of light.
*See also* TACHYON

### TAU

Thousand Astronomical Units, a possible space mission to explore deep space beyond the Solar System some time next century, using an unmanned spacecraft

## Taurids
Meteor shower visible in October and November, with its **radiant** in Taurus

## Taurus
Constellation on the ecliptic in the northern hemisphere, notable for including the **Pleiades**, the **Hyades** and the bright star **Aldebaran**, Alpha Tauri.
*(Genitive is **Tauri**; means the 'bull')*

## tektite
Glassy blobs found scattered on the Earth's surface in distinct geographical regions and usually ranging in size up to a few centimetres across. Tektites seem to have been shaped aerodynamically by a passage while warm through the Earth's atmosphere, but their origin is by no means certain. Meteorite impacts on the Moon are one postulated source although some process involving their being formed in the upper atmosphere from material ejected from the Earth by impact or from volcanoes is more favourably regarded by most scientists

## telescope
Any device for concentrating electromagnetic radiation for human study. Optical telescopes do this by presenting a larger light-collecting area to incoming light than the human eye can, and by using photographic methods to collect light over longer periods than the near-instantaneous period over which the eye forms an image. In the last four centuries, massive ingenuity has been devoted to refining telescopes, with many types produced to resolve objects close together in the sky, give distortion-free images of large areas of the sky, and carry out other tasks. Making telescopes is an art and science at the forefront of modern technology. A telescope's optics must be accurate to much less than the wavelength of light if they are to produce usable images. Telescope makers use advanced materials to produce large areas of high-quality optics capable of coping with temperature variations and other problems. Modern telescopes also involve computer controls and telecommunications links, often allowing astronomers to use them from thousands of kilometres away. Telescopes have also been developed for use in space and on the Earth across virtually the whole of the electromagnetic spectrum, including radio, microwave, X-ray, infra-red and ultraviolet frequencies. The term is also applied to machines for detecting gravity waves, neutrinos, cosmic rays and other astronomically rewarding phenomena – a usage which is technically dubious but which is true to the word's Greek origins from the words for 'seeing at a distance,' even if the seeing takes an unanticipated form

## Telescopium
Small constellation of the southern hemisphere, so-called for a supposed

resemblance to a telescope.
*(Genitive is **Telescopii**)*

### Telesto
Tiny satellite of Saturn in the same orbit as **Tethys**

### terahertz
Frequency band with wavelengths of 0.1-1mm, first observed from the Earth's surface in 2000 using a special detector on a telescope in the US. Star formation is a special target for observations in this region.

### terminator
The line between dark and light on a planetary or satellite surface

### terrestrial planets
The rocky, Earth-like planets of the inner solar system, Mercury, Venus, the Earth, the Moon and Mars

### Tethys
Satellite of Saturn discovered in 1684 by **Cassini**. Tethys orbits Saturn in a circular 1.9 day orbit 295,000km from the planet and is just over 500km across. With a density close to 1gm/cc, Tethys consists mainly of ice. Its surface is heavily cratered and features deep, wide valleys, the latter being regarded as evidence of past geological activity

### Thebe
Tiny satellite of Jupiter discovered from **Voyager 1** images

### thermal radiation
Radiation emitted by a body by virtue of its surface temperature, like sunlight from the Sun's surface or heat from a flame. Its opposite is non-thermal radiation, which includes all emissions caused by non-temperature-related effects, and includes emissions like **Cerenkov** radiation

### thermonuclear reactions
Nuclear reactions in which atomic nuclei are fused together to make heavier types. Thermonuclear reactions drive stars (as well as hydrogen bombs and possible fusion power reactors), because the creation of nuclei up to iron releases energy. Nuclei beyond iron can only be produced by absorbing energy, which is why they are rare by comparison with lighter species

### Thorne-Zytkow Object
Stars looking like normal **red giants** or **supergiants** but containing a neutron star at their core. Such objects, proposed by US astronomers Kip Thorne and Anna Zytkow, might form in double stars of which one member degenerates into a neutron star. None are known to have been observed

### thought experiment
An experiment in which the experimenter follows a chain of events

mentally rather than by deed

### tidal bulges
The bulges in the Earth's oceans caused by the tidal actions of the Sun and Moon

### tidal force
Force exerted on one astronomical body by another and tending to alter its shape. Tides were first identified in the Earth-Moon system by observations of obvious changes in sea level, but have since been observed in the Earth's atmosphere and solid body, as well as in the Moon. They are also an important part of the interactions between closely orbiting stars, colliding galaxies and other astronomical bodies on all scales

### tide
Shift in the distribution of the Earth's waters under the gravitational influence of the Moon and (to a lesser extent) the Sun, and, by analogy, similar gravitational effects in other astronomical systems

### tilted component telescope
Telescope which uses an arrangement of several mirrors to avoid the loss or distortion of incoming light caused by a secondary mirror placed in front of the primary

### time dilation
Variation in the apparent rate at which time passes as measured by clocks moving with relative velocities which are a significant fraction of the velocity of light. Time dilation is a consequence of the **Special Theory of Relativity** and its precise size can be obtained from the **Lorentz Transformations**, which itemise the effects of special relativity at velocities close to that of light. The effect of time dilation is to make clocks travelling at high velocities appear to run slow as seen by a stationary observer. Thus a space traveller making a long journey at velocities close to that of light could come back still young to find that her or his friends had long since died of old age

### timelike path
A route through spacetime involving a velocity less than that of light. Timelike paths are the only ones we known of actual objects taking, apart from **photons** and other particles which travel at exactly the velocity of light. Timelike paths are so-called because they involve using more time to cover less space than hypothetical **space-like paths**, in which objects can exceed the velocity of light

### Titan
The largest satellite of Saturn, and in the solar system. Titan was discovered by **Huygens** in 1655 and is over 5 000km across, just larger than Mercury. It takes 16 days to complete an orbit some 1.2 million km from Saturn. As the densest of Saturn's satellites, with a density of

1.9gm/cc, Titan is thought to have a rocky interior. It is also the only solar system satellite known to have a dense atmosphere in which lightning has been observed. It contains hydrogen, methane, acetylene and other complex organic molecules and its chemistry may resemble that of the young Earth's atmosphere. Titan appears to have a solid surface and the large amounts of hydrocarbons in its atmosphere have led to speculations that it may have lakes or even oceans of liquid hydrocarbons There are also large amounts of nitrogen in the atmosphere of Titan. The interior of Titan is less familiar. Titan may have been subject to important geological change and may contain significant amounts of ice and even water. Some observers regard Titan as a smaller version of the Earth, stalled at an earlier evolutionary stage by its position in the outer solar system away from significant supplies of solar energy. Titan is due to be visited by the **ESA's Huygens space probe** in the year 2004

## Titania
Satellite of Uranus discovered in 1787 by **William Herschel**. It orbits Uranus in 8.7 days in a near-circular orbit in the plane of Uranus's equator, 438,000km from the planet and is just over 1000km in diameter. **Voyager 2**'s 1986 flyby of Uranus revealed Titania as a heavily cratered world with deep, wide rift valleys hundreds of kilometres long, possibly formed by thawing and freezing of water with accompanying expansion and contraction

## Titius-Bode Law
Synonym for **Bode's Law**, called Titius-Bode by purists because it was recorded by Titius of Wittemberg (although even he seems not to have thought of it first) in 1766 before Bode popularised it

## Tombaugh, Clyde (1906-1997)
US astronomer best known for discovering Pluto in 1930

## Toros
Small, stony asteroid capable of making close approaches to the Earth

## Torr
Unit of pressure equal to 1mm of Mercury and now obsolete. Named after Evangelista Torricelli (1806-1647), the Italian scientist who discovered the principle of the barometer and so provided the means of measuring atmospheric pressure

## total eclipse
An eclipse of the Sun in which the Moon completely covers the Sun's disc, or of the Moon in which the Earth's shadow completely covers the visible face of the Moon

## Transient Lunar Phenomena
Short-lived appearances of colour, obscurations and other effects seen on the Moon and regarded by some as evidence of residual volcanic

activity there. Despite many plausible observations, especially one by the Soviet astronomer Nikolai Kozirev in 1958 and from Apollo 11 in 1969, few scientists now take Transient Lunar Phenomena seriously and most regard them mainly as evidence of poor observational method. They have been observed preferentially at some sites, especially the crater Aristarchus, site of the 1958 observation, an indication that they may be genuine but hard to observe. Tides set on the Moon by the Earth could trigger lunar volcanic action, a possibility increased by an apparent grouping of TLPs at some times of the lunar month. Apart from vulcanism, fluorescence of lunar soil under the influence of solar radiation is another possible explanation for TLPs

### transit
Passage of Mercury or Venus across the face of the Sun, as seen from the Earth, or of any astronomical body across the meridian. Transits of Mercury and Venus were observed closely in early attempts to discover the size of the astronomical unit, and hence the scale of the solar system, by timing transits as seen from different points on the Earth, whose distance apart was known

### transit telescope
Telescope set up to observe objects as they cross the meridian. Transit telescopes are used mainly to allow the exact positions of objects in the sky to be determined, a role now partly usurped by photography. Modern ones run under automatic computer control

### transparency
The property of allowing radiation to pass. In astronomy the transparency of the Earth's atmosphere is important because it determines the ability of astronomers to observe from Earth rather than from space. The Earth's atmosphere transmits mainly visible light, some infrared light, and some radio, microwave and millimetre wavelength radiation

### Trapezium
a group of four stars in the Orion nebula

### Trapezium Systems
Group of stars, named after and including the **Trapezium**, involving four companions orbiting each other mutually. 11 such systems were known at the time of writing and they seem to be unstable, leading to one member being ejected from the system or going into orbit around another, to form a system consisting of two binary stars with one member itself being a binary

### Triangulum
Small constellation of the northern hemisphere, predictably enough having three main stars arranged in a triangle.
*(Genitive is **Trianguli**)*

## Triangulum Australe
Small constellation of the southern hemisphere, predictably enough
having three main stars arranged in a triangle.
*(Genitive is **Trianguli Australis**)*

## trigonometric parallax
The parallax of a star determined by measurement of its position in the
sky – using trigonometrical methods – rather than by spectroscopic
techniques. Such parallaxes are 'true' parallaxes, whereas spectroscopic
ones are at one remove from the parallax method and derive from
results it has produced

## Triple Alpha Process
Process occurring in very hot stars whereby three alpha particles are
fused into a Carbon-12 nucleus. The Triple Alpha Process occurs at
over 100 million K and occurs via an intermediate step in which two
alphas are added together to form a Beryllium nucleus

## Triton
Satellite of Neptune discovered by Lassell in 1846. Triton has a
circular, retrograde orbit 355,000km from Neptune and takes 5.9 days
to complete. An icy planet (although the ices at its surface may be
dominated by solid nitrogen rather than water ice) resembling Pluto and
Charon, and some 4000km across, Triton is in a decaying orbit which
will apparently lead to its destruction by tidal forces in under 100
million years. Triton seems to have a thin methane atmosphere. There
has been speculation that it may be one of a clutch of thousands of such
bodies in the outer reaches of the early solar system, the rest being
expelled into the **Kuiper Belt** or the **Oort Cloud** by gravitational
perturbation. Its surface features indicate a past when it may have been
warmer than now, with liquids present, as well as faulting that suggests
that Triton may have been geologically active at some point in its past

## Trojans
Asteroids occupying two of the **Lagrangian** points in the orbit of
Jupiter, orbiting the Sun 60° ahead of Jupiter (the Greek camp) or
behind it (the Trojan camp). Asteroid 624 Hektor is the largest member
of the group, apparently measuring about 100 by 300km, and was the
first to be discovered. Despite the existence of the two camps, the term
Trojan is usually applied to both groups. An asteroid, 1990MB, has also
been detected 60° behind Mars and others could exist in the
Langrangian points of the orbits of other planets

## Tropical Year
The Year measured from equinox to equinox, and equal to 365.24 days.
By analogy the Tropical Month is 27.32 days, the time taken for the
Moon to return after one month to the celestial equator

## tropopause
The dividing line in the Earth's atmosphere between the **troposphere**

and the **stratosphere**. The tropopause is the site of a temperature inversion between temperatures well below freezing at the top of the troposphere to temperatures of up to 30° in the stratosphere

### troposphere
The lowest layer of the Earth's atmosphere, extending to about 12km above sea level

### Tsiolovsky, Konstantin (1857-1935)
Russian scientist and inventor who had the first modern ideas about spaceflight, especially the use of rockets for long space flights. **'Beyond the Planet Earth'**, published in 1920, is his best-known book. He said that 'The Earth is the cradle of mankind, but one cannot remain in the cradle forever.'

### twinkling
*Lay term for*   SCINTILLATION

### Tucana
Constellation of the Toucan in the southern hemisphere, the site of most of the **Small Magellanic Cloud**.
*(Genitive is **Tucanae**; means the 'Toucan')*

### tunnelling
**Relativistic effect** whereby electrons might travel through rather than over the gravitational wall around a black hole, especially one of low mass

### Tunguska Event
Impact of some astronomical object, probably an asteroid or the head of a small comet, at Tunguksa in Siberia on June 30 1908. The impact, involving an incoming mass of about 100,000 tonnes, has been thought not to have involved a solid body because it caused a large atmospheric disturbance detectable all around the world and much surface damage, including perhaps 2000 square kilometres of demolished trees, but left no impact crater. But tree resin in the area has been found to contain solid particles whose composition is close to that of stony meteorites, encouraging the asteroid theory rather than the initial notion that Tunguska was struck by the head of a comet

### Tycho
*See*   BRAHE, TYCHO DE

# Uu

## UFO
Unidentified Flying Object. Hundreds of UFOs have been studied over
the last few decades but no concrete evidence has emerged for the idea
that they are due to visits by interstellar travellers. Instead,
comparatively dull explanations have usually been found for the UFOs
which it has been possible to investigate in detail, revealing more about
public ignorance of the night sky than about alien holiday habits

## Uhuru
The astronomy satellite Explorer 42, launched in 1970 for X-ray
observations. The word is Swahili for Freedom.
*See* SMALL ASTRONOMY SATELLITE

## UKIRT
The United Kingdom Infra-Red Telescope, a 3.8m telescope at Mauna
Kea, Hawaii, used for infra-red astronomy, mostly by British
astronomers

## ultraviolet light
Light in the 5-400 nanometre wavelength band, between visible light
and X-rays. Ultraviolet light does not penetrate the Earth's atmosphere,
so that ultraviolet astronomy has to be practised from space. Being more
energetic than visible light, UV carries information about hotter stars
and more energetic galaxies and nebulae than does visible light. The
International Ultraviolet Explorer has so far been the most productive
UV observatory in space, although cheap balloon-borne experiments are
also capable of yielding useful results. Lyman, a planned UV space
telescope for the 1990s, should add vastly to knowledge of the field,
especially in the far ultraviolet, the region of shortest-wavelength UV
light, which is least familiar to astronomers

## Ulysses
**ESA/NASA** space mission originally known as ISPM, the International
Solar Polar Mission, launched in October 1990. Its instruments are
designed to yield information on the solar wind, the solar magnetic field
in interplanetary space, solar radio and plasma emissions, flare particles
and X-rays, galactic cosmic rays (those not emitted by the Sun) in the
solar system, and neutral dust and gas of solar system and interstellar
origin in the solar system, as well as **gamma-ray bursts** from outside
the solar system. It travelled from the Earth to Jupiter in 14 months,
where Jupiter's gravitation was used to push it into a trajectory taking it
over the Sun's South Pole after 45 months in space, back through the

plane of the **ecliptic** in 50 months, and over the Sun's north pole after 56 months. This journey provided the first direct information on wide expanses of the solar system above and below the ecliptic never before visited by spacecraft. Its astonishing journey continued with a flight over the Sun's south polar region in 2000 and a return flight over its north polar region in 2001.

## umbra
Latin for shadow. Has two main uses among astronomers – for the dark central zone of a sunspot and for the dark centre part of the Earth's or Moon's shadow at an eclipse

## Umbriel
Satellite of Uranus discovered by Lassell in 1851. Umbriel has a 4.1 day, near-circular orbit in the plane of Uranus's equator, at an average distance of 267,000km from the planet. **Voyager 2**'s 1986 visit to Uranus reveals Umbriel as a dark, crater-covered world with one or more bright patches, possibly sites where impacts have brought ice to the surface. Umbriel's spectrum is also rich in lines indicating the presence of water. Umbriel is about 1200km in diameter

## uncertainty principle
The maxim of **quantum mechanics** that both the position and velocity of a particle can never be definitely determined

## Unified Field Theory
Union of the laws governing gravitation, electromagnetic fields and atomic forces. A Unified Field Theory is an ambition of present-day physics which may be achieved within the next few years and would have large effects on thinking in cosmology. GUTs (Grand Unified Theories) are replacing Unified Field Theory in physicists' jargon and are close to them in meaning

## Universal Law of Gravitation
The law of gravitation set out by **Newton** and applying to every object in the universe. It states that every body in the universe exerts an attraction on every other, proportional to the product of their masses (their masses multiplied together) divided by the square of the distance between them. The gravitational constant G gives the force between any pair of objects whose masses and separation are known, and equals $6.672 \times 10^{11} \text{kg}^{-1} \text{m}^3 \text{s}^{-2}$. There has been much speculation among cosmologists about the possibility that G varies over time, which if true would have a severe effect on our ideas about the past evolution and future development of the universe

## universe
The total existing amount of mass, space and radiation, and the proper study of astronomers and cosmologists. Viewed on the scale of the whole universe, a small number of simple issues dominate what we see – the fact that the universe is expanding from the big bang and that

matter within it tends to form into galaxies – often themselves distributed in clusters – and within galaxies into stars – often binary or multiple. But in recent years intellectual concern over whether the universe will continue to expand indefinitely or may contract, and over the possibility that perhaps 90% of matter in the universe may be dark rather than the visible material so far studied by astronomers, reminds us that huge discoveries remain to be made about the universe on the largest scale

## Uraniburg

**Brahe's** observatory on the Danish island of Hveen, where the precise observations which allowed our modern ideas about the solar system to be produced were carried out between 1576 and 1597

## Uranus

The seventh planet of the solar system, discovered in 1781 by **William Herschel**. Uranus was the first planet to be discovered, rather than simply being observed in the night sky, and its presence was a huge shock to contemporary science. It is now known that earlier astronomers including **Flamsteed** had also charted Uranus – which can just be seen as a naked-eye object – and failed to register it as a planet. Uranus takes 84 years to orbit the Sun – it is still fewer than three Uranus years since we found out about it – and has an average distance of 19AU from the Sun. Uranus is one of the giant gas planets, 15 times as massive as the Earth and 52,000km in diameter. Its day of 16 hours is the oddest in the solar system, since the axis of Uranus's rotation is at 98° to the plane of its orbit. This means that Uranus is in effect rotating 'backwards.' Explanations for this behaviour must cope with the fact that Uranus's large satellites **Miranda, Ariel, Umbriel, Titania** and **Oberon** orbit the planet exactly in the plane of its equator. Uranus also has a system of ten dark, narrow rings extending out to 51,200km from the planet, discovered in 1977 by observers in an airborne observatory high in the Earth's atmosphere. Our knowledge of Uranus was expanded vastly in 1986 by a flyby of the planet by the US spacecraft **Voyager 2**. Its images show Uranus as a planet almost bare of the spectacular cloud features found on Jupiter and Saturn. Uranus has a magnetic field comparable in strength to the Earth's, tilted steeply both to its angle of rotation and to its orbit. Voyager 2 also revealed ten small satellites orbiting closer to Uranus than the five satellites previously known, some of which seem to have a role in shaping the ring system. Uranus also has an extensive magnetospheric system. Uranus's atmosphere seems to be dominated by hydrogen, helium and methane, and there are also more complex molecules like acetylene. Below the clouds, Uranus may have an icy mantle (possibly including solid ammonia) and perhaps a rocky core. The planet has a density of about 1.2gm/cc

### Urey, Harold Clayton (1893-1981)
US chemist who worked extensively on chemical problems of astronomical significance. He discovered **Deuterium**, for which he won the Nobel Prize in chemistry, and worked widely on the chemistry of meteorites and other solar system objects

### Ursa Major
The constellation of the Great Bear in the northern hemisphere. Includes the very conspicuous star grouping called the Plough in Britain and the Big Dipper in North America, two of whose stars, the pointers, show the way to the Pole Star.
*(Genitive is **Ursae Majoris**)*

### Ursa Minor
Constellation of the Little Bear in the northern hemisphere, including the Pole Star, (Polaris or Alpha Ursae Minoris and the Northern celestial pole)

### Utopia Planitia
Plain on the surface of Mars where the landing craft of the US space probe **Viking 2** landed to make observations in 1976

### UV
*See* ULTRAVIOLET

# Vv

### Valles Marineris
Massive rift valley on Mars, called after the US **Mariner** spacecraft used for Mars exploration

### Van Allen Belts
Zones of ionised particles surrounding the Earth. The Van Allen Belts (called after US scientist James Van Allen, born 1914) were among the first scientific discoveries of the space age, as they were found by the first US satellite, Explorer 1. There are two main Van Allen belts, one lying mainly 3,000-6,000km above sea level at the equator and the other 20,000-30,000km above sea level at the equator. The particles are trapped there by the Earth's magnetic field, which brings them into the Earth's upper atmosphere in the polar regions, where their interaction with molecules of air causes the aurora. The inner belt consists mainly of **protons** and the outer of **electrons**. Within the inner belt a layer of heavier cosmic ray nuclei was discovered in 1993

### variable stars
Stars with a fluctuating output of light (or other electromagnetic radiation). Many types of variable stars are known. The most spectacular kind of variation is that of **novae** and **supernovae**, which are not counted as mainstream variables. Apart from these, the principal kinds include eclipsing binaries such as the prominent variable **Algol** in Perseus, which vary because they consist of two stars which periodically cut off each other's light from observers on the Earth, and **Cepheids, RR Lyrae stars**, and **R Coronae Borealis** stars. Variability is often associated with interactions between members of double star pairs, and includes high-energy variability seen in X-rays rather than visible light. Main-sequence stars like the Sun are rarely variable: stars off the main sequence, especially those near the beginning and end of their lives, are the usual candidates for variability. Despite our sophisticated understanding of the nature of variable star types, their light curves are still one of the major observational targets open to amateur astronomers with modest telescopes.
*For the unique method used to name variables, see* STAR CLASSIFICATION

### Vatican Advanced Technology Telescope (VATT)
1.8m telescope in Arizona, US, run by the Vatican Observatory

### Vega[1]
The fifth brightest star in the sky, Alpha Lyrae, with an apparent

magnitude of 0.04 and an absolute magnitude of 0.5. Vega is 26.5 light years from Earth and of spectral type A0

## Vega[2]

Pair of Soviet spacecraft, Vega 1 and 2, sent to **Halley's Comet** in 1986 and thereafter placed in orbits around the Sun between the Earth and Venus for studies of the solar wind and other aspects of the inner solar system. They also carried landers and balloons sent to explore the surface and atmosphere of Venus

## Veil Nebula

Nebula which forms part of the large Cygnus Loop, a celebrated supernova remnant

## Vela[1]

Large constellation of the Southern hemisphere, crossed by the Milky Way. Vela is one of the constellations formed by the breakup of the huge constellation Argo Navis, and its name means the sails.
*(Genitive is Velorum)*

## Vela[2]

Series of US spy satellites used for detecting nuclear weapons explosions, and used in astronomy to observe celestial X-rays

## Vela Pulsar

One of the most rapid **pulsars** known, apparently symptomatic of a neutron star some 10,000 years old. The pulsar in Vela pulses in optical, X-ray and radio wavelengths

## velocity of light

In a vacuum, light moves at almost 300,000km a second, as does all other electromagnetic radiation. This is much more than a mere measure of distance covered in a given amount of time because c, the velocity of light, appears in the fundamental equations of relativity as the factor linking mass with the amount of energy to which it is equivalent, and as a basic speed limit for all objects in the universe

## Venera

Series of Soviet space probes to Venus and the inner solar system which started in 1961. This lengthy programme had its first success with Venera 4, which returned data from the atmosphere of Venus in 1967. Venera 5 and 6 carried out similar missions while Venera 7 and 8 returned data from the surface of Venus. Venera 9 transmitted the first photograph of the surface of Venus: Venera 10 sent more. Venera 11 and 12 had similar missions but more sophisticated instruments, while Venera 13 and 14 carried out successful analysis of surface samples. Veneras 15 and 16, launched in 1983, used radar to produce maps of the surface of Venus

## Venus

The second planet of the solar system, and the closest in size to the

Earth, 82 per cent as massive as the Earth. Venus orbits the Sun in 225 days, at an average distance of 0.72AU (108 million km), and has no satellites. Venus is swathed in clouds and has a high albedo, so that it can outshine anything in the sky apart from the Sun and Moon, reaching a magnitude of -4.4. Because of its nearness in mass and size (a radius of 6,050km to the Earth's 6,378) to the Earth, Venus was long regarded as the Earth's 'twin'. But space missions to Venus have shown that it bears little resemblance to the Earth in terms of surface conditions – which is just as well for us. Its surface temperature can be over 700K. Venus rotates on its axis in a retrograde direction every 244 days. Its atmosphere is some 400 km deep and has a complex structure and wind systems. It contains large amounts of sulphur in chemical compounds and in elemental form, as well as nitrogen, rare gases and carbon dioxide. Water is rare but there is a theory that it might once have been abundant. Atmospheric surface pressures on Venus run up nearly 100 times that at sea level on the Earth. The surface of Venus has plains, highlands and rift valleys, which have been mapped by radar **(Magellan)** . Almost all our information about Venus has been obtained by spacecraft, especially the close radar mapping carried out by Magellan and information from probes sent into the planet's atmosphere and onto its surface by parachute from US and Soviet spacecraft, mainly in the **Venera** series. Venusian surface features are named mainly in honour of real, mythological and fictional women

### Venus Orbiting Imaging Radar
*See* MAGELLAN

### Vernal Equinox
The spring **equinox**, on or about March 21

### Very Large Array (VLA)
Radio telescope used for interferometry and consisting of 27 antennae, each 26m across, arranged in a Y shape of variable geometry in the New Mexico desert in the United States

### Very Large Telescope (VLT)
Telescope on Cerro Paranal, a 2635m mountain in Chile, run by the **European Southern Observatory** and consisting of four 8.2m telescopes called Antu, Kueyen, Melipal and Yepun, the words in the native Mapuche language for the Sun, Moon, Southern Cross and Sirius. They can be used separately or in combination.

### Very Long Baseline Array (VLBA)
Series of radio telescopes based across the United States, including sites in Hawaii and Puerto Rico, allowing observations to be carried out by **interferometry** to create a radio telescope effectively 8,000 km across

### Very Long Baseline Interferometry (VLBI)
*See* INTERFEROMETRY

## Very Massive Object (VMO)

Possible form of **dark matter**, consisting of aggregations of material up to a million times as massive as the Sun. Such objects would form very bright but short-lived stars which by now would have collapsed to black holes. The **gravitational lensing** they caused to passing starlight might allow them to be detected

## vesicle

Tiny gas bubble found in lava rocks on the Earth and other planets

## Vesta

Asteroid 4, the second or third largest of the asteroids, some 525km in diameter and of comparatively light colour. An oval-shaped object which rotates on its axis in about 9 hours, Vesta has a surface with a complex pattern of markings

## Vidicon

TV-camera type tube, used in astronomy and on spacecraft. Vidicons work by means of photoconductivity, whereby the electrical conductivity of a surface varies according to the amount of light shining on it

## Viking

Pair of US space probes sent to Mars in 1975 and arriving in 1976. Viking 1 and 2 each consisted of a lander and an orbiter. The Vikings supplied tens of thousands of photographs of the Martian surface, from orbit and from ground level, as well as data on the composition of the polar caps and atmosphere of Mars. They are popularly remembered for a series of experiments designed to test for the presence or absence of life on Mars – which yielded no results encouraging to believers in Martians. The Vikings were a technological development of the US Mariner spacecraft sent to Mars, and there is a possibility of later Vikings which would rove the surface of Mars instead of remaining static there

## violet shift

*Little-used synonym for* BLUESHIFT

## Virgo

Large constellation crossed by the ecliptic and spread across the celestial equator. Noted objects within Virgo include the bright star **Spica, Alpha Virginis, Virgo A,** a radio source identified with the elliptical galaxy M87, and the massive **Virgo** cluster, consisting of thousands of galaxies of many kinds at a distance of about 20 million parsecs from Earth. Members of the cluster are also found beyond the boundaries of the constellation
*(Genitive is **Virginis**: means the 'Virgin')*

## visible

The range of electromagnetic radiation to which average human eyes are sensitive is generally termed 'the visible,' and taken to be in the 380-780nm wavelength range. Individuals differ in the range of light to which their eyes are sensitive

## visual binary
Double star whose components can be distinguished by direct optical observation rather than by **spectroscopic** or other indirect methods

## VLA
*See* VERY LARGE ARRAY

## VLBA
*See* VERY LONG BASELINE ARRAY

## VLBI
Very Long Baseline Interferometry.
*See* INTERFEROMETRY

## VLT
*See* VERY LARGE TELESCOPE

## VMO
*See* VERY MASSIVE OBJECT

## VOIR
*See* MAGELLAN

## Volans
Small constellation of the southern hemisphere.
*(Genitive is **Volantis**; means the 'flying fish')*

## Von Neumann Machine
Machine whose abilities include the skills needed to reproduce itself from commonly available materials. Von Neumann machines have been proposed as a possible tool for interstellar exploration, and could be released by humans or other species. One possible complication is that they might obey their programming and, once let loose, turn entire galaxies into millions of Von Neumann machines in periods of time far less than the lifetime of a galaxy. Named for John von Neumann (1903-1957), Hungarian-born US mathematician and engineer who among much else was one of the founders of computing

## Voyager
Pair of US spacecraft used for the exploration of the outer solar system. Voyager 1 was launched in 1977 and reached Jupiter in March 1979 and Saturn in November 1980. Voyager 2 was also launched in 1977 and travelled through the solar system behind Voyager 1, reaching Jupiter and Saturn in July 1979 and August 1981 respectively. Voyager 2 then flew past Uranus in 1986 and Neptune in 1989, making the Voyagers the source of an overwhelming proportion of our knowledge of the giant planets. Both are now leaving the solar system, equipped with greetings from Earth for any living creatures they might encounter

## Vulpecula
Constellation of the little fox, found in the northern hemisphere and
crossed by the Milky Way. Contains the well-known Dumbbell Nebula
M27, a planetary nebula
*(Genitive is **Vulpeculae**)*

# Ww

## W (Star Type)
*See* WOLF-RAYET STARS

## waterhole
Term applied by **exobiologists** to the 18-21cm wavelength region in
radio astronomy. This waveband encompasses the principal radio
emissions due to hydrogen and the hydroxyl ion, the components of
water. Because of the overwhelming importance of hydrogen as a
component of the universe, the waterhole could be a logical waveband
for transmissions designed for interstellar reception, especially if, as on
the Earth, water is of widespread importance as a constituent of living
beings

## wavelength
The distance from peak to peak of a wave, whether of matter or of
radiation. Multiplying wavelength by frequency yields a wave's
velocity

## weak force
*See* FORCES

## Weakly Interacting Massive Particles (WIMP)
A postulated type of matter proposed as a candidate type of **dark
matter** within galaxies

## weird terrain
Jumbled, hilly region of the surface of Mercury, apparently shaped by
seismic waves set up by a massive meteorite impact

## Whirlpool Galaxy
Spectacular spiral galaxy M51 in Canes Venatici

## white dwarf
One of the possible remnants which can be formed from stars after they
cease producing energy by **fusion**. If less than 1.4 solar masses of
material remain after the star leaves the main sequence and loses mass,
it will collapse into a white dwarf when the outward **radiation pressure**
which holds active stars up is removed. White dwarfs are held up
instead by the mutual repulsion between the electrons in their atoms.
They emit small amounts of residual heat and when this is gone reach
the **black dwarf** stage – or they will, since the process takes so long
that no star in the universe has completed it yet. The coolest white
dwarfs are still at about 3,500°. White dwarf material has a density of
many tonnes per cc. The interior of a white dwarf can be active because

of sloshing vibrations as heat seeps to the surface from the interior, causing their brightness to vary over a timescale of hours

## white hole
The exact opposite of a **black hole**, a **singularity** from which matter emerges instead of being sucked in. White holes are speculative constructs, unlike black holes which have a solid theoretical backing. They open up the possibility of allowing matter to be sent to alternative universes

## white light
Light containing a perfect or near-perfect mix of the colours of the visible **spectrum** appears white to the eye. By analogy a radio or other **electromagnetic** signal containing a broad mix of frequencies rather than a few spikes of favoured frequencies can also be termed white

## Wide-Field Infrared Explorer (WIRE)
Planned NASA satellite for infrared astronomy, using a 30cm telescope cooled by solid hydrogen and planned for launch in 1997 at the time of writing

## Widmanstatten Pattern
Criss-cross pattern observed in iron meteorites under the microscope. The patterns are thought to be produced by very slow cooling over millions of years

## Wien's Displacement Law
Law prescribing the way in which the frequency of the most intense emissions from a hot body increases as its temperature rises. The maximum frequency in hertz equals absolute temperature multiplied by $5.88 \times 10^{-10}$

## Wilson, Robert Woodrow (born 1936)
US physicist and co-discoverer with **Arno Penzias** of the **cosmic background radiation**

## Wilson-Bappu Effect
Empirical link whereby the absolute magnitudes of stars of types G, K and M are related to the width of a particular set of **spectral lines** due to calcium, the CaII lines. This allows their distances to be obtained from examining their spectra and measuring their apparent magnitudes as seen from Earth

## WIMP
*See* WEAKLY INTERACTING MASSIVE PARTICLES

## Wind
NASA satellite for exploring the solar wind, launched in 1995 to take up a position at the **L1 point** in the Earth-Moon system. Its instruments look at protons, electrons and the other components of the solar wind as well as gamma rays and magnetic fields

### window
Property of the Earth's atmosphere whereby radiation of particular wavelengths is able to reach the Earth's surface. There are windows for some radio, infrared and other wavelengths as well as for visible light

### winter solstice
For the northern hemisphere, the moment at which the Sun is at its southernmost, making the shortest day of the year, on or around December 22. For the southern hemisphere the shortest day falls when the Sun is at its northernmost point in the sky, giving a winter solstice on or around June 21

### WIRE
*See* WIDE-FIELD INFRARED EXPLORER

### Wolf-Rayet Stars
Stars with a peculiar spectrum indicating that they are surrounded by dense gas clouds and are suffering **nova-like** mass loss at a rapid rate. The Wolf-Rayets are among the hottest stars known with surface temperatures of up to 100,000K and are sometimes regarded as belonging to a category, the W stars, hotter than the **O stars** which are the hottest in the standard sequence of **spectral types**

### Wolf Sunspot Number
System for assessing the number of visible sunspots at a given time, by counting the number of individual spots and spot groups visible. A completely clear Sun would score zero on Wolf's scale and at maximum in the solar cycle the score can be about 200

### World Line
Line in **spacetime** connecting the points occupied by a real object

### wormhole
Temporary path which might in theory exist to connect **black holes** in different universes

# Xx Yy Zz

## XMM

X-ray astronomy satellite, the X-Ray Mirror Mission, planned for launch by **ESA** late in the 20th century. At the time of writing XMM was one of ESA's high priority 'cornerstone' missions. It is designed to provide high-quality spectra of the many different types of object in the X-ray sky. It would carry three X-ray telescopes and an optical telescope to allow simultaneous viewing of the same objects as are being seen in X-rays

## XMM-Newton

ESA spacecraft originally called XMM for X-ray multi-mirror, the biggest X-ray telescope ever launched. Put into orbit in 1999, it has x-ray cameras and spectrometers as well as an optical telescope. It should observe 1,000,000 objects in its planned 10-year life. Its three x-ray telescopes each use an array of 58 gold-covered mirrors to form high-resolution images

## X-rays

Electromagnetic radiation in the $10^{-9} - 10^{-13}$m wavelength region, overlapping longer wavelength gamma rays and shorter wavelength ultraviolet radiation. X-ray astronomy is a new science because X-rays are unable to penetrate the Earth's atmosphere, necessitating satellites or at least balloons or sounding rockets to allow them to be observed. X-ray astronomy has been one of the most fruitful branches of the science for some years, because it allows previously invisible effects of great fundamental importance to be observed. The X-ray sky contains many familiar objects, like the Sun, whose corona is an intense X-ray source. But most of the objects which dominate the X-ray sky are faint in visible light, so that important new science can be done in X-rays. The centres of galaxies, including our own, are powerful X-ray emitters, and so are the regions surrounding neutron stars, black holes and other highly condensed objects, so that **pulsars** are observed in X-rays as well as in other wavelengths. The first satellite for detailed, long-term X-ray astronomy observations was launched in 1970 **(Small Astronomical Satellite)**, and the total observational base of X-ray astronomy is still far less than that for optical or radio astronomy, so that the field is still ripe for major discoveries. X-rays emitted by material orbiting **black holes** are the main way in which black holes can be detected and indirectly observed.

## X-ray burster

Type of X-ray source probably consisting of a **neutron star** drawing material from a companion star and emitting bursts of X-rays as the material builds up near its surface and is sucked down to it at intervals of a few hours or days

## X-ray fluorescence spectroscopy

Chemical analysis technique which makes use of X-rays emitted by different elements after bombardment by the X-rays produced by a source carried within the instrument. Used inter alia on the experiments carried to the surface of Mars on the **Viking spacecraft**

## X-ray telescope

X-rays cannot be focused by conventional lenses and mirrors. So telescopes for X-ray astronomy depend on unusual technology. The most common design makes use of **grazing incidence**, in which the X-rays are reflected at a low angle from a succession of surfaces of some material which does not absorb them, bringing them gradually to a focus to form the image. New materials may allow genuine X-ray lenses and mirrors to be made. In addition, it is now proving possible to make X-ray telescopes of conventional design by using mirrors made of thin sandwiches in which light and heavy atoms alternate. These materials reflect X-rays as glass reflects light.
*See* SKY AND TELESCOPE MAGAZINE, MARCH 1988

## XTE

The X-ray Timing Explorer, a NASA satellite launched on December 30, 1995. It is designed to produce accurate X-ray **spectra** and measure short-term variation in the output of X-ray sources

## XUV

The extreme ultra-violet region of the **electromagnetic spectrum, in the $10^{-9}$–$10^{-10}$m wavelength range**

## year

The period of just over 365 days in which the Earth makes an orbit of the Sun. The word is used by analogy for the time taken for other planets to orbit to the Sun, although 'orbital period' is less ambiguous. The year has been defined in a large number of ways. The solar or tropical year, the usual measure of the year, is 365.242194 days and is the time taken for the Sun to return to the first point of Aries, where it crosses the celestial equator heading north. The sidereal year is the time taken for the Sun to return to the same point in the sky relative to the fixed stars, and equals 365.25636 days. The anomalistic year is the time between two perigees of the Earth's orbit, 365.25964 days. And the eclipse year, the time taken for the Sun to return to the node of the Moon's orbit, is 365.62003 days

## Yerkes telescope

40-inch refractor in Williams Bay, Wisconsin, USA, completed in 1897 and the largest refracting telescope ever.

## Yohkoh
Japanese/UK/USA satellite launched in 1991 for X-ray observations of the Sun, especially solar flares and other violent phenomena in the Sun's atmosphere. The name is Japanese for Sunbeam and the satellite is operated from the Institute for Space and Astronomical Sciences in Tokyo

## zap pits
Pits formed in moonrock by micrometeorite impact, measuring 1mm or less in size

## Zeeman Effect
Also called Zeeman Splitting, the phenomenon whereby strong magnetic fields cause spectral lines to split into separate components. The Zeeman Effect can be used to determine the strength of stellar magnetic fields. Pieter Zeeman (1865-1943), a Netherlands physicist, discovered the effect in 1896 and it was used early in the 20th century to measure the powerful magnetic fields in sunspots. It began being applied to measurements of other stars in 1946

## zenith
The point on the celestial sphere directly above the observer, 90° above the **horizon** and 180° from the **nadir**

## zero gravity experiments
Experiments in biology, materials science, physics, medicine and other sciences carried out in orbit at a velocity high enough to cancel the influence of the Earth's gravitation. More generally called microgravity experiments because in practice the gravitation obtainable in orbit is still not zero, typically amounting to $10^{-3} - 10^{-6}$ of that at the Earth's surface

## Zodiac
The band of sky 9° to either side of the ecliptic in which the Moon and planets are usually found. The twelve constellations of the Zodiac as used by astrologers tell only part of the story, since the Sun also travels through **Ophiuchus** each year and the other planets also visit it

## Zodiacal Light
Faint glow visible along the Zodiac (especially at dawn and dusk, and under very good observing conditions), caused by dusty material in the plane of the solar system scattering sunlight to an observer on the Earth. The Zodiacal Light has been cited as evidence that some of the material deposited in the inner solar system by comets is large enough to avoid being dispersed by radiation pressure

# Bibliography

A wide range of sources has been used in the compilation of this
Dictionary, including books, journals and magazines as well as press
information from such bodies as the European Space Agency, NASA
and PPARC in the UK. Among magazine sources, it is essential to
acknowledge *Sky and Telescope*, based in Cambridge, Massachusetts,
which is simply the one-stop source for up to date astronomy
information and which was invaluable in the updating of my own text.
The books listed here were all useful, but Jay M Pasachoff's
**'Contemporary Astronomy'** and its companion volume, **'Astronomy:
From the Earth to the Universe',** were especially valuable and the
data on the brightest and nearest stars comes from them.

Astronomers use online resources extensively. Sites worth a look
because of their extensive links to other astronomy content include: *Sky
and Telescope* at **www.skypub.com**: a lengthy list of astronomy sites
run by the *Carnegie Institute of Washington* at
**www.ciw.edu/Astro_hot.html**: the (UK) *Royal Astronomical Society*,
**www.ras.org.uk**: and for space missions, *NASA*, **www.nasa.gov** and
the *European Space Agency*, **www.esa.int.**

*Beatty, J Kelly, O'Leary, Brian* and *Chaikin, Andrew*
**The New Solar System**
(CUP 1981)

*Brandt, John C* and *Chapman*
**Rendezvous in Space: The Science of Comets**
(Freeman 1992)

*Cattermole, Peter*
**Venus: The Geological Story**
(UCL Press 1994)

*Cooper, Henry SF*
**The Evening Star**
(Johns Hopkins 1994)

*Darton, Mike* and *Clark, John*
**Dent Dictionary of Measurement**
(Dent 1994)

*Francis, Peter*
**The Planets**
(Penguin 1981)

*Grosser, Morton*
**The Discovery of Neptune**
(Dover 1978)

*Hearnshaw, J B*
**The Analysis of Starlight**
(CUP 1986)

*Hoskin, Michael (editor)*
**The Cambridge Illustrated History of Astronomy**
Cambridge University Press 1997

*Hunt, Garry* and *Moore, Patrick*
**Atlas of Uranus**
(CUP 1989)

*Hutchison, Robert* and *Graham, Andrew*
**Meteorites**
(British Museum (Natural History) 1992)

*Kaufman, William J*
**The Cosmic Frontiers of General Relativity**
(Penguin 1979)

*Kaufmann III, William J* and *Freedman, Roger A*
**Universe**
W H Freeman, 5th edition 1998

*Kaye, G W C* and *Laby, T H*
**Tables of Physical and Chemical Constants**
(many editions from 1911 to date including Longman 1966)

*Koestler, Arthur*
**The Sleepwalkers**
(many editions by Penguin et al)

*Krauss, Lawrence*
**The Fifth Essence**
(Vintage 1989)

*Littmann, Mark*
**Planets Beyond: Discovering the Outer Solar System**
(Wiley 1990)

*Mitton, Simon*
**Daytime Star**
(Faber 1981)

*Muir, Hazel (ed)*
**Larousse Dictionary of Scientists**
(Larousse 1994)

*Pasachoff, Jay M*
**Astronomy: From the Earth to the Universe**
(Saunders College Publishing 1979)

*Pasachoff, Jay M*
**Contemporary Astronomy, 4th edition**
(Saunders College Publishing 1989)

*Peterson, Ivars*
**Newton's Clock: Chaos in the Solar System**
(Freeman 1993)

*Rees, Sir Martin*
**Perspectives in Astrophysical Cosmology**
(Lezioni Lincee/CUP 1995)

*Ronan, Colin A*
**Cambridge Illustrated History of the World's Science**
(CUP 1983)

*Walker, Peter*
**Chambers Science and Technology Dictionary**
(Chambers 1988)

*Washburn, Mark*
**Mars at Last!**
(Abacus 1977)

*Westfall, Richard S*
**Never at Rest: A Biography of Isaac Newton**
(CUP 1983)

*Williams, Trevor (ed)*
**Collins Biographical Dictionary of Scientists**
(Harper Collins 1994)

*Yenne, Bill*
**Encyclopedia of US Spacecraft**
(Hamlyn 1985)

**Also of value were**: *Popular Astronomy*, the publication of the Society for Popular Astronomy, the *Quarterly Journal of the Royal Astronomical Society* and its successor publication, *Astronomy and Geophysics.*